Sports Illustrated
BASEBALL

THE SPORTS ILLUSTRATED LIBRARY

BOOKS ON TEAM SPORTS

*Baseball	Football: Defense	Ice Hockey
*Basketball	Football: Offense	Pitching
Curling: Techniques	Football: Quarterback	*Soccer
and Strategy		Volleyball

BOOKS ON INDIVIDUAL SPORTS

*Bowling	Skiing	*Women's Gymnastics
Fly Fishing	Squash	I: The Floor Exercise
*Golf	Table Tennis	Event
Horseback Riding	*Tennis	*Women's Gymnastics
Judo	Track: Running Events	II: The Vaulting,
*Racquetball	Track: Field Events	Balance Beam and
*Running for	*Tumbling	Uneven Parallel Bars
Women	Wrestling	Events

BOOKS ON WATER SPORTS

*Canoeing	Small Boat Sailing
*Scuba Diving	Swimming and Diving
Skin Diving and Snorkeling	

SPECIAL BOOKS

*Backpacking	Training with Weights
Dog Training	

*Expanded Format

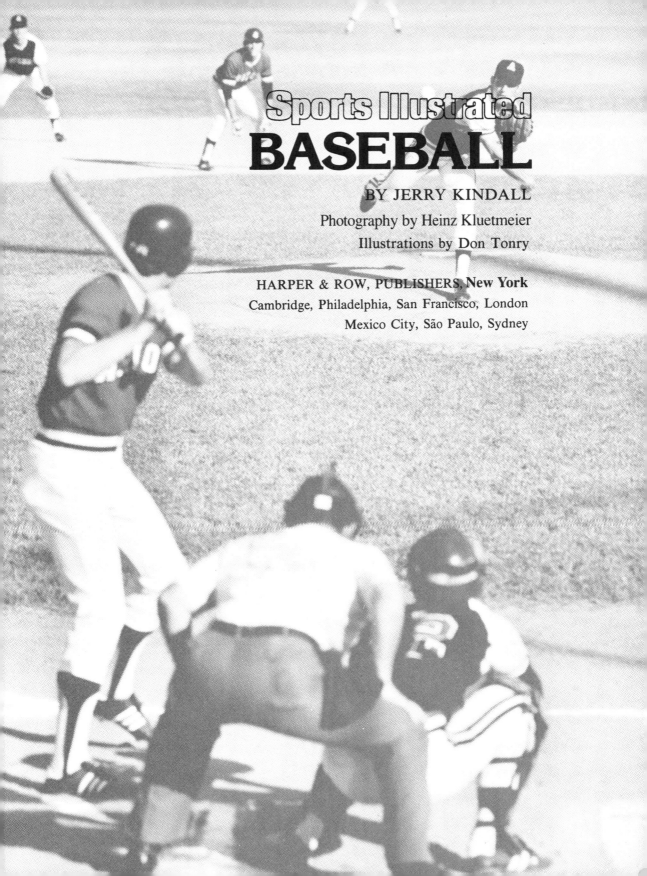

Sports Illustrated
BASEBALL

BY JERRY KINDALL

Photography by Heinz Kluetmeier

Illustrations by Don Tonry

HARPER & ROW, PUBLISHERS, New York
Cambridge, Philadelphia, San Francisco, London
Mexico City, São Paulo, Sydney

Acknowledgments

To the late Dick Siebert, former baseball coach at the University of Minnesota, for his mastery in teaching and sharing baseball.

To Jim Wing, associate head baseball coach at the University of Arizona, for his excellence in coaching and unparalleled kindness to players and co-workers.

To Jerry Stitt, assistant baseball coach at the University of Arizona, for his long hours of capable instruction and teaching.

To Arizona Wildcat baseball players, past and present, for their commitment to excellence in practice as well as in games.

To Dr. Paul and Barbara Schnur, for the use of their lovely home on Oak Creek.

To Mrs. Pat Buergey, a most capable and friendly secretary.

To Bill Jaspersohn, editor, Sports Illustrated Library, for his kind and patient counsel to a rookie author.

To J. C. Percell, noted baseball historian and librarian.

To Harold Kindall, for his legacy of interest in baseball—and unqualified devotion to his family.

To my children, Betsy, Doug, Bruce, and Martha, for providing me a loving and supportive "home plate."

This book—and the author—are dedicated to my wife, Georgia.

Picture credits: King Features Syndicate, Inc.: p. 12; Joe Vitti: pp. 40 (top, bottom), 62, 64 (bottom), 74, 131, 220 (top), 225, 230. *Sports Illustrated* pictures by: Andy Hayt: pp. 20, 158 (top), 183 (left); Peter Read Miller: pp. 32, 232, 254; Ronald C. Modra: pp. 42, 58, 66, 184, 256; Walter Iooss, Jr.: pp. 108, 110, 158 (right); Neil Leifer: p. 144; Steve Goldstein: p. 158 (left); Tony Tomsic: pp. 168, 253; Richard Mackson: p. 250. All other photographs by Heinz Kluetmeier. Picture researcher, Carolyn Keith. Diagram on p. 221 by Georgia Froom. All other diagrams by Don Tonry.

Designer: C. Linda Dingler

Library of Congress Cataloging in Publication Data

Kindall, Jerry.
    Sports illustrated baseball.
    1. Baseball. I. Title.
GV867.K56   1983   796.357'2   82-48670
ISBN 0-06-015079-3
ISBN 0-06-091055-0 (pbk.)

85 86 10 9 8 7 6 5 4 3
85 86 10 9 8 7 6 5 4 3

Contents

Preface

Why another baseball book? There seems to be a proliferation of "how to" manuals in recent years to instruct the player, the coach, the fan—yes, even the fan. Because baseball requires such precise and sophisticated skills (try hitting a round ball squarely with a round bat), mastering this game remains a mystery to most people.

The intent of this baseball book is multifold: to strip away the mystery of playing and coaching this most difficult of all team sports; to provide a workable system of organization and planning when learning its four essential skills—running, throwing, hitting, and fielding; to provide certain keys to player, coach, and fan for unlocking the gates to better performance, understanding, and enjoyment of this marvelous sport; and to lay a solid foundation of fundamentals upon which the reader can build a lifelong interest in the sport of baseball.

This is a layman's book, covering all baseball interests: high school, college, amateur, recreational, and professional. One of baseball's enduring qualities is that certain common threads interweave its fabric. From Williamsport, Pennsylvania, to Dodger Stadium, from Taiwan to Cuba, no matter the level, these common threads stand out and define the good player, the successful coach, the knowledgeable fan.

If there is a prevailing characteristic by which I want my team, the University of Arizona Wildcats, to be recognized, it's in the execution of sound baseball fundamentals. I believe that in each of the four skills of the game there are certain basic techniques that can be taught to players and will lead to this characteristic. Further, I believe these techniques should be applied at all levels of play: from the day a youngster tries out for his first Little League team to the day he retires proudly wearing a World Series ring.

Whether you are a baseball player or a coach, this book will detail for you the fundamentals of every skill and position in the sport, and then show you how to apply those fundamentals to the strategies and situations that arise during actual play.

One outstanding feature of this book is its illustrations. The photographs, taken by the experts at *Sports Illustrated,* bring a dimension of instruction that few such books provide. Any reader's understanding of baseball can be significantly broadened by a careful analysis of each picture.

Whatever your approach to this book—as eager young player, concerned coach or parent, serious-minded professional, devoted fan, or casual observer —I hope you find what you're looking for: a better understanding of baseball.

J.K.
University of Arizona

Sports Illustrated
BASEBALL

1

Baseball History and Changes

On July 4, 1976, the United States celebrated its bicentennial. Fittingly, our country's birthday was marked throughout baseball parks and stadiums that weekend with gala fireworks displays and proud renditions of the national anthem. The game of baseball has grown up with America and is wrapped in historical significance beginning 154 years ago. The first game of baseball was played at Harvard University in 1829. Ten years later, Abner Doubleday laid out the dimensions of the first baseball field in Cooperstown, New York. In 1869, the first professional team, the Cincinnati Red Stockings, was organized; and seven years later, in 1876, the National League was formed. The American League was born in 1901. In 1947, the first College World Series was played in Kalamazoo, Michigan. And in 1982, major-league baseball set an all-time attendance record of over 44 million fans!

For well over a century, baseball has maintained a remarkable hold on the American sports fan's attention. While the world and society have tumbled through changes that muddle historians' brains and defy remaining logic, baseball has somehow kept an almost eternal quality: a sense of comfort and consistency that appeals deeply to

13

Baseball immortal Ty Cobb of the early Detroit Tigers hows the contrast between the uniforms of today and 916.

the nature of the American public. The game itself is so pure, so established, that even the 90-foot distance between the bases has not changed an inch since Alexander Cartright established it in 1845, almost a century and a half ago.

Its critics' gibes notwithstanding, baseball is no idle pastime dreamed up by a bunch of loafers on a lazy, hot July afternoon in a pasture by the railroad tracks. It is a social phenomenon that, in its own way, gives as accurate an insight into American life as the most scholarly history text. I remember the late "Pepper" Martin of the St. Louis Cardinals' "Gashouse Gang" forever impressing on my consciousness what baseball meant to him, and to millions like him. In 1956, which was my rookie year with the Chicago Cubs, Pepper, as our third-base coach, asked for five minutes during a team meeting at Cincinnati's old Crosley Field. Instead of telling us what to expect from the Reds, he gave an impassioned speech on the privilege of being a baseball player. With tears in his eyes, he reminded us that millions of people longed to be in our place. Then he referred us to the sign painted on the right-field wall at Crosley Field. As we left the clubhouse and came onto the field near the third-base dugout, I dare say we all looked at that sign. It was a quote by former President Herbert Hoover. It said: "The rigid voluntary rules of right and wrong, as applied in American sports, are second only to religion in strengthening the morals of the American people . . . and baseball is the greatest of all team sports."

My introduction to baseball came via my dad, a fine athlete himself and a knowledgeable fan. I grew up in St. Paul, Minnesota, and when time and money allowed, Dad would take my brothers, the neighborhood kids, and me to Lexington Park to watch the St. Paul Saints, a triple-A farm club of the Brooklyn Dodgers. It is easy to remember the warm sun on the wooden left-field bleachers, the scramble for foul balls, the visits through the fence with the visiting team bullpen batteries, the pride I felt when the Saints won and Campanella, Snider, Zimmer, and Labine did well. That was thirty-five years ago. Twenty years before that, youngsters had the same feelings as I. And twenty years later, I saw the same light of pleasure and thrill in my own children's eyes. Different ball parks, different players, different cities, vastly different times—but the same feelings. I suspect that that's what will make baseball prevail another century or more in America's life. Ty Cobb meant as much to my dad as Alvin Dark meant to me, and Dave Winfield means to my sons.

Of course there have been changes, and baseball *has* kept up with the times. But the baseball fan recognizes and appreciates the underlying consistency and continuity that this sport, more than any other, gives its players and its public.

SOME OF THE CHANGES

Ball Parks

The cozy confines of Ebbets Field, the Polo Grounds, Forbes Field, Crosley Field, and Sportsman's Park have been replaced by the spacious concrete-and-steel monuments called Dodger Stadium, Candlestick Park, Three Rivers Stadium, Riverfront Stadium, and Busch Stadium. Add to these arenas the Astrodome, the Kingdome, the Metrodome, the Big A, and Veterans Stadium, and many would say that the old brick-and-steel ball parks of the past are artifacts. Perhaps. But Wrigley Field, Fenway Park, and Tiger Stadium have never looked so good. And the neat, well-kept, on-campus college ball parks around the country have a special baseball flavor that has endured for decades.

The Hubert H. Humphrey Metrodome in Minneapolis—newest of the indoor baseball stadiums.

The introduction of artificial turf by the Houston Astros in the early 1960s seemed to herald a new and significant era in baseball. Today, of the twenty-six major-league teams, no fewer than nine have installed "the rug." But wait—the other seventeen clubs have had over twenty years to "catch up," and yet natural grass is still the preferred surface in two of every three big-league parks.

Uniforms

Did you notice that picture of Ty Cobb at the opening of this chapter? That baggy old-time uniform is a laugher, right? "Give me the modern uni any day!" I can hear my college players saying now, and I must admit that I, too, would rather wear the present-day Steve Sax model than the 1920 Rogers Hornsby threads. But let's take a closer look.

Ty Cobb's hair was shorter than today's modern player, but his hat had a visor very similar to the streamlined model of the Eighties. Apparently there were sun fields even in those days.

His baseball shirt had longer sleeves than those worn today, but the Detroit emblem is over the left breast, the same place Bill Buckner wears the Cubs symbol. And though Ty is wearing a heavier, woolen sweat shirt under his baseball shirt, it serves the same function as sweat shirts today.

The baseball pants are essentially the same knickers style we wear today, but Cobb wears his higher than most. I wouldn't be surprised if he had more low pitches called balls rather than strikes that way.

Same system of baseball stockings today as in the Twenties: the outer dark stockings with stirrups for some protection, and the inner white sanitary hose to guard against chafing and infection.

And, finally, those shoes. If my eyes aren't blurred from looking so far back in history, I think I see the "Georgia Peach" wearing the same type of metal spikes on the bottom of his shoes as "Stan the Man" did in the Fifties, "Say, Hey" did in the Sixties, "Brooks" did in the Seventies, and "Mr. October" does in the Eighties.

Gloves

Quite a contrast between the glove Cobb wore and the huge, streamlined models we have today. But the basic configuration of web, pocket, fingers, thumb, and heel hasn't changed. And, interestingly, the major-league record for putouts in one season is held by John Donahue of the Chicago White Sox,

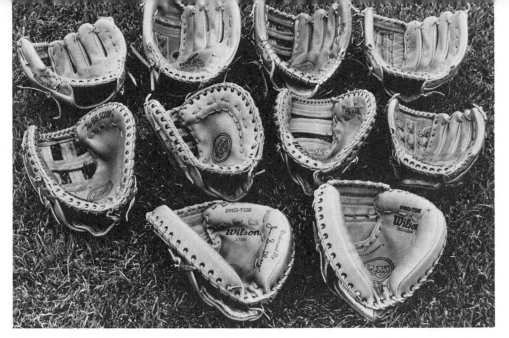

Compared to Ty Cobb's tiny glove, today's models seem like bushel baskets.

whose first baseman's glove was designed well enough to make 1,846 catches in . . . 1907. Too, the major-league career record for assists belongs to Luis Aparicio who began fielding ground balls for the White Sox twenty-seven years ago when the gloves were more like Ty's than like those of the 1980s.

Bats

In amateur baseball, bats represent the biggest change in recent years. The introduction of aluminum bats has saved considerable money in baseball budgets but has also brought a rather distorted measure of a hitter's effectiveness compared to his using a wooden bat. And yet, the same rules on length, circumference, taper, and style apply to both the aluminum and wooden bats. In pro baseball, Dale Murphy has the same selection of bats available today that Ty Cobb had sixty years ago. And one of the favorite models of today's big boppers is the K55 Louisville Slugger, the same bat with which Milwaukee Brewer manager Harvey Kuenn won the American League batting title in 1959 with the Detroit Tigers.

General Equipment

There are certainly more gimmicks and fads today than there were fifty, thirty, ten, even five years ago. Experts are forever searching for means to improve performance and pick up an edge over the opponent. No longer is it possible to carry a dozen balls and several bats out to the field and expect a good practice. At the University of Arizona, at each practice and game we have six pitching machines representing three different brand models; three full tunnel cages; eight pitching mounds; a videotape camera recorder with instant-replay capabilities; several dozen bats and at least five dozen baseballs.

Please don't misunderstand. I'm grateful for the excellent facilities and equipment at our disposal. It does help our team's performance, and we try to utilize every bit of it, especially the weight machines, which have been particularly beneficial. But then I think of extraordinary players like Al Kaline, Ernie Banks, Nolan Ryan, Rickey Henderson, Pedro Guerrero, Hal McRae, and many others who learned baseball on sandlots and whose only pitching machine was a tired father's arm. Would they, I wonder, have made it any faster or farther in the majors if the gimmicks, fads, and machines had been available to them when they first fell in love with baseball? Maybe. But the conclusion I find myself reaching is that there are more important things to baseball than stadiums, equipment, and appearances.

For the nearly 150 years that have passed since Doubleday and Cartright gave some system to the game of baseball, there has been a strong undercurrent

The aluminum bat represents the biggest and most dramatic change in baseball equipment today.

A modern-day equipment manager surrounded by the tools of his trade.

of something constant and true that has held the game together for players and fans alike. I'm not sure I can define exactly what that undercurrent is, but I know it's there. Maybe it's what makes Ty Cobb's uniform, the longer we look at it, seem more like Steve Sax's Dodger blue, or what makes fans feel they enjoy an afternoon at Fenway Park more than a night at the Metrodome. The fact is that Babe Ruth's single-season home-run record will never have an asterisk beside it, and Lou Gehrig's consecutive-game mark may stand for another fifty years. And perhaps most important, there will always be a chance for a young player to make it to the majors whether his parents can afford a pitching machine or not.

Baseball hasn't changed as much as we think.

2

Hitting and Bunting

There are literally millions of "batters" through-out baseball who do all the right things up to the moment the pitcher delivers the ball, but then when the pitch is released, suddenly fade. Of all the millions of baseball players in the world, relatively few can call themselves "hitters"—that is, players prepared to hit anything the pitcher dares throw in the 17-inch-wide rectangle between the armpits and the knees known as the "strike zone."

How do batters become hitters? There are no simple answers that will assure a .400 batting average. And yet, there seem to be certain consistent qualities that, day after day, season after season, prevail among the good hitters in baseball. Let's try to identify, define, and implement those qualities so that you can separate yourself as a hitter from the crowd of batters surrounding the bat rack.

QUALIFICATIONS

Hitting a baseball isn't easy; in fact, it's probably the single most difficult sports skill to master. To hit a fast-pitched, often curving, round ball with a round bat, and hit it solidly, takes a perfect

21

George Foster, one of baseball's true home-run hitters, generates much of his power through explosive hip rotation.

combination of courage, body balance, eye-hand coordination, strength, and split-second muscle reaction.

Whether you're a Little Leaguer or a major-leaguer, if you want to be a good hitter, you must first thoroughly understand the fundamentals and mechanics of hitting. Rare is the player who can walk up to the plate and, without thought or practice, find success as a hitter. Hitting is such a complex and difficult process that anxiety and frustration will set in quickly unless you have some foundation of instruction to build on. Simply put: If you ignore any of the fundamentals of hitting, the entire action falls apart!

Second, to be a good hitter, you must have a measure of physical strength. I have never seen a good hitter at the advanced levels of baseball who was weak and anemic. To accelerate a bat from a resting position to a speed that will literally overpower the pitched ball in the short distance of the swing requires a great amount of hands-wrist-forearm and upper-body strength. Weight training programs, which more and more are strengthening players in every sport, are the chief factor behind the general surge of home runs and extra-base hits these days in baseball. While you *can* become stronger by swinging a bat more, you also need the strength and flexibility development provided through regular use of Nautilus, Universal, and free weight systems.

Third, to be successful as a hitter, you need good eyesight. A 90-mile-per-hour fastball allows you less than half a second to make up your mind whether or not you want to swing at that pitch. If your eyes can't quickly pick up the path of the pitch and lack the depth perception to ascertain whether the ball is high, low, inside, outside, curving, straight, fast, or slow, you have absolutely no chance of hitting it! If you're a young hitter, don't be discouraged if your natural eyesight checks out poorly when examined. Many good major-league hitters wear glasses or contact lenses and have overcome the problem of relatively poor natural vision.

Finally, you must be willing to practice, practice, practice. Ted Williams, considered by most baseball experts to be the best *natural* hitter ever, supplemented his great eyesight, extraordinarily strong wrists and forearms, and acute knowledge of hitting with an eagerness for practice and long hours of drills that puts most modern-day hitters to shame. Williams, whose career with the Boston Red Sox spanned twenty-one years and produced a .344 lifetime batting average, remarked that through all those years he would take batting practice until his hands literally bled from constantly swinging the bat. Once you understand the proper fundamentals and techniques and your strength and eyesight are up to par, there is no easy way out if you want to improve your hitting. Like Ted Williams did, you just have to get out there and *practice.*

PHILOSOPHY OF HITTING

Any worthwhile activity must have a purpose. The same goes for hitting a baseball. A good athlete or team will succeed more often if there are goals to which they aspire—some consistent motivation that will give substance to both their bodies and minds as they approach the task. As a hitter, you should ask yourself: "What am I trying to accomplish with this bat? When do I decide to foresake one method and try another? What criteria can I use that will indicate I am making progress?"

In his book *The Science of Hitting,* Ted Williams offers a sound three-point philosophy for a young hitter, formulating what his approach to hitting should be. He calls them "The Three Rules to Hit By."

1. *Get a good pitch to hit.* Although my first four years in pro baseball were in the National League with the Chicago Cubs, I did get to see Ted Williams in spring training as he concluded his illustrious career with the Boston Red Sox. I marveled at how he lived by this rule, even in spring training games. He seldom swung at a pitch that was outside the strike zone by the smallest margin. And when he did swing, chances are he hit a line drive. His point, of course, is that swinging at bad pitches is self-defeating. It's hard enough to hit to begin with, so why penalize yourself by swinging at balls outside the strike zone?

2. *Proper thinking.* Most hitters do not concentrate hard enough on the variables that face them each time they step up to the plate. What is the pitcher's best pitch? What did he throw to me last time? What are my strengths? My weaknesses? What does this pitcher normally throw on the first pitch? On a 3-and-1 count? A 2-and-0 count? Perhaps the most consistent hitter we ever had at Arizona was Brad Mills, now with the Montreal Expos. Brad kept a small black book with him on the bench at all times; in it he recorded *every pitch* the opposing pitcher threw to him, with a note on how effective that pitch was in the situation. Mills was thinking properly!

3. *Be quick with the bat.* At the instant you decide to swing at the ball, any slow or unnecessary movement of the bat will be the difference between success and failure. A weak ground ball or easy pop fly can be a sharp line drive if the bat is an instant or two quicker through its swing.

Our philosophy of hitting at Arizona is built largely on aggressiveness: We want our hitters in a positive, eager frame of mind as they approach the plate. As explained in Chapter 13 on offensive strategy, we feel we will win far more games swinging the bat than waiting out the pitcher for walks. This positive approach to hitting is so much a key that you must feel absolute confidence in your ability to hit the ball hard. Without that confidence, you boost the pitcher's natural edge dramatically. Let's face it, the pitcher wins the battle over the hitter nearly 70 percent of the time anyway, so an all-out hitting philosophy fosters the feeling that "Yes, I *can* do better! Yes, I *will* do better! Yes, I *am* better! *Give me the bat!*"

Still, when I say "be aggressive as a hitter," I don't mean take a random, reckless, all-out swing from the heels at any pitch that suits your fancy. The aggressiveness that I'm talking about and that leads to hitting success is a calculated, *controlled* full swing at the *right pitch,* and at the *right time.* Remember Ted Williams's first rule: *Get a good pitch to hit.* When that pitch crosses the plate, you must be ready, physically and mentally, to give it your very best swing and not waste the moment with a weak, halfhearted wave. You coaches can make your hitters more aggressive and self-confident through your encouragement, support, and enthusiasm as well as your hitting instruction.

Another fundamental approach we take to hitting at the University of Arizona is to hit hard ground balls rather than deep fly balls. Your chances of reaching base are much improved if you hit the ball sharply on the ground rather than up in the air. Consider: A ground ball requires that the defense execute three distinct and sometimes difficult acts: (1) fielding the ball cleanly; (2) throwing the ball; and (3) catching the ball. Since a pop fly need only be *fielded* for the defense to register an out, when you hit a ball in the air, in a way you're doing the defense a favor.

To further make this point, a few years ago I had my coaching staff chart every fair ball hit by Arizona and its opponents at both the varsity and junior-varsity level for an entire season. The charts proved revealing. Of the 1,759 fair balls hit, 377 were line drives, 869 were ground balls, and 513 were fly balls. As you might expect, the line drives resulted in the best on-base average for the hitters: 84 percent. The 869 ground balls resulted in a 42-percent on-base average, while the 513 fly balls got the hitters on base 29 percent of the time. Thus, as a batter, you have a 13-percent better chance to reach base by hitting a ground ball than by hitting a fly ball.

The other, more dramatic conclusion is that clearly *you can raise your batting average if you concentrate on hitting ground balls.* Of the 513 fly balls charted, 146 fell safely, including home runs and long extra-base hits. The fly-ball batting average was .285. Of the 869 ground balls charted, 276 were base hits for a .318 batting average, or a difference of *33 points!* * You are far better

*I should note that that particular year our team hit .348—an unusually high team average—so the averages quoted above are high. But year after year, I expect that a ground-ball batting average will still be significantly higher than that for fly balls.

off, then, trying to hit the top half of the ball for a hard grounder than you are uppercutting and trying to hit the ball out of the park. To hit the ball on the ground, I advocate a slight downward arc to the swing as if you were swinging an ax at a spot on a tree somewhere between 2 and 4 feet above the ground. If you can swing this way consistently, you will hit more line drives and strike out less, since most strikeouts occur when the bat passes under the flight of the pitch, particularly on fastballs.

So much for a philosophy of hitting. Try to keep it in mind as you study the specific techniques and mechanics of hitting outlined in this chapter.

THE BAT

Your first decision as a hitter is the selection of the proper bat—the right size, weight, and length. Most young hitters use a bat that is too big and/or too heavy. Choose a bat that feels comfortable in your hands—whether its handle is thin, medium, or thick—and then gauge if it is the best possible weight and length. There are some general guidelines for bat selection that players and coaches should keep in mind.

- For players between 10 and 14 years of age, select a bat 28 to 32 inches long.
- For players between 15 and 17 years of age, the bat should be from 32 to 34 inches long.
- For college and professional players, the bat should be from 34 to 36 inches long.

The weight of the bat should be approximately 1 or 2 ounces less than its length. A 33-inch bat, for example, should weigh 31 or 32 ounces for proper balance.

An easy way to test if your bat is too heavy is to hold it by the handle at arm's length horizontally in front of you with your strongest hand. If the hitting end of the bat begins to waver and drop before ten seconds elapse, the bat is probably too heavy.

THE GRIP

The bat should be held in your fingers, not your palms. The middle knuckles of your top hand should be lined up as close as possible to the middle knuckles

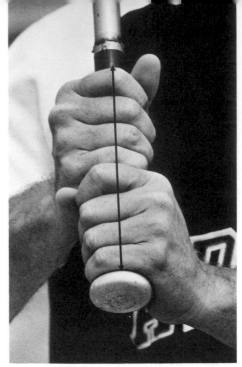

The grip on the bat should be with the fingers rather than the palms of the hands. Aligning the middle knuckles helps provide a faster swing.

of your bottom hand, usually somewhere between the base and middle knuckles of the bottom hand. If you rotate your hands on the bat so that the base knuckles near alignment, you end up locking your wrists and severely limiting the bat's speed in the actual swing. By keeping your middle knuckles near alignment throughout the swing, the bat will have a fast, whiplike action because the wrists are free. As you await the pitch, your grip should be somewhat firm but relaxed to prevent tension and tightness from being transferred up from your arms to your shoulders. It is not uncommon to see hitters

A

The closed stance (A): The hitter can protect the outside part of the plate.

The open stance (B): used by most pull hitters whose strength is the pitch on the inside part of the plate.

The even stance (C): favored by most hitters because it provides good plate coverage on virtually every swing (D).

wringing the bat so tightly that every muscle stands out in both arms as they wait for the pitch. This tension will slow the hitter when the time comes to explode the hands forward to start the swing.

THE STANCE

There are many stances from which to choose. With some, the hitter is compensating for a weakness, while with others he is hoping to maximize his strengths as he takes his place in the batter's box. Some hitters like the *closed stance,* with the front foot closer to the plate than the back foot, which allows them to protect the outside part of the plate and also curbs the natural urge to pull away from the pitch. Others prefer the *open stance,* with the back foot closer to the plate, which gives them the best view of the pitch and will facilitate hitting the inside pitch with power. Most hitters assume the normal *straightaway* or *even stance,* which allows them to adjust to pitches on both the inside and outside edges of the strike zone. Whichever stance you choose, you should be certain you can do the following as you begin your swing:

1.   *Cover the plate well.* You must be able to reach every part of the strike zone with the bat's prime hitting surface. Outside of professional baseball, nearly every hitter uses an aluminum bat, which has considerably more prime hitting surface than a wooden bat. Whereas the wooden bat has 4 to 4½ inches of "good wood," the aluminum bat has up to 6 inches of "good metal" for best impact against the ball. Whichever bat you choose, your stance should afford optimum use of the prime hitting surface.

C   D

2. *Maintain good balance.* If your stance places too much weight on your back or front foot, or on your heels, or limits your vision, or tips your shoulders, or locks your knees, or causes any other problems that affect your control and balance, it will also lead to a poor swing. Your stance must give you a comfortable, almost relaxed, sense of ease and balance as you await the pitch.

3. *Have maximum hip, shoulder, arm, and hand freedom* to accelerate the bat into the strike zone to meet the ball.

Any stance that can meet these three requirements is acceptable. Young hitters are tempted to emulate their heroes, but few of us would be able to hit from the same stance as Carl Yastrzemski, Brian Downing, or Reggie Smith. Coaches have a tendency to teach a favorite stance because it worked for *them.* But you must find what works best for *you,* and much of this can only be done by trial and error. So, hitting becomes a series of experiments, until a combination of grip, stance, bat angle, stride, and swing finally begins to click for you.

The Constants

Recognizing that stances are different and that what works well for one hitter can be disastrous for another, we still need some point of departure, some standard, through which to illustrate good hitting technique. There are some constants that every good hitter seems to include in his stance. If we were to study the ten best hitters in baseball and consolidate their strengths into one composite stance, I think we would see the following:

1. The feet spread about 6 to 8 inches wider than the shoulders, the front foot opened slightly toward the pitcher at about 45 degrees.

2. Slightly more weight on the rear foot and more weight forward on the balls of the feet, with the heels only lightly touching the ground; knees and hips flexed slightly to ensure a smooth stride.

3. Hips and shoulders level, with the front shoulder tucked in slightly toward the plate.

4. The head steady, eyes level, and chin tucked in on the front shoulder. It is important that the head be turned toward the pitcher as far as possible without straining the neck, to get a clear view of the pitch. A common fault among young hitters is trying to see the pitch without fully turning the head, which allows them to see only with the front eye while part of the rear eye's vision is obscured by the bridge of the nose. This poor position of the head also tilts the eyes off the horizontal plane and distorts their focus on the ball.

5. The hands comfortably away from the body about 8 to 12 inches and on the same plane as the back shoulder. This puts the hands at the top of the

strike zone and paves the way for swinging with a slight downward arc. The elbows comfortably bent, the back elbow about 6 to 8 inches away from the body.

6.   The bat angle, as the hitter takes his stance, should be about midway between horizontal and vertical. This lessens the distance the hitting surface of the bat must travel during the swing so that solid contact with the ball can occur in front of the plate with the arms extended.

Whatever preparatory routine you go through before assuming your stance—digging in with your rear foot, taking practice swings or deep breaths, resting the bat on your shoulder—when the pitcher delivers the pitch, the above stance will prepare you nicely for your stride, swing, and follow-through.

THE STRIDE

This is the part of hitting that confuses many hitters and causes the most problems. Perhaps the best way to introduce the mechanics of a proper stride is to build on this concept: *Keep your hands and weight back as long as possible.* Nearly every young hitter has a tendency to stride too soon, lunging forward and away from the plate as he strides. His head, front shoulder, and hands then move forward prematurely and prevent him from having a good swing at a breaking or an off-speed pitch, or any pitch on the outside part of the plate. Although it sounds contradictory, it's a fact of hitting that the longer you wait, the quicker you'll be. If you can keep your stride back until the last instant, that will keep your hands and weight back longer, and when you do swing, you will be quicker with the bat. To keep from striding too soon, turn your front hip and shoulder inward, toward the plate, as the pitcher begins his delivery. Don't stride yet; merely cock your hips and shoulders back about 2 inches and transfer a bit more weight to your back foot. Your head remains still and your hands in the same relative position, although they do move back slightly as the front shoulder turns in.

Try to delay your stride until the pitch is about one-third of the way to the plate. Then, as you stride toward the pitch with your front foot, cock your hips inward and take your hands back, away from the ball, about 5 inches. This inward turn, or cocking, of the hips and hands occurs simultaneously with the beginning of your stride. It also sets the power and weight back over the rear foot and, in a way, "loads the gun" to explode. To understand this simultaneous motion, imagine there is a rubber band tied between your front wrist and front ankle. During your stance, this rubber band is very slightly taut. If your hands were to go forward *with* the stride, there would be very little "snap" to the hands as they brought the bat into the strike zone. But if your hands were to draw back as the left foot strode forward, the rubber band's tension would increase and give your hands a great amount of "snap" as they brought the bat forward into the swing. Cocking the hips and hands backward as the stride begins keeps the weight over the rear foot, prevents an early stride and lunge at the ball, and improves bat speed. Your hands should cock *back*. Not down. Not up. By hitching your hands either down or up, you remove them from the horizontal plane and increase your margin for error in the swing.

Your stride should be low, light, and short—between 8 to 12 inches—and in the same place every time. Practice a soft stride almost as if your front foot is testing thin ice while most of your weight remains on your rear foot. The inside of your big toe should land first to assure that you don't lunge forward too soon and waste your power and bat speed.

At this instant in the stride, you still don't know if the pitch will be inside, outside, high, low, fast, or breaking, so your hands and weight *must* remain back to explode to the ball when you make the decision to swing. It is a mistake to think or teach that you stride *into* the outside pitch, *away* from the inside pitch, and *straight* toward the pitcher on the pitch down the middle. The truth is that when a ball is traveling 85 or 90 miles per hour, you cannot delay your stride until you know whether the pitch is inside, outside, or down the middle. You must stride and cock your hips and hands *before* you discern the location of the pitch and keep your upper body and hands held back until you know.

THE SWING

When you decide to start your swing, begin by "exploding" your hands toward the ball. If you stride and cock your hands properly an instant before, your hands will have the necessary power and "snap" to accelerate the bat rapidly

A

B

C

D

forward into the strike zone with good leverage. Keep your head down, your eyes fastened on the ball, and your chin tucked on your front shoulder as the swing begins. Your front arm straightens and your rear elbow remains bent and close to your body to provide a tight, powerful arc to the bat as it enters the strike zone. Your weight begins to transfer from your rear leg to your front leg as your hips begin exploding open, which gives a torquelike power to your hands and bat. Your rear foot pivots on its ball to allow the hips more freedom as they open.

Now the bat is literally whipping through the strike zone and into the ball. Again, it should be moving in a slight downward arc so that it hits the ball on the top half and produces a hard ground ball or line drive. As the bat drives through the strike zone, your weight further transfers over your braced front leg, your rear foot continues pivoting up on its ball, and the hips continue to open. Your arms should extend and eyes look down at the V formed by the arms and hands at the point of contact. Note that a batter's head remains virtually in the same position throughout the stance, stride, and swing. This means the hips, shoulders, arms, hands, and bat have all rotated around a vertical axis, thus increasing balance and bat control, and also generating more power. An equation applies here: A still head equals a quick bat.

THE FOLLOW-THROUGH

After you hit the ball, your wrists break and roll over, which allows the bat to complete its swing and wind up over the front shoulder. Your chin is now tucked on your rear shoulder while your eyes are still on the point of contact. Your hips and shoulders have rotated explosively around the vertical axis of the body, and your rear foot is fully pivoted up on the ball of the foot. You should have neither lifted up nor dragged your rear foot during the swing.

E

As the hitter focuses on the pitch from a comfortable stance, he makes a split-second decision during his stride to swing at the ball (A). By cocking his hands and hips as he strides, he sets his power and strength over the rear leg (B). The swing itself moves in a slight downward arc, the hips rotate open, and the hitter's weight begins transferring to the front leg (C). When bat meets ball, his eyes are still on the ball, his arms are extended, and his bat is moving at maximum speed (D). After contact, the hitter's wrists "roll over" and he follows through (E).

HITTING THE BALL WHERE IT IS PITCHED

I mentioned earlier how nearly impossible it is to stride differently for pitches inside and outside, because a hitter has so little reaction time—less than half a second. And yet the good hitter does try to hit the outside pitch to the opposite field, the pitch down the middle to center field, and to pull the inside pitch. Mike Schmidt of the Phillies concedes that he became a much better hitter when he began "going with the pitch"—that is, hitting the ball where it was pitched.

Good hip and hand action will permit you to go with the pitch. Far too many hitters try to pull everything, and thus become easy outs when the pitcher can keep the ball away from them. On an inside strike, try to pull the ball toward left field if you're a right-handed batter, toward right field if you're a lefty, and get the bat out in front of the plate for contact. To do this, you must rotate your hips extremely fast in an arc of about 110 degrees from start to finish of your swing, and bring your hands around quickly so that the bat can contact the ball in front of the plate. After the swing, if you are a right-handed hitter, your belt buckle should be pointed toward left field.

When the pitch is over the middle of the plate, delay the movement of your hips slightly before beginning your swing, then rotate them about 90 degrees through the swing. The bat contacts the ball over the front edge of the plate and your belt buckle points toward center field at the conclusion of the swing. Your hips still "explode" open, but not as soon or as far as on the inside pitch.

For a pitch over the outside corner of the plate, take the same stride as always but keep your hips and hands back even longer than before and explode the hips open only about 75 degrees, making contact with the ball over the back edge of the plate. After the swing, your belt buckle should be pointing toward the opposite field.

All-star third baseman Mike Schmidt combines power with a high batting average.

The key to hitting the ball where it is pitched is keeping your weight back until you see where the pitch will be. Quick hips and quick hands can then handle any pitch.

The same key applies in hitting the curve ball or the off-speed pitch. The longer you can wait before committing your hips and hands forward, the more clearly you can read the pitch and adjust your swing.

COMMON HITTING FAULTS AND CURES

Having seen literally thousands of young hitters in twenty years of playing and sixteen years of coaching baseball, I count three common mistakes that hitters make over and over again. Of course, there are other faults as well, but those are usually the result of one or several of these basic faults.

Collapsing the Rear Side

In this case, your back shoulder dips downward as the swing begins, which throws your front shoulder up and away, carries your head up, and causes your eyes to lose focus on the ball. Your rear elbow drops, dragging the hitting surface of the bat down into a sweeping push through the strike zone. When these things occur in sequence, the result is a weak uppercut swing with little or no eye contact on the ball during its last 20 feet to the plate.

Cure: Keep your rear elbow higher in the stance and point your front shoulder at the pitch as long as possible before beginning your swing. These adjustments will keep your shoulders level and your eyes on the ball throughout the swing and help create the early stages of a proper swing.

A common hitting fault among young hitters is dropping the rear shoulder as the swing begins.

Poor Hip Pivot

If you complete your swing with your hips locked and stiff, instead of the hips exploding open anywhere from 75 to 110 degrees, they will have opened barely 50 degrees. This means that any power and bat speed must be generated by your arms and upper body, and few hitters have arms strong enough to compensate for the loss of power that quick hips provide. When the hips pivot poorly, the bat speed diminishes and your swing is consistently weak and late.

Cure: The hips cannot be activated in the swing until the rear foot pivots up on the ball of the foot. This action turns the rear knee toward the pitcher and frees the muscles in the upper legs and stomach area to pull the hips around and provide the necessary rotary power to the entire body. The hip drill explained later in this chapter can help overcome this fundamental hitting fault.

Overstriding and Lunging

A multitude of hitting problems follow when you overstride and transfer your weight to the front foot too soon. Whereas most good hitters control their stride by limiting it to approximately 8 to 12 inches, the overstrider strides up to 24 inches, forcing him to bring his hands forward early, drag his rear foot forward, and move his head forward, causing him to lose eye focus on the ball. Instead of conserving his power by cocking his hips and hands as the good hitter does, the overstrider has dissipated his power, neutralized his hip action, and has only his arms left to push the bat at the ball. Instead of the "rubber band principle"

A poor hip pivot (left) is perhaps the most widespread hitting fault, while overstriding (right) leads to lunging, which in turn leads to an overall breakdown of good hitting fundamentals.

that produces a stride in unison with cocking the hands and hips (see pp. 29–30), the overstrider seems to have an imaginary iron chain shackling his front ankle to his front wrist.

Cure: If you overstride, or lunge, you must learn to keep your weight on your rear foot longer. Turning your body inward will help, along with widening your stance. In batting practice, put an object such as a bat or glove no more than 12 inches in front of your front foot to limit the length of your stride. Keeping your head still throughout the entire swing will help keep your weight back longer. And finally, hitting flat-footed in batting practice will help convince you of the need to keep your weight over the rear foot.

HITTING DRILLS

It is one thing to talk or read about hitting techniques, quite another thing to put these fundamentals and principles into actual practice. At the University of Arizona, we believe in isolating certain parts of hitting, concentrating fully on one component until we are certain the hitter understands and shows progress before moving on to the next component and doing the same.

The following drills isolate certain key parts of hitting and allow full concentration on that specific technique for as long as the coach chooses. If you practice these drills in sequence, you will see the parts emerge and join into the total act of hitting.

The Stance and Inward-Turn Drill

All the hitters stand in front of the coach as if he were the pitcher, each hitter with a bat held against his back through the crook of each elbow. Each hitter assumes his stance, which gives the coach the opportunity to check the placement of feet, knees, hips, shoulders, head, and eyes. Then the coach winds up and "delivers," without, of course, throwing the ball. As the coach/pitcher in the windup or stretch begins reaching back with his pitching arm, he shouts, "Inward turn!" and the hitters turn their front shoulders and front hips inward toward the plate about 2 inches. No other part of the hitters' bodies should move, particularly the head. This slight, almost imperceptible movement gives the hitter the feeling of transferring his weight slightly back into a "cocking" position and prevents him from striding too soon. Do this drill twenty or twenty-five times before proceeding to the next drill.

The Stride Drill

This follows naturally from the first drill and presents the second component of hitting. Again, with the hitters holding bats behind their backs, the coach/pitcher goes through the windup or stretch. As the coach reaches back with his pitching hand, he shouts, "Inward turn!" and then continues the delivery. As the pitching hand comes down and across the body just after the ball *would have been released,* the coach shouts, "Stride!" At that command, the hitters take a low, quick, soft stride 8 to 12 inches forward and *simultaneously* cock back their front hips and front shoulders. They stride as if testing thin ice and cock their hips and shoulders to keep their weight back. Their heads remain still and their eyes focused intently on the imaginary ball after it has left the coach/pitcher's hand. This stride drill gives the hitters the distinct feeling of controlling and limiting their stride while keeping the upper body back and conserving all their power until they begin their actual swing. Repeat this drill twenty to twenty-five times, taking care that the hitters time their stride a split second after the imaginary ball has left the pitcher's hand.

The Hip Drill

To begin with, the hitters stand in the same position with their bats behind them and then place their front feet out to what they consider to be their best stride

The Stance and Inward-Turn Drill. The hitter's weight remains approximately 60 percent over the rear leg.

The Stride Drill. The stride should measure between 8 and 12 inches. The hitter's weight remains 60 percent over the rear leg.

The Hip Drill. Explosive hip movement occurs by pivoting on the ball of the rear foot.

—8 to 12 inches. Without moving their feet, and on their own time, they then whip their hips open ten or twelve times, *making sure* they pivot well up on the ball of the rear foot. This isolates and emphasizes the importance of the hips in the swing.

Next, they assume their stances, each with a bat still held behind his back, and the coach/pitcher begins his windup or stretch. The command "Inward turn" can be shortened to "Turn!" then "Stride!" at the appropriate moments, followed an instant later by a shout of "Hips!" Now the hips whip open as the rear foot pivots up on the ball of that foot. The players' heads should remain in essentially the same place throughout this three-part drill to give them the feeling of not overstriding or lunging.

Repeat the drill twenty times, and then add imaginary pitches to different locations over the plate. Instead of "Turn," "Stride," and "Hips," the coach/ pitcher shouts "Inside," "Middle," or "Outside!" If the command is "Inside," the hitters explode their hips all the way so their belt buckles finish the swing pointing toward left field if they're right-handed hitters, right field if they're lefties. Their hips thus have "pulled" that imaginary inside pitch. If the command is "Middle," the hitters whip their hips only 90 degrees so their belt buckles point toward center field. If the command is "Outside," the hitters delay the action of their hips an instant, then whip them through about a 75-degree arc, after which their belt buckles point toward the opposite field.

In the mass bat-swing drill, stance, stride, swing, and follow-through all come together.

The Mass Bat-Swing Drill

Here's where the hitters put it all together. After each removes his bat from behind his back, the hitters assume their regular stances, spaced a safe distance apart from each other and facing the coach/pitcher. By now, the proper inward turn, stride, and hip movement are all firmly fixed in their minds, and the timing of each with the pitcher's delivery is familiar. In this drill, as the coach/pitcher releases the imaginary pitch, he shouts one of six commands: "Low and inside," "High and inside," "Down the middle," "Low and outside," "High and outside," or "Ball!" On any of the first five commands, the hitters incorporate the inward turn, stride, hip movement, and slight downward arc to their swing into that area of the strike zone. On the command "Ball," they stride and simultaneously cock their hips and hands, but hold their swings, keeping the hands and weight back.

Throughout these sequential drills, the coach can check the hitters on the important components of good hitting. I suggest that these drills be done every day during the first week of practice with all players. Each player then has a solid foundation upon which he can build as the season progresses.

OTHER DRILLS

It isn't easy to organize an effective batting-practice session and use the available time wisely. Many teams have limited facilities and equipment, which imposes further restrictions. Still, there is no excuse for having only one player hitting at home plate while everyone else stands around idly. The following drills all have great value and can be executed on other parts of the field while the regular batting practice is being conducted at home plate. I am very much

The soft-toss drill is useful for frequent repetitions under close supervision.

an advocate of *station drills* that can keep everyone usefully busy during a baseball practice. The enterprising coach can take these drills and fit them into his practice plan so that all hitters have equal and sufficient time at each station to work on hitting technique.

The Soft-Toss Drill

A teammate kneels about 12 feet from the hitter and at a 45-degree angle away from the direction of the swing. The hitter stands about 12 feet from a screen or barrier into which he will hit the ball. The partner tosses the ball softly underhanded into the hitter's strike zone for the full swing. The hitter drives the ball straight ahead into the screen. The virtue of this drill is that the tosser can direct "pitches" very accurately and provide many repetitions in a short time. All parts of good hitting form can be practiced in this drill, particularly the slight down-arc swing.

The One-Knee Drill

This drill isolates good hand use in the swing, and is excellent proof of the need for a strong top hand in order to whip the bat through the strike zone rather than sweep it. The hitter stands about 12 feet away from a screen or backstop and kneels on his rear knee with his front leg bent at approximately a 90-degree angle. A teammate takes a position about 12 feet in front and to the side of the hitter and tosses balls underhanded into the hitter's reduced strike zone. The proper grip, strong top hand, down-arc swing, and quick hands are important in this drill, and the inward turn and hand-cocking as the teammate tosses the ball should also be incorporated. The hitter will tire rather quickly in this drill, so I suggest no more than ten or twelve swings before changing places with the teammate.

In the one-knee drill, the player develops strength in his hands and forearms and also learns to swing with a slight downward arc.

The short-toss drill simulates a pitch from the same angle as game conditions.

Hitting from tees—a historic drill that still pays dividends.

The Short-Toss Drill

Perhaps the single most useful hitting drill I know is what we at Arizona call "short toss." It can be done inside a batting cage or up against a wide and high backstop or net. The hitter takes his position about 15 feet in front of his teammate or coach, who is seated or crouched behind a protective screen through which he can see, but which *must* be strong enough to prevent the batted ball from coming through. With a supply of old or taped balls, the teammate or coach flips a ball over the top of the protective screen with a three-quarter overhand motion into the strike zone, and the hitter drives the ball back into the screen or net. The obvious advantage of this drill is that the tossed ball is coming at the same angle as a regular pitch, and yet the coach or teammate is close enough to throw consistent strikes. The thrower must flip the ball with some velocity or the drill loses its benefit and realism. All aspects of hitting can be practiced in this drill, and many swings can be repeated in a short time.

Tees

Batting tees provide one of the oldest, yet one of the most basic and useful, drills in baseball. Generally, tees are not too expensive to purchase and there are a good many different models available in sporting-goods stores. If not, they can easily be constructed from 5-gallon pails, ready-mixed cement, metal rods, and quarter-inch rubber hose. With tees of varying heights, one hitter can get several hundred swings in a short time. By positioning his stance differently in relation to the tee, he can simulate pitches inside, outside, and down the middle, and have valuable practice time for all components of his swing.

BUNTING

The key to victory in many games is a runner advanced into scoring position via a bunt. When a manager or coach has a particularly effective pitcher on the mound that day, his offensive strategy could well revolve around the bunt game, or "short game" as it's called. Every batter on the team, whether he is the home-run slugger or the weakest hitter, must know the proper technique to execute what should be one of the easiest skills in baseball: the bunt.

Terry Francona prepares to "lay one down." Note how his top hand cradles the bat to cushion the impact of the ball.

The Grip

The top hand slides up to the halfway position on the bat, with the thumb and index finger forming a cradle within which the bat can rest. The thumb is on top and parallel to the bat, with the fingers curled underneath and pointing back toward the handle. The top hand holds the bat lightly to cushion the ball on impact; don't clutch the bat tightly or you minimize control. The bottom hand slides up the handle slightly and also assumes a light, relaxed grip. Angle the bat slightly upward at the top of the strike zone with your arms held comfortably out in front of your body and your elbows bent.

Foot and Body Position

There are two acceptable positions for the feet when preparing for the sacrifice bunt. The first and classic one is to turn the body fully facing the pitcher and bring the rear foot up parallel with the front foot. The feet should be spread more than shoulders' width apart, with the weight on the balls of the feet and knees bent for smoothness and control. This position can be quickly and easily assumed as the pitcher begins his delivery, and it provides excellent plate coverage. Its only drawback is that it does tip off the defense rather early that a bunt is being attempted.

The second method is preferred by most present-day bunters because it disguises their intention a bit longer and keeps the first and third basemen from charging quite so quickly. As the pitcher delivers, instead of moving your feet from their original position in the hitter's stance, you pivot on the balls of your feet and turn your hips and shoulders open to the pitch. By bending at the knees and hips and placing 60 percent of your weight on your left foot, you are now in a good position to control the bat and body for the sacrifice bunt. Another advantage is that this method allows for the fake-bunt-and-slash technique, which you can use when the first and third basemen are charging hard, and when advancing the runner with a bunt would be difficult. All this entails is drawing the bat back quickly from the bunting position and slashing the ball with a quick hard swing from a choked-up position achieved by bringing the hands together. Because your feet have not moved from their original hitter's stance, you can easily and quickly adapt to the fake bunt and slash.

No matter which of the two positions you assume for this sacrifice bunt, there are certain basic techniques that apply to both:

1.   This is a sacrifice bunt. You are giving yourself up to advance the more important runner on base, so you must square early enough to be in full control of the bat and your body's balance, and you must not try to run before the bunt is safely down.

2.   The best direction to bunt is down the first-base line with a runner on first base, and down the third-base line with runners on first and second.

3.   Start the bat at the top of the strike zone and lower your body for a low strike by bending your knees more than your hips. Also, by keeping the bat at the top of the strike zone, you'll sight the pitch better and avoid the temptation to bunt a high pitch, which is easy to pop up. You should not raise your bat to bunt any pitch.

4.   Do not poke or punch at the ball; wait for the pitch and tap it lightly. Make every effort to bunt the top half of the ball. Some bunters find it helpful to imagine a long spike protruding from the bat and attempt to catch the ball on the end of the spike. By tapping the bunt lightly, the bat cushions the ball's impact and the ball will be somewhat deadened as it rolls out toward the infield.

5.   Your hips, shoulders, head, and especially your eyes must be fully facing the pitch.

6.   The bat must be held over and in front of the plate for best coverage. Knowing the sacrifice bunt is on, you should take a position in the front of the batter's box to assure that the bat is in fair territory when the ball is bunted.

7.   Bunt only strikes! Not only are pitches outside the strike zone difficult to bunt, but a walk to a bunter advances the runner without sacrificing an out.

8.   Try to keep the head of the bat above the level of the handle when bunting. This will lessen the chances of a popped up bunt.

9.   The bottom hand controls the angle of the bat for bunts down the first- or third-base lines.

The Squeeze Bunt

The squeeze bunt's effectiveness depends on the element of surprise, so you must delay squaring your upper body until the pitcher releases the ball. Thereafter, the squeeze-bunt techniques are the same as those for the sacrifice—except that on the suicide squeeze, you *must* bunt the ball regardless of where the pitch is.

Base-Hit Bunts

Whenever the third baseman, first baseman, or second baseman is playing deep, you have a good chance for a base-hit bunt. The strategy is much different from the sacrifice bunt, so you must not show your intent until the pitcher releases the ball. Most base-hit bunt attempts are toward third base because of the longer throw required to retire the runner.

Technique for the Right-Handed Bunter

As the pitcher releases the ball, drop your right foot back quickly and take what I call a short "jab" step forward with your left foot. At the same time, bring the bat into position by sliding your top hand up just as you did for the sacrifice bunt. In doing so, you have good control of both the bat and your body and you are also moving toward first base when you bunt the ball. Your intention is to bunt near the third-base line so the ball will either stay barely fair for a hit, or roll foul. You must not give the pitcher a chance to field the base-hit bunt!

The key to bunting right-handed is not how fast you run but how well you place the ball down the third-base line.

The left-handed batter's base-hit bunt down the third-base line requires absolute body and bat control lest the batter leave the box too soon.

Technique for the Left-Handed Bunter

Your technique is a bit different for the base-hit bunt. As the pitcher delivers the ball, take a short jab step toward the mound with your right foot while sliding your top hand up to the middle of the bat for good control. You must hesitate until the ball is bunted before crossing the left leg over and sprinting toward first base. The mistake most left-handed bunters make is that they begin running before the ball is bunted, giving them little or no control of the bat. For both the right- and left-handed bunters, location of the bunt is more important than speed afoot. No matter how fast you can run or how quickly you can get out of the batter's box, if the bunt is popped up or rolled back to the pitcher, you will be out.

Situations

When the first baseman and second baseman are playing deep and a left-handed pitcher is on the mound, the situation invites a base-hit bunt to the right side past the pitcher. If you're a right-handed bunter, use the same footwork and timing you used for your earlier base-hit bunt toward third base, but now angle your bat toward first base, keep your hands closer together near the middle of the bat, and "push" the ball hard toward the second baseman. If this bunt gets by the pitcher, you will probably be safe.

    If you're a left-handed bunter, you, too, should use the same footwork, hand position, and timing as before, but point the bat at the pitcher and "drag," or carry, the ball hard toward the second baseman as you cross over with the left foot out of the batter's box. You must get the bunt past the pitcher, so look for an inside pitch and bunt the ball fairly hard.

The Bunting Game

The "short," or bunting, game is especially effective in a close, low-scoring game. When the infield is damp, or the infielders and pitcher slow afoot, a good bunting attack can break open a game for the offense. In recent years, the bunting game seems to have lost credibility in baseball. This is a big mistake. A hustling, alert team capable of bunting well can tip the scales from defeat to victory.

3

Baserunning

For all the distances involved—400 feet to center field; 345 feet down the lines; 127 feet, 3⅜ inches from home to second base; 90 feet from base to base; 140 feet from shortstop to first base—baseball is still a game of inches. Consider, for example, the difference between a ball or strike in a close game, a foul or fair batted ball down the line, an out or a home run at the fence. In each case, a few inches either way can decide a game, or even a season.

Still, nowhere is the game of inches more dramatically enacted than on the bases and at home plate. No single play arouses more dispute than when an umpire calls a runner safe or out—*by inches!* It would seem that if a team's base runners could increase their speed by, say, a foot —or even 6 inches—they could sway in their favor the outcome of more games. In fact, if an average team could reduce its close outs on the bases by 25 percent, it would change from a middle of-the-pack also-ran to a champion. Look at it this way: For a major-leaguer, the difference between hitting .250 and hitting .300 is a matter of one hit more every twenty times at bat. Think of the numerous times a base runner is called out by a whisker; think of the effect a greater on-base per-

47

Premier base runner Tim Raines executes an explosive crossover step on his way to stealing another base.

centage from him could have on him, his teammates, and his team. But to raise that percentage, he'll have to find a way to pick up an added 12 inches every time he runs that 90 feet. How can he do it? How can he—and you—be "safe" on the bases more often than "out"? To answer that question, let's first examine what constitutes good running form.

PROPER RUNNING FORM

It's very simple: Effective running requires good technique from every muscle in your body. A swimming coach would never tell his team, "Forget technique. Just get from one end of the pool to the other as fast as you can." Wildly thrashing your arms and legs is not going to help you win a swimming race any more than poor running form will help you stretch a double to a triple, or score from first base on a long single.

It is an unhappy fact that we cannot increase our running speed significantly after the age of 16 or 18. But remember, all we are hoping to do is pick up one extra foot in 90—and that can, with effort, be done. Furthermore, in the early developmental years of a person's body—from ages 8 to 16—even more improvement will be seen with the practice and utilization of the following techniques:

1. Run with your head up, your eyes on the target, and a "loose" chin. When you grit your teeth and tighten your jaw, that tension transfers down the cords of the neck into your shoulders and restricts necessary shoulder action. Do not bob your head up and down, or from side to side, or in any way divert the head's position from a straight line toward the target.

2. Run with your shoulders level and allow your arms to pump freely straight ahead and swinging out, down, and back from the shoulder. The arms

High leg lift, forward lean, full arm action, and a loose, relaxed upper body are the marks of good running form.

act as pistons that drive the upper body straight ahead and should form approximately a 90-degree angle at the elbow. As your arms pump rapidly ahead and back in a push-pull movement, your elbows should remain close to your sides to prevent your arms from flapping. As your arms pump forward, your hands should go no higher than the shoulders; if your hands proceed up past the shoulders, part of the momentum generated by the pistonlike pumping of the arms is dissipated upward rather than continued forward. As your arms pump backward, your hands should go no further than the hips before they begin their forward thrust. Both hands should be loosely cupped rather than tightly clenched. This prevents tension and tightness from being transferred up the arms to the shoulders and upper body. Besides not pumping higher than the shoulder, the hands should not swing past the midline of your body. All action should be directed forward, not sideways, so that the upper body doesn't zigzag. The faster and more efficiently your arms pump, the more your legs do the same.

3.   Your hips should be level throughout the running action. Keep your knees bent and lift them high—up to the level of the hips; then extend each lower leg as far as possible toward the target. By lifting your knees high, you can lengthen your stride and cover more ground. Your legs should not leap and glide, but rise, stretch, and thrust forward powerfully.

4.   You should land on the ball of your foot, and your toes should be pointing straight ahead or slightly in with each stride. The best way to place your feet is along a straight line toward the target. You can practice your foot placement by running up and down the base line. Run with your left foot on the left of the line and your right foot on the right of the line.

5.   Your body should be leaning forward about 18 to 20 degrees as you begin stretching your lead leg into its stride.

BREAKING FROM THE BATTER'S BOX

After you hit the ball, let your upper body follow through in the swing and discard the bat immediately. Congratulations. You have just become a base runner, and if you batted from the right side, your first step should be a driving push-off taken with your rear (right) foot toward first base. If you're a lefty, your first step after the swing is with your left (rear) foot. Whether left- or right-handed, batters commonly make the mistake of taking that first step toward the pitcher's mound or toward the first-base dugout, which is a distinct waste of time. Since you're running toward first base, *do so from your very first*

Whether you're a lefty or a righty, in leaving the batter's box, start with a short chopping stride with your rear leg, followed by a flurry of short strides until you reach full speed.

step! Your first several strides should be short and choppy with your body somewhat low to pick up momentum as quickly as possible. After three or four steps, you should be in full stride and going at maximum speed.

To determine whether you should run straight to the bag or swing out to your right and make the turn at first base, you must know if the ball will be fielded in the infield, so look briefly to your left once you've reached full speed. If the ball appears likely to be fielded, you must, of course, try to beat the infielder's throw, so turn your eyes back to the bag. On a close throw, often a runner's inclination is to take a long, desperate leap at the bag from 10 or 12 feet away. This is a big mistake. You'll find that you reach the bag far more quickly if you turn that long, floating leap into two quick strides across the bag, and an umpire will more likely call you safe on a tie throw. Too, you lose momentum when you launch into the air like a bird, whereas you maintain or even gain momentum with an additional stride. And if an umpire's last visual impression is of you floating through the air as the ball nears the first baseman's glove, his call will likely be "Out!"

In general, when running to first base, try to make yourself run *95* feet *through* the bag, not 90 feet *to* it. This will eliminate any tendency to slow down as you reach the bag, which, needless to say, can be fatal. Hit the front of the bag with either foot and as your next stride carries you over the bag, glance quickly over your right shoulder to see if the throw has gotten past the first baseman. If it has and the ball has rolled far enough, you know immediately, without the first-base coach telling you, and can advance to second base. If you are safe and the first baseman catches the ball, bring yourself under control quickly, return to the bag, and watch for a possible bad throw from the first baseman to the pitcher.

On close plays at first base, many young base runners will slide headlong into the bag, hoping to beat the throw. This is a mistake, not only because it's injurious but also because it's slower. Believe me, you will reach the bag faster by running through it and also give the umpire a better perspective for a favorable call.

The only time it is proper to slide into first base is to avoid a tag. As you approach first base, keep your eyes on the front edge of the bag. If you see the first baseman's foot coming off the bag to catch a high or wide throw, then slide either feet- or headfirst to avoid the first baseman's sweeping tag. Tag plays at first base happen more often than we think, but if you're an alert runner watching that first baseman's foot, you can avoid them and raise your on-base percentage another notch.

MAKING THE TURN AT FIRST BASE: THE 12-FOOT ARC

As soon as you determine that the ball is through the infield, swing out to your right approximately 12 feet into foul territory and, as you near first base, begin

On crossing first base, the smart base runner glances quickly over his right shoulder to see if the ball has gotten past the first baseman. If it has, he advances to second base.

your left turn by pushing hard off your right foot and leaning left. You can hit the inside corner of first base with either foot and use the bag to drive your body hard toward second base. The 12-foot arc is enough to give you body control without affecting your speed or causing you to stumble as you make the turn, and more important, puts you in a straight path from first to second base. Anything less than a 12-foot arc will carry you out toward right field as you make your turn, and anything more than a 12-foot arc is wasted time and effort. Ideally, you should hit first base with your right foot so that your next stride with your left foot is straight toward second base. But if you can't, don't risk stumbling and losing time trying to stagger your steps. Go for the front inside corner of the bag with either foot.

As an agressive, alert runner, you can force errors in the outfield by running full-speed as you make your turn at first base and continuing toward second until the outfielder fields the ball cleanly and throws to second base. On a single to left field, for example, you can go nearly halfway to second base before breaking to a stop and retreating to first base. On a single to center field, you could worry the outfielder into a fumble or bad throw by going one-third of the way toward second base. Of course, you must be more cautious on a ball hit to right field, because a quick throw the short distance from the right fielder to the first baseman could pick you off if your turn is too long. In any case, run full-speed on a ball hit to the outfield, make the 12-foot arc across first base, and challenge the outfielder to hold you to a single. When you return to first base, retreat with your eyes on the ball and your chest facing the throw from the outfield. A bad throw to second base could allow you to advance.

Swinging out into a 12-foot arc on a base hit puts you on a straight course toward second base.

THE LEAD AT FIRST BASE

The Primary Lead

The primary lead is the first lead taken while the pitcher still has the ball. It can vary in length from 5 feet against a left-handed pitcher with an extremely good pick-off move, to 15 feet against a right-handed pitcher. The secondary lead is the extension of the primary lead as the pitcher delivers the ball to home plate.

Before you begin your primary lead, you should stand with your left foot on first base and your right foot forward and toward second. Then check the following three things:

1. *The ball.* Where is it? Do not begin your lead until you are certain the pitcher, not the first baseman, has the ball.

2. *The coach.* Is there a sign? What is the play?

3. *The defense.* Where are they playing? Will a line drive in the hole get through or is the shortstop playing this hitter to pull? Are the outfielders deep or shallow? How many outs?

With these checkpoints satisfied, you now take a "quick and early" primary lead—that is, you want to establish your 15-foot lead and be set before the pitcher concludes his stretch. If the pitcher sees you already at your maximum lead when he comes to his set position, you are a threat and must be watched carefully. But if you are only beginning your lead as the pitcher comes to his set position, he has no worry and can concentrate fully on the hitter. Additionally, if you can take your lead while the pitcher is peering in for the catcher's sign, there is less chance of the pitcher making a quick pick-off move.

With a right-handed pitcher on the mound, *strive* for a 15-foot primary lead. This will place you 3 to 5 feet closer to second base than most leads we see in baseball games these days, and that extra distance is the difference between being safe and out most of the time! As your first move, take what is known as a quick *drop step* toward second base with your left foot. Keep your knees comfortably bent and your weight forward on the balls of your feet. Following that, take a fairly long *lead step* with your right foot toward second base, but still keep your weight over your *left* leg. That way, if the pitcher tries to pick you off now, you can easily shift your weight back toward first base for your return. If there's no pick-off attempt, though, your next move is to shuffle your left foot quickly up to your right foot and then lead out quickly again with your right foot.

E D   C

When establishing a 15-foot lead at first base, first take a drop-back step with your left foot (B), and thereafter, keeping your weight primarily over

In all, the choreography for the primary lead is as follows: Drop back left; right foot lead; left foot shuffle; right foot lead; left foot shuffle; right foot lead; left foot shuffle. Perform these steps in a continuous, fluid movement with no pause. Keep your knees bent, your weight on the balls of your feet, your head up, and more weight on your left leg than on your right. You are most vulnerable to the pick-off when your feet are together, so minimize the time for the left-foot shuffle. After the initial drop step left, those three right-foot leads and left-foot shuffles will take you to a point where your right foot is 15 feet from first base.

A 15-foot primary lead against a right-handed pitcher is a threat to the defense, but it is also somewhat risky because getting back to first base safely on a pick-off attempt is no simple matter. As a runner, always try to maintain good balance and control so you can react either to the right (for a steal) or to the left (on a pick-off attempt). Keep your feet spread slightly more than a shoulders' width apart, your knees always flexed, your back straight, and your head up. Your right foot should be dropped back slightly and opened up toward second base to facilitate the crossover step toward second on a steal attempt. Let your arms hang loosely from your shoulders and in front of your body. If you are *not* stealing on the next pitch, 60 percent of your weight is over your left foot to help you quickly make the crossover step back toward the bag on a pick-off. If you *are* stealing on the pitch, 60 percent of your weight should be over your right foot. In either case, you must disguise your weight distribution and not lean in either direction and tip the pitcher off.

When a pick-off attempt occurs, you must not run but *dive* back to first

B A

your left foot, lead out with your right and shuffle with your left
three times (C), (D), (E).

base from that long a lead. To dive properly, first throw your upper body
toward first base while pivoting on the ball of your left foot, then cross over
with your right foot and dive back to the base, reaching for the *outfield corner
of the bag* with your right hand. From a shorter lead (10 or 12 feet), you can
step back to the bag with a crossover right and long stride left to the bag's
outfield corner, but a pick-off attempt on a 15-foot primary lead almost always
demands that you take a crossover step with your right foot and dive back.

The Secondary Lead

Most of the time, of course, when the pitcher delivers to the plate, you are not
stealing or breaking on the hit-and-run. The secondary lead at this point is
important to mobilize your body and move you closer toward second base so
that you can advance on a batted ball, wild pitch, or passed ball. But you must
also be able to return to first base safely after the secondary lead in the event
of a line drive to the infield or a pick-off attempt by the catcher.

Once you are certain the pitcher is delivering to the plate, switch your
attention from the pitcher to the strike zone at home plate and simultaneously
take several long shuffle steps toward second base while still pointing your chest
toward home and still crouched. As the pitch enters the strike zone, you should
be completing your second or third shuffle and your weight should be on your
right foot. At that instant, you must read what is happening at the plate and
react immediately. If the ball is hit on the ground, you cross over with your
left foot and break for second base. If the hit is a line drive with fewer than

two outs, freeze to see if it will be caught. On a fly ball, advance cautiously to see if the ball will be caught and, if so, retreat to first base. On a wild pitch or passed ball, take that same crossover step and advance to second base. If the batter takes the pitch or swings and misses, take a crossover step with your right foot and hustle back to first. Of course, on two outs, advance on *any* batted ball.

An aggressive, yet controlled, secondary lead will help you pick up several feet and improve your ability to beat a force play at second base, break up a double play, or advance to third base or home on a base hit.

STEALING SECOND BASE

As a base runner, you should always study the pitcher's mannerisms intently in hopes of picking up some telltale sign that he intends to pitch home. Some common giveaway points are the pitcher's heel, his lead shoulder, his knee, his head, his elbow, or his hands when resting in the set position. After assuming your primary lead, watch for that tip-off that tells you the pitcher is committed to deliver to the plate.

Most base runners use the crossover step as their first move toward second base in the steal attempt. If you do, throw your upper body vigorously toward second base, reach out with your left arm, and pivot on the ball of your right foot while pushing off hard toward second base with your left foot. Several things are important in this first explosive move:

After you establish your lead, your base-stealing position places 60 percent of your weight over your right foot. When you are certain the pitcher is delivering the pitch home, throw your upper body toward second base as you pivot on your right foot and push off hard with your left (B). Next, make your first stride a crossover step with your left leg and tilt your body

F E   **D**

1. Stay somewhat low during your first stride.

2. Step first with your left foot directly toward second base, not toward the mound or shortstop.

3. Your arms should instantly begin powering your body in coordination with your legs.

Make your first several strides toward second base short, driving, choppy ones until you attain full speed. After two or three strides, look at the plate to see what is happening to the pitch. Our rule at Arizona is "Two steps and LOOK!" Turning your head slightly will tell you whether you should (1) continue, (2) stop (on a pop fly), (3) break up a double play (on a ground ball), (4) go on to third base (on a base hit), or (5) round second base (on a passed ball or wild pitch). I am distressed by how many runners are tricked into double plays or held somewhere between bases because they do not know where the ball is, particularly since turning the head after the second stride and reading the ball off the bat is such a simple matter. An important rally was cut short and the game lost in a recent American League divisional playoff because the stealing runner was tricked into sliding into second base while the third baseman caught a pop fly and doubled that runner off first base.

There will be times when you break prematurely for second base while the pitcher is picking you off. The best option then is to go full-speed toward second base and try to either beat the first baseman's throw or force a bad throw. Such situations generally occur when a left-handed pitcher is on the mound and has a deceptive move to first base.

forward to a 40-degree angle (C). Your first several strides should be short, powerful, and choppy until you gain full speed; then your strides lengthen (D) and (E). After two or three strides, check the ball's location by glancing toward home plate (F).

C B   A

Record-setting base stealer Rickey Henderson achieves full speed shortly after his powerful crossover step.

On a hit-and-run, your role as runner at first base is very simple: *You must absolutely not get picked off.* Be certain the pitcher has delivered to the plate before breaking for second base, then take two steps and look toward the plate. Obviously, your coach has decided that you're more likely to advance using the hit-and-run than the straight steal, so don't ruin the strategy by carelessness.

GOING FROM FIRST BASE TO THIRD BASE

The best time to advance from first base to third base is with one out. Do not take chances when there is nobody out (a big inning may be in store), or with two outs (at second base, you are still in scoring position). But with one out and your team ahead, tied, or one run down, the risk is good because if you reach third, you can score on an error, ground ball, fly ball, squeeze play, wild pitch, or passed ball. Also the infield must play in, which increases the batter's chances of hitting past them safely.

As you break for second base on a batted ball and see the ball go through the infield, immediately swing out to your right and make a 12-foot arc into second base. If the ball is within your view in left field or left center, make up your own mind whether or not to keep going to third base. If you go, the 12-foot arc will permit you to hit the inside corner of second in stride with either foot and point you in a straight line toward third base. If, however, the ball is hit to center field or right field and out of your view, look for the third-base coach's sign. Take your first look about 25 feet from second base, then focus on the bag, and as your foot hits it, take your second look at the third-base coach.

Advancing from first to third base is not so much a function of your speed as it is a function of your secondary lead, your 12-foot arc and turn at second base, your accurate reading of the batted ball's flight, and your third-base coach's signs.

LEADS AT SECOND BASE

Once you reach second base, you have advanced into scoring position and now must be careful to assure every opportunity of reaching home. You embarrass yourself and, worse, kill the rally if you let yourself get picked off at second base.

With fewer than two outs, take your lead off second base in a straight line toward third. Your primary lead can normally be up to 20 feet without danger, because the shortstop and second baseman won't be holding you tight at the bag. Your stance in the primary lead is similar to the one you assumed at first base. Watch the pitcher and, out of the corner of your left eye, watch the second baseman lest he break for a pick-off attempt. Your third-base coach is responsible for alerting you back to second base if the shortstop breaks behind you to the bag for a pick-off. If neither middle infielder decides to hold you, your third-base coach can then talk you into a longer primary lead, perhaps up to 30 feet, and the choreography would be the same as at first base: right foot lead; left foot shuffle; right foot lead; left foot shuffle.

When the pitcher delivers to the plate, take your secondary lead by shuffling several times toward third base with your chest pointing toward home and your eyes focused intently on the strike zone. As the pitch enters the strike zone, you should be completing your second shuffle with your weight on the right foot.

With fewer than two outs, do not try to advance on a routine or hard-hit ground ball to your right, since either the shortstop could field it and make the throw to third to retire you, or the third baseman could field it and tag you before you reach third base or catch you in a rundown. All of these are "sucker plays," and such unwise baserunning can kill the inning for your team at bat. How to avoid the sucker play? Quite simple. As you complete your secondary lead and the ball is hit, you should be able to read the direction of the batted ball because you are facing the plate. If the ground ball is hit at you or to your left, *except to the pitcher,* you advance to third base. If the ground ball is hit hard or routinely to your right, hold and retreat to second base with your chest pointing toward the play. Of course, if that ground ball to your right gets through the infield, advance to third base. Too, if a ground ball hit to your right is a high chopper or slow roller, you can gauge that and advance safely. Concentrate, apply the ground-ball-location rule, and you should always be able to decide when to advance to third base with fewer than two outs.

STEALING THIRD BASE

The best time to steal third base is with one out and your team ahead, tied, or one run behind. The great base stealers—Maury Wills, Lou Brock, Rickey Henderson, Tim Raines, Lonnie Smith, Willie Wilson—all feel that stealing third base is generally easier than stealing second, because the pitcher, middle infielders, and third baseman are more concerned with the batter than the runner, thus permitting a much longer lead. The two important musts for stealing third base are: You *must* have a good lead and you *must* have a good jump. Having only one of the two is not enough. By increasing your primary lead from 18 or 20 feet to 25 or 28 feet and keeping your body moving toward third base as the pitcher commits his delivery to the plate, you guarantee a quicker jump and a shorter run for the steal.

THE TWO-OUT LEAD AT SECOND BASE

In the chapter on offensive strategy, I discuss the percentages when a team is attempting to score base runners from second base. With two outs, you generally have less than a 30-percent chance of scoring from second base on a base hit, which leads to the conclusion that your third-base coach should send you home on virtually any ball that gets into the outfield. This strategy works providing your team is ahead, tied, or one run behind.

With two outs, in order to give yourself at second base the best possible jump on a batted ball, begin your lead 15 feet toward third base *and* 12 feet back from the bag. There is little danger that you will be picked off, because

Two types of leads at second base. The less-than-two-out lead provides the best way to advance to third base, while the two-out lead provides the fastest way to score.

12-Foot 2-Out Lead

15-Foot Less Than 2-Out Lead

you can get back easily from this rather short distance. As the pitcher delivers, begin a jogging lead toward the third-base line with your chest toward third base and your head and eyes turned toward home plate. As the pitch enters the strike zone, you will be 20 to 25 feet toward third base *and* your momentum will be well under way in that direction. If the batter swings and hits the ball in any way—a ground ball, fly ball, line drive, or foul ball—you instantly shift into high gear and head for third base. Your 12-foot arc is already established so your turn at third base should be tight and fast, and your trip home full-speed and straight down the line. You'll find that you score much faster taking the two-out lead than the normal one where you can't swing out into a 12-foot arc until after the ball is hit and you begin advancing. But, caution! Taking a two-out lead, if the pitch is not hit, you must slam to a stop and hustle back to second base to avoid a catcher pick-off. Because you are actually jogging during your secondary lead, your distance from second base and your body's position (facing third) make you quite vulnerable.

THE BASE RUNNER AT THIRD BASE

You have reached third base and now are only 90 feet from completing your long journey around the diamond. No matter how you got there, you can probably thank the contributions, perhaps even the sacrifices, of one or two of your teammates. There are a number of ways for you to score now, and if your team is wise, it is ready to use them all.

Your first concern at third base is not to do anything foolish to negate all the work it took to get you there. *Never get picked off at third base!* The opposition's pitcher, catcher, and third baseman are not dummies, and if you're a sleeping base runner, you could suffer great embarrassment and your team a significant setback if you get picked off.

A lead at third base has several rules.

First rule: *Your primary lead should be only as far toward home plate as the third baseman is from the bag.* If the third baseman is only 3 feet from third, that is the extent of your primary lead. If he is 12 feet off the bag when the pitcher comes to his set or begins his windup, you can be 12 feet down the line. The same with each increment, up to a limit of 20 feet.

Second Rule: *Always take your primary and secondary leads in foul territory.* If a batted ball hits you while you are on the base line or in fair territory, you are automatically out; whereas if you are in foul territory when the batted ball strikes you, there is no penalty.

At third base, take your lead in foul territory, return to the bag in fair territory.

Third rule: *If you lead off the bag in foul territory, come back to the bag in fair territory.* Once the pitch hits the catcher's mitt, jam your right foot in the ground to stop your secondary lead, then turn and retreat to third base in fair territory in the event of a catcher pick-off. By retreating in fair ground, you obscure the catcher's view toward the bag, and if the catcher throws to the third baseman, the ball may hit you and allow you to score.

The Primary Lead at Third Base

Once you've established your primary lead in foul ground equidistant from the bag with the third baseman, your position should essentially be the same as when you took your lead at first base—that is, facing the pitcher, your feet spread more than a shoulders' width apart, your weight on the balls of your feet, etc. (see pp. 53–55). From this position, you can get back to the bag if there is a pitcher pick-off attempt, or you can begin your secondary lead once you are certain the pitcher is delivering the pitch.

The Secondary Lead

When making a secondary lead off third base, point your chest toward the mound, keep your eyes turned toward home plate, and step first toward the plate with your left foot, following it with a series of shuffle steps. As you begin your shuffles, it is important that you fix your eyes intently on the strike zone, where, of course, the ball will come in contact with the bat. Time your shuffles so that as the pitch enters the strike zone, most of your weight is on your right foot and you can react instantly to what may happen at the plate. Taking this type of aggressive, yet controlled, lead, you can also practice the "down angle" concept of scoring on a ground ball, wherein with one out and your team ahead, tied, or one run down, you can score on most ground balls even with the infield playing in to cut that run off at the plate. Here's how it works.

Let's say the pitcher is delivering from the set position, and the third baseman is allowing you a 15-foot primary lead. When the ball is pitched, and the batter swings, and the ball leaves the bat at a downward angle, your secondary lead will have carried you 25 to 28 feet down the line from third base, or slightly more than 60 feet from home plate. At that instant, if your weight is primarily on your right foot and you see the ball go "down angle," you can break home immediately using a crossover left stride and beat most infielders' throws home. Of course, if the ground ball is hit to the pitcher or hit hard at an infielder playing shallow, you will likely be out. But most ground balls are hit to an infielder's right or left and many are slowly hit, and this majority of ground balls will allow you to score, so long as you read the "down angle" immediately.

Now, from your proper secondary lead with fewer than two outs, if you read "line drive" off the bat, freeze and hustle back to third base if the line drive is caught. If you read "up angle" off the bat, meaning fly ball, immediately retreat to third base and tag up for the possible score after the catch.

Tagging Up at Third Base

As soon as a fly ball or pop fly leaves the infield, you should be back on third base, ready to score when the ball is caught. Never start prematurely toward home on the assumption that the ball will fall in safely. The outfielder may make a great running or diving catch and you will be forced to return to third base and probably won't score. Better for you to assume every fly ball or line drive will be caught, and return to the bag. If the ball does fall in safely, you score easily; and if it is caught, you have tagged up and can still score.

To tag up properly, plant your left foot on the bag, point your right foot toward home, your body nearly toward home, but turn your eyes, head, and chest toward the play, and lean in a modified sprinter's crouch. On a deep fly ball, wait until the ball is definitely in the outfielder's glove before pushing off hard with your left foot and sprinting home. If the play will be close at home plate, you should start your push off the bag when the ball is approximately 3 feet above the outfielder's glove. By the time your foot actually leaves the bag, the ball will be contacting the outfielder's glove.

When tagging up at third base, use the bag as a sprinter does a starting block: to drive your body forward. But beware leaving the bag before the catch!

With fewer than two outs, you should tag up on all medium-to-deep fly balls, even if they're foul. Do not depend on the third-base coach to tell you when to leave the bag. Make that decision yourself as you watch the fielder catch the fly ball.

Scoring on the Squeeze Play

As a runner at third base, you must not tip off the suicide-squeeze bunt by breaking home too early. Take your normal primary and secondary leads, but don't break full-speed for home until the pitcher's stride foot comes down in the delivery. By then, it is too late for the pitcher to change his pitch to prevent the batter from bunting the ball.

In this suicide-squeeze attempt, the runner on third is careful not to tip off the play by leaving too early. He takes his normal secondary lead, then breaks for home when the pitcher's stride foot hits the ground.

Stealing Home

The best time to steal home plate is with two outs; a left-handed pitcher on the mound, who, in the middle of his windup, will be turning his back on you at third base; and a right-handed hitter at the plate. It is possible, of course, to steal home with a right-handed pitcher on the mound, but he also must be delivering from the windup. Stealing home with the pitcher in the stretch is virtually impossible because he can stop you from getting a big enough primary lead by stepping off the pitcher's rubber.

I'll admit we did win a key game in our 1980 NCAA championship drive when our runner on third base missed a sign and attempted to steal home with a right-handed pitcher in the set position and looking right at him. Our runner made it home safely when the thunderstruck pitcher threw a wild pitch. However, the best technique for stealing home is to increase your primary lead by edging down the line as far as possible before the pitcher begins his windup. You should be at least 28 feet down the line and moving if you intend to steal home on that pitch. When the pitcher raises his hands to begin his windup, break full-speed for home. The batter should stay in his stance—perhaps even fake a bunt—until you begin your slide and then leap back out of the way.

Stealing home is a risky, last-ditch attempt to score the run. Two outs, a weak hitter, a fast base runner, a left-handed pitcher, late innings, a tied game —these are the circumstances in which stealing home may be a team's best strategy.

GENERAL REMINDERS FOR THE BASE RUNNER

1. There is no such thing as an automatic out. Go full-speed in every situation.

2. Watch the runner ahead of you. Don't run with your head down.

3. The on-deck hitter alone is responsible for signaling the scoring base runner. Give both verbal and visual signs to him to slide or to score standing up.

4. Never get tagged out easily in the base lines. Always force a rundown.

5. When you are about to be tagged out in a rundown, drop low and try to scramble under the tag.

6. When you are on third base and a wild pitch occurs with nobody out, you must be 100-percent sure you can score; with one out, 75-percent sure; with two outs, 30-percent sure.

7.   Always run full-speed from home to first base. The way you cover that 90 feet tells how badly you want to win!

8.   If there is an outfield throw on a runner ahead of you, read the height of the throw as soon as you can, and if it misses the cutoff man, go on to second base.

9.   Always touch first base. Sometimes the first baseman will drop the throw.

10.   When you are on first base and are the lead man in a double steal with two outs, never get tagged out at second base before your teammate at third has a chance to score. Stop and get in a rundown if necessary. With fewer than two outs, go all the way and try to steal the bag.

11.   You are the runner on second base with nobody out. Tag up on any catch in the outfield, questionable or certain, if it is deep enough to allow you to advance after the catch. With one out, tag up on the certain catch, but move halfway toward third base on the questionable catch.

12.   When you are on base and being bunted over, look to see that the ball takes a "down angle" off the bat, and break when you are sure the ball is on the ground. Do not get picked off by either the pitcher or the catcher.

SLIDING

Sliding is not as natural an action as running or throwing, and requires, first, technique and, second, diligent practice. Many players never become good sliders for fear of injury; whenever they are forced to slide, they become tentative, which, of course, is exactly when injuries and "strawberries" (abrasions of the knee or hip) occur. When a slider holds back or interrupts the correct sliding technique, parts of the body become tense and restricted, and instead of a smooth slide, well . . . the body moves something like a bicycle over train tracks.

Tim Raines completes a steal of second base with a perfect figure-4 slide.

Correct sliding is really controlled falling. Don't leap, broad-jump, or tumble into a slide. Don't even slow down preparing for one. Instead, keep your body as close to the ground as possible as you lean, and begin falling backward first onto the outer surface of your knee and lower leg; next, the outer surface of your thigh and hip; and finally, your back. As you begin your controlled fall backward, the speed that you have attained while running will slide you the rest of the way across the ground.

The "Figure-4 Slide"

The most basic, most effective, and easiest slide to learn is the figure-4 slide, often called the "bent-leg slide." It is also the safest and requires a minimum of technique. You must first decide from which leg you will launch your slide; that leg becomes the "tuck leg" (the one on which you actually slide). It doesn't

Which is your strong side for sliding? This simple drill will tell you, since we all instinctively tuck one or the other leg upon falling.

matter which leg you use; either is acceptable, and a useful drill will determine which leg is most natural for you. Sit on the ground with your legs extended and your arms stretched out behind you to support your upper body as you lean back. Then raise yourself up on your hands and feet and fall backward while tucking one leg underneath the other. Every slider naturally tucks one or the other leg, and that becomes his strong side. This method also reminds us that sliding itself should be no more painful than falling backward in this simple drill. Repeat this drill a number of times using the following techniques, which are important to the figure-4 slide:

1. Your lead leg on top should be slightly flexed at the knee and should be extended toward the base with toes up. Your lead leg makes first contact with the base.
2. Your hands should be thrown back rather than used to brace your body and slow down the momentum of the slide.
3. Your head should be held up and watching the base.
4. Your tuck leg and lead leg should together form a perfect 4.

This basic and most effective slide configuration is primarily used to beat close plays at a base, and can also be changed into a "pop-up slide," when your lead foot, hitting the base, uses it as a brace and your momentum carries you back up to your feet. Besides allowing you to get to your feet quickly and scramble to the next base when the ball gets by the infielder, the pop-up slide is helpful when the play is not close or the throw is high and you want to get to the base fast, stop, and be ready to advance.

Sliding practice can be a discouraging experience for young players until they learn the proper techniques and gain confidence. Practice sessions should never be conducted in baseball shoes where a spike could catch in the ground

Before you practice sliding, pad the vulnerable parts of your body.

and cause a twisted ankle or knee. Instead, slide in tennis shoes or stockinged feet on soft grass, or in the traditional sliding pit—an area of heavy, soft sand. At Arizona, we practice sliding on heavy cardboard placed over the outfield grass. In bad weather, we place the cardboard on a gym floor. The cardboard provides a slick, smooth surface that gives the player an actual sensation of sliding. Its one drawback is that friction wears out uniforms or sweat pants rapidly. Try wearing one or several pairs of old practice pants over your uniform, and elbow or kneepads slipped over your knees and ankles—the places where "burns" may occur. With enough heavy cardboard pieces available, you and your team can form three or four lines, place a loose base at each sliding station, and slide fifteen or twenty times in ten minutes. You should begin your run about 40 feet from the cardboard, slide under the watchful eye of the coach, and return to the line while a teammate begins his run.

Hook Slide

The hook slide away from the tag is used when the throw has barely beaten the runner and the fielder has reached to the other side of the base for the ball. The slider wants to hook the bag with his toe as his body fades away from the tag. A hook slide to the strong side (the tuck leg) is a fairly easy variation of the basic figure-4 slide. Begin your figure-4 slide 3 or 4 feet to the open side of the base away from the tag. As you approach the base, roll your upper body away from the tag and reach for the corner of the bag with your lead foot. Your

The hook slide to the strong side is a variation of the basic figure-4.

The weak-side hook slide is quicker and safer if you use your hand to touch the bag.

momentum will carry you around and away from the tag while your lead foot anchors to the bag.

I have discovered very few players capable of a hook slide to their weak side. Generally, players attempting to hook to their weak side slow down and get mixed up in their footwork, or miss the base altogether, or get injured. At Arizona, we have found it best, when an evasive slide is necessary to the weak side, to instruct the slider to stay with the basic figure-4, aim the slide 4 feet away from the side of the base where the tag will occur, and catch the bag with his hand as he slides by. The players seem to have much more confidence attempting this slide than a hook slide to their weak side.

A clever "backdoor slide" can be used when the tag is waiting ahead of you. Execute a figure-4 slide well away from the bag and reach for the bag with your hand as you would in the weak-side figure-4. When the infielder makes the mistake of reaching out to tag that hand, though, pull it away, roll over toward the bag, and slip the other hand behind the tag.

The Headfirst Slide

This slide has become more frequent and popular in recent years. Runners use it to dive back to a base on a pick-off attempt when taking a long and aggressive lead. Runners also use it when advancing to second and third base, because it is faster than any feetfirst slide in that the momentum of the runner's upper body is already forward when he slides headfirst. Additionally, it is easier to maneuver the hands to avoid a tag than it is the feet. Pete Rose has made the headfirst slide respectable, and more players, amateur and professional, are using it.

We teach the headfirst slide at Arizona for the same reasons, and because not everyone can slide well feetfirst. Also, since helmets and batting gloves have

The Headfirst Slide: quickest way by far to reach a base and avoid the tag. With practice, you can overcome the natural fear of throwing yourself headlong onto the ground.

become part of a base runner's equipment, there is no longer the danger of head or hand injuries that there once was in using this slide.

The technique is simple, and you can use either foot to launch yourself. Do not take a high leap through the air, but rather a straight, low, horizontal dive to the base. In fact, the closer you can stay to the ground, the better your slide will be. Make the dive with your palms down but your fingers up to avoid jamming them into the dirt. Your first contact with the ground should be with the heels of your hands, and almost simultaneously your chest. If these two contact points absorb the brunt of the shock, the rest of your body should not feel the hurt. Slide to the open side of the bag away from the tag and use only one hand to touch the bag. Seldom will you use the headfirst method to slide straight into the bag, but rather to avoid a close tag at either side. I do not recommend headfirst slides into home plate because of catchers' tendencies to block runners out. Nor do I recommend that it be used in a force play at second base to break up a double play.

As Pete Rose has proven, the headfirst slide is often the mark of a hustling, scrappy player, and its successful use can spark and ignite both players and fans.

BREAKING UP THE DOUBLE PLAY

At all levels below professional baseball, the rules have been tightened to help prevent injury to the defensive pivot man on the double play. No longer are blocks, rolls, slashes, reaches, and kicks permitted in the slide when breaking up a double play. These are good rules and will help do away with the serious knee and ankle injuries that all too frequently occur to the shortstop and second baseman. The rules do permit a normal slide within 3 feet of either side of the bag, and a good hard figure-4 at the pivot man's feet will often serve to disrupt his throw without hurting him. Never, though, should a slider attempt to spike or injure a defensive player.

THE ROLE OF THE BASE COACHES

Many games have been won because the first- and third-base coaches exercised intelligent and decisive judgment in either holding or sending runners. Good base coaches are essential to a winning team effort, and their contributions can be just as important as those of the players in the lineup.

If you are a third-base coach, get to know the speed and mental capacity of each of your players, as well as the defensive strengths and weaknesses of your opponents. More than merely a traffic cop, you must be a kind of human computer, able to make the right split-second decision after the appropriate information has been fed into your brain. You must know the percentages of each possible play and calculate the best decision based on the defense, the runners, the score, the batter, the inning, the outs, the field, and more. (See "Offensive Strategy," chapter 13.)

Some third-base coaches relay signs from the bench coach to the hitters and runners on their teams, and this responsibility, added to their other duties, requires coaches who are poised and quick-thinking under the pressure of game conditions.

Although runners are generally responsible for knowing when to advance, sometimes they cannot see the ball or the defense, and that's when the help of a third-base coach is vital. Let's say the ball has been hit to right or center field and you think that your base runner on first can make it all the way to third. As a base coach, you are allowed to move out of either of the coaching boxes once the ball is hit and set yourself in line with the runner's vision. In this case, you would move out toward the left-field line so the runner could clearly see your arm circling to tell him to keep coming to third base.

Your signals as a base coach must be clear and emphatic so that there is no misunderstanding of what you mean. It helps if you couple your visual signals with verbal commands. The more animated you are as a third-base coach, the less likely your players will misunderstand your signals.

When a base runner is leading off second base, he is responsible for watching the second baseman, but you as the third-base coach are responsible for warning him of the shortstop's position and any possible pick-offs between the shortstop and the pitcher. If the runner at second base is not threatened, he can increase his lead one more step with each "OK" that you shout. When the runner reaches the limit of a safe lead, you then call "Stay!" or "Right there!" and, if a pick-off attempt occurs, holler "Back!" These verbal commands should be short, clear, and loud.

You should instruct your runners to keep running and think extra base if you are not giving them a distinct visual signal. For instance, when a runner is scoring from second base, you should move down the line toward home plate as much as halfway so you can reserve your decision as long as possible before either holding the runner at third or waving him home to score. As soon as you make that decision, start shouting and waving your arms—but make your signals precise. If you want the runner to stop, throw up both arms and yell "Back!" But if you want the runner to score, windmill your left arm rapidly, point home with your right arm, and yell "Go, go!" If the runner is approaching third and the play will be close, it is best if you kneel or flop down on your stomach toward the side of the base away from the throw and scream "Slide!" while throwing your arms to that side. If the throw is not close and the runner can come into third base standing up, throw up one arm in the stop position, point to the bag with the other arm, and call "Stay!"

The third-base coaching box is not a place for a shy, timid person. Animation, alertness, and, most important, good judgment are essential for the job, and a loud voice helps so that you can constantly remind runners on second and third of the game situation.

If you're the first-base coach, although you're not as responsible as your third-base counterpart for helping the runners advance, you, too, must be alert and encouraging to the batters and base runners. It is you, with your advice and support at first base, who helps a runner's successful advance to second, third, and home. You can also help a batter/runner "Watch the bag, not the ball!" or "Hustle!" or "Round the bag!" or "Go for two!" or "Stay!" You are

At key moments, the third-base coach becomes the eyes and ears of the base runner.

responsible for helping the runner at first base find the ball before the leadoff, watching for a pitcher or catcher pick-off when the first baseman is playing behind the runner; watching the second baseman in a bunt situation; and instructing the runner at first base when to tag up on a fly ball or pop foul.

The best first-base coach I have ever seen was a seldom-used pitcher whose alert, enthusiastic contributions to the team from the first-base box helped Arizona win the 1980 NCAA championship.

As you can see, baserunning is a lot more complicated and sophisticated than it appears. But if I had to reduce the intricacies of baserunning into a formula, I would write $S + C + GJ + T\&F = R$, which, translated, means equal parts of speed plus concentration plus good judgment plus technique and fundamentals equals . . . *runs!*

Throwing

The human body contains 374 paired muscles, and throwing, that most complicated of all baseball skills, uses most of them. And yet, propelling a ball with speed and accuracy over the distances the game requires takes more than muscular strength. In fact, relying primarily on brute force to throw a baseball reduces not only the accuracy of the throw but generally the velocity as well. There are techniques in throwing as important to a baseball player as proper bowing and finger placement are to a concert violinist.

THE GRIP

There are four long and four short seams on a baseball. When gripping a ball, place your index and middle fingers over one of the four long seams and then spread the two fingers approximately three quarters of an inch apart. Place the inner side of your thumb on the underside of the ball so that it is in line with your middle finger, and hold the ball loosely almost in your fingertips. Your grip should form a V-shaped space between the ball and the juncture of your thumb and index finger. Holding the ball in this fashion and releas-

77

This grip for catchers, infielders, and outfielders assures an accurate throw with maximum velocity.

ing it with a three-quarter overhand throwing motion will cause it to rotate with all four long seams spinning on a horizontal axis, which gives the ball maximum lift and accuracy. Unless you're a pitcher, you should always grip the ball this way. Practice the grip so that it becomes instinctive. Anything other than the correct grip is ultimately a mistake and will lead to bad throws.

ARM ACTION

In the act of throwing, if you drop your throwing arm down to your side with your elbow close to your body, your arm will be forced to sling the ball, and your throw will be weak and inaccurate. Instead, keep your elbow up, your shoulders level, and your wrist cocked with your fingers behind and on top of the ball. By doing this, your arm will have a much more efficient range of action through the throwing motion and your throws will be crisper and more accurate.

If you study the mechanics of a proper three-quarter overhand throw, you'll see that arm and body form three 90-degree angles that work in concert as the arm moves through the throw.

1. The first 90-degree angle is formed at the wrist as the ball is laid back, or cocked, and the throw begins.

2. The second 90-degree angle is formed at the elbow as the forearm moves forward and down in a vertical plane and the upper arm remains hori-

zontal until the forearm straightens out upon release. The key to making this part of the throw effective is keeping the elbow up.

    3.   The third 90-degree angle is formed between the upper arm and torso. Important for an effective throw now is keeping the shoulders level.

As you release the ball from a point over and in front of your head, your fingers should be behind the ball and pulling down hard on it to impart the four-seam rotation. Your lead, or glove, arm is important now, too, as it provides a certain downthrust to your body, which keeps the throwing arm high.

THE STRIDE

After catching a ball, position your body so your shoulders are lined up with your target as you begin your throw. Your body needs some kind of thrust in order to build arm speed for the throw, so *stride* toward your target. As you begin your stride, your front shoulder should be pointing toward the target and your rear, or pivot, foot placed perpendicular to it so that the foot's entire inner

Good throwing form includes striding 4 to 6 inches to the left of an imaginary line running from the pivot foot toward the target; bending the stride leg; a strong push off the pivot foot; free rotation of the hips opening toward the target; the glove arm pulled down; level shoulders; throwing arm and elbow up; and proper grip and release. Note the three 90-degree angles at wrist, elbow, and shoulder.

A

B

surface, from the heel to the big toe, is providing maximum push. Your stride foot should land flat, with your toes pointing directly toward the target and about 6 inches to the left of an imaginary line running to the target from the pivot foot. This permits your hips and shoulders to open quickly and gives more freedom to your arm as, elbow up, it follows through. If your stride is to the right of the imaginary line toward the target, your hips will be restricted and unable to open as quickly or as far, thus forcing your throwing arm down into a sidearm release.

The length of your stride will vary with the distance of your throw. An outfielder's stride and arm arc are necessarily longer than an infielder's because the former's throws must travel up to 300 feet; and yet, all the mechanics and techniques for each player are essentially the same. A catcher's stride and arm arc are the shortest because he is forced to throw quickly from his receiver's

An outfielder's stride and arm arc (A, B) are longer than an infielder's (C), and the catcher's (D) are the shortest of the three.

C

D

crouch on steal attempts. This need to unload quickly with a limited stride and arm arc requires that the catcher's arm generally be the strongest on the team.

THE RELEASE

If your grip, stride, and arm action are all correct, the way you release the ball can guarantee a strong, accurate throw. As your elbow leads the wrist, which is cocked back with the ball in the proper grip, your arm straightens and you release the ball with a downward snap of the wrist and downward pull of the index and middle fingers. Release the ball in front of your body as your hand starts down across your trunk in the follow-through. Generally, a player with long, strong fingers and a strong wrist will make the best release.

THE FOLLOW-THROUGH

The act of throwing, though, doesn't stop with release of the ball. If you don't follow through, your throw will lose much of its speed and accuracy. Upon releasing the ball, your throwing arm should be allowed to continue its downward, diagonal sweep across the front of the body and behind the opposite hip. Your lead, or glove, arm has already moved down, across, and behind the body in a rapid, pendulumlike motion. Your hips and shoulders continue through their motion and your pivot foot comes forward, pulled by the momentum of the upper body after the release. Both feet are now somewhat parallel, spread, and pointing toward the target.

OTHER THROWS

The mechanics described above apply to the three-quarter overhand throw, which is fundamental to all positions. When time allows, the three-quarter technique is unquestionably the best for guaranteeing the strongest and most accurate throw. There are times, however, when you won't be permitted the luxury of this throw, and then sidearm and underhand throws come in handy.

The Sidearm Throw

The sidearm throw requires a strong wrist snap and places an additional strain on the elbow and shoulder, but it is useful when you find yourself going far to your right or left for a ground ball, or fielding a slow-hit ball on the run. The technique is to bring the ball quickly out of your glove and release it sidearm at a level between your belt and your knees. Obviously, you can't get as much speed or distance on this throw, so use it only when time does not allow straightening for the three-quarter overhand throw.

The Underhand Throw

The underhand throw is used when a ground ball—such as a bunt or batted ball that has stopped rolling—must be fielded close to the ground and released immediately. The throw is executed with virtually the wrist alone and will not travel far at all. Furthermore, the way the ball is released causes it to begin sinking almost immediately, making it difficult to catch. The strain on the arm for both the sidearm and underhand throws is quite great because the body does not straighten up and utilize other muscles.

CARE OF THE ARM

A player unable to throw will have a difficult time finding any reward or satisfaction from baseball. It seems incongruous that so many players and coaches pay such attention to the care of equipment—bats, balls, gloves, etc. —yet have so little regard for the health and strength of the players' arms. To ensure healthy arms, every player and coach should have some idea of how to throw properly and efficiently. After all, a team's defensive success is built upon the players' ability to throw hard and straight, and a team that can't retire batters on the simplest, most routine plays because they can't throw well is in for a long season.

Every player and coach should be careful not to cause injury to this delicate, complicated instrument. Adequate stretching and warm-up are imperative before throwing a baseball full-speed, and coaches should allow sufficient time in their practices and pregame warm-ups to assure that their players are properly prepared. Far too many players, both amateur and pro, have lost the opportunity to enjoy baseball due to careless use of their arms, and far too many coaches have literally ruined the careers of budding youngsters by forcing them to throw with pain, or not allowing them enough warm-up time. If any pain develops in your arm, particularly in the joint areas—wrist, elbow, or shoulder —stop throwing and consult your doctor or trainer.

Finally, every player, at no matter what level—Little League, high school, college, the majors—whether in games or in practice, should *always use the*

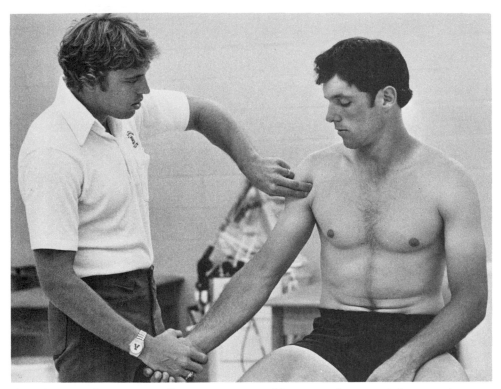

A trainer or doctor can diagnose arm problems, such as an injury to the shoulder's rotator cuff.

correct mechanics when throwing. Face it: If you grip the ball across the long seams in practice, you'll probably do the same in a game situation, and the tricky business of rotating the ball in your glove and bare hand to achieve proper grip will have become second nature. Alternately, if you have any smarts as an infielder, catcher, or outfielder, you won't risk arm injury throwing "junk" pitches during practice. Really: Forget the trick stuff. After all, do you throw curves or knucklers in a game? Of course you don't. Save your arm. Set an example for your teammates. Try to throw properly *all the time,* in games *and* in practice.

Some players are gifted with strong arms from birth, while others will never have Dave Winfield's "gun" no matter how hard they try. So be it. In baseball, all players are *not* created equal. Still, no matter what your gifts, you can improve your throwing by applying the right fundamentals and techniques. And who knows? Your dead-on-the-money, late-inning perfect throw might even save your team a ball game.

5

General Infield Play

A solid, smoothly functioning infield is essential to a team's success—and with good reason. Over a long season, half of the fair batted balls are hit on the ground, and to retire a batter on an infield grounder takes a combination of specific skills and fundamentals. In a recent season at the University of Arizona, we charted *every* fair batted ball at both varsity and junior-varsity games to determine the frequency of grounders, fly balls, pop flies, and line drives. Ground balls accounted for 49 percent of the total, which leads to an obvious conclusion: If you're an infielder, you must be able to handle grounders properly if your team expects to win.

SELECTION OF AN INFIELDER'S GLOVE

Most young infielders have a tendency to choose too large a glove. The adage "Bigger is better" is a mistake in this case and can lead to poor execution of infield skills. It's best to use a glove that feels like part of your hand and not an awkward, unfeeling extension of it. When the ball hits the

bin Yount has everything in perfect control as he
gins the act of fielding a ground ball.

glove's pocket, you should feel exactly where the ball is so you can transfer it quickly to your throwing hand to complete the play. One of the worst experiences you can have as an infielder is groping for the ball somewhere in the depths of a vast glove while the runner speeds to the base. A smaller glove prevents this. Further, when removing the ball from your glove with your throwing hand, you should come out with the proper grip across the long seams (see p. 77). A ball rattling around in a large glove is more difficult to secure, and may result in your throwing a sinker, slider, or change-up across the diamond to first base.

Consider these four factors in a glove for playing second base, shortstop, or third base:

1. Select a glove with squared fingers that will allow a wide pocket when the glove is placed on the ground.
2. Select a glove with a solid web rather than an open "H" type web. This will prevent your fingers from slipping through any open spaces in the web and becoming entangled when reaching for the ball.
3. Break the glove in so that the pocket is wider than it is long. Rather than extending vertically from the web to the heel, the pocket should extend across the glove from thumb to little finger, thus giving you more pocket area when fielding a ground ball.
4. Choose a glove that accommodates your *whole* bare hand and *all five* fingers. It's fashionable these days to wear a batter's glove on the fielding hand before putting on the fielder's glove and placing the index finger outside the glove. Avoid this "fashion." A batter's glove prevents you from "feeling" the ball effectively when it enters your glove. And for greatest security and control, the sensitive nerve endings of your fingertips, particularly the index finger's, should be as close to the ball as possible as it settles into your glove. An index finger outside the glove restricts the flexibility of both glove and finger.

A second baseman, particularly, should learn to use a relatively small glove that allows him to remove the ball quickly for the throw. A shortstop's or third baseman's may be slightly larger, but still easily controllable. Remember: A good infielder catches the ball with his *hand,* not his glove.

MENTAL PREPARATION FOR THE INFIELDER

It almost goes without saying that a confident infielder is a successful one. If you lack confidence as an infielder, your movements will be tentative and uncertain when the ball is hit in your direction, which will likely result in an error or bad throw. One of the signs hanging in our locker room at Arizona reads, "Hard Practice Builds Confidence; Confidence Builds Success." Consistency under game conditions comes from diligent practice. When you know you've put in those necessary long practice hours, your mind will convince your body you're ready for even the toughest grounder. Moreover, that inner confidence will be reflected to your teammates—most importantly, your pitcher—and the entire team will benefit. The confident infielder is a leader.

But confidence isn't your only mental preparation. There are a host of other variables you should consider before your pitcher even throws the ball. Is yours the home team or the visitor? What's the score? The inning? The speed of the batter? The speed of the base runners? Your pitcher's degree of fatigue? Is he relying today on fastballs or breaking pitches? The infield grass: Is it long? Wet? What's the wind direction and wind speed, the sun's location, the location of your teammates in relation to yourself? All this information must be programmed correctly in your mind so if the ball is hit to you, you know the right decision almost automatically and can make the play. Don't daydream. Don't let your attention wander. You do, and you almost guarantee an error if the ball is hit to you. Be smart. Concentrate. Always look ahead and preprogram all variables that might affect you.

PHYSICAL PREPARATION FOR THE INFIELDER

To facilitate the correct movement when the ball is hit, there are two body positions you should assume: one before the pitch, the *set position;* and the other as the pitch is delivered, the *ready position.*

The Set Position

Spread your feet slightly more than shoulders' width apart to provide a comfortable and balanced base of support. Turn your toes out slightly to make it easier for you to move laterally, and drop your throwing-side foot back a bit to make it easier to break to your bare-hand side. Bend your knees comfortably and distribute approximately 60 percent of your weight on the balls of your feet with your heels lightly on the ground. Keep your back straight, your hands resting on your knees, your head up, and your eyes surveying the entire scene: the pitcher, catcher, batter, base runners. Once in the set position, activate your computer brain, and while your catcher is flashing the pitch signal to your pitcher and he begins his delivery, feed into your brain all necessary information. The set position helps prepare both your mind and body well in advance for any quick movements you may have to make when the ball is hit.

The Ready Position

When the pitcher releases the ball to the plate, take the *ready position*. The difference between the set and ready positions is slight but significant. Your weight is transferred even more to the balls of your feet (approximately 75 percent) while your heels remain very lightly touching the ground, and your center of gravity lowers as your knees bend more. Move your hands from your knees to your stomach level while keeping your back straight, head up, and eyes focused intently on the strike zone at home plate. Don't try to follow the ball from the pitcher's hand to the batter; instead, focus on the strike zone out of which the ball may be hit toward you. In this position, you are "ready" to explode your muscles forward, backward, up, down, right, or left, depending on where the ball is hit.

The ready position, or slight variations thereof, is a familiar defensive posture in other sports, too, such as basketball or football. But remember, it's impossible to hold the ready position effectively for more than a few seconds before your muscles begin to tighten and fatigues sets in, so your transition from set to ready should not be too long before the ball is pitched. You may prefer to take several small steps toward the plate as your pitcher begins his delivery and then widen your stance to the ready position as the ball approaches the hitter. This is fine, and provides needed flow and rhythm to your body as it "readies" itself.

THE INFIELDER'S FIRST MOVEMENT TO THE GROUND BALL

The batter swings. A ground ball comes bouncing toward you. As it does, you in turn should move from the ready position *toward the ball*. Don't straighten up and wait for the ball to reach you; that causes your weight to shift back from the balls of your feet to your heels, where the body's balance is more precarious. By staying low and moving in to meet the ball, you keep your body under control for that crucial moment when the ball enters your glove. No matter

In the *set position* (A), the infielder screens all the variables before the pitch, and then, as the pitcher releases the ball, switches to the *ready position* (B) for optimum movement when the ball is hit. On a grounder, his first movement is *toward* the ball (C). He stays low, keeps his body movement controlled, his glove forward, his eyes focused intently on the ball (D) while deciding whether to field it on the short or long hop. As the ball approaches, he widens his stance (E) to permit his knees to bend and his glove to play *below* the ball. Then, as he prepares to "funnel" the ball (F), his feet are spread, his seat down, his hands low and in front of him, and his eyes on the ball. He brings the ball up through the "funnel" (G,H), closes

his throwing hand over it in the proper grip, and with his right foot begins the shuffle step known as a "crowhop." His shoulders are now lined up with the target (I); he grips the ball across the long seams and throws it (J) with a three-quarter overhand motion.

whether the ground ball is hit directly at you or slightly to your right or left, glide toward the ball, keeping comfortably low to the ground and the ball directly in front of you. (Some coaches tell their infielders to "charge the ball," but don't, because a reckless rush forward increases your chance of error.) As you near the ball, decide if you're going to field it at the *high point* of its bounce or on the *short hop* just as it leaves the ground. In either case, if your concentration and visual focus on the ball are good and your body is under control, you must still remember to *play below the ball.* The most common (and embarrassing) error you can make is letting the ball roll under your glove. It's much easier to raise your glove at the last instant for an unexpected bad hop than to try to lower it if the ball stays down.

As you take your last steps toward the ball, include what I call a "crow-hop"—that is, a quick shuffle-type step to widen the distance between your feet —then get your body low to the ground by bending your knees. Your body must be under near-perfect control as the ball enters your glove, and the following techniques should be applied:

1. Your feet should be spread more than shoulders' width apart and your weight should be forward on the balls of your feet.

2. Your seat should be down by bending your knees, not your hips. The good infielder lowers his body at the knees, keeping his back relatively straight.

3. *Both* hands should be out in front of you where you can see the ball enter the glove. Your form is correct when hands and feet are equidistant from each other. Your glove should be at roughly a 45-degree angle off the ground and completely open, with the bare hand alongside, ready to help control the ball.

4. Your shoulders should be squared off to the path of the ball and your body entirely in front of it, so if a bad hop occurs, the ball will at least be blocked.

5. You should keep your eyes on the ball as it enters the glove. As your bare hand begins gripping the ball for the throw, it's time to execute what I call the "funnel principle" to assure maximum control of body and ball in completing the throw. Imagine a large funnel, its point touching your navel, it's mouth

Using the "funnel principle" keeps the body and hands in position to react to bad hops and still make the play.

spreading toward the ground. To lower the funnel to the ground requires bending your knees rather than your back. Then, as the ball enters the "funnel" (the glove), bring your hands directly up to your navel while transferring the ball to your throwing hand and beginning to turn your body with a quick shuffling crowhop step into the proper throwing position. The funnel principle enables you to keep your body directly in front of the ball throughout the fielding action, and allows you an instant longer to transfer the ball to your throwing hand and properly grip it across the long seams. It's a mistake to begin turning your body and glove angle before the ball reaches the glove, because a bad or unexpected hop can cause the ball to skip past you altogether. The funnel principle helps keep your body and hands in position to block that bad hop, recover, and make the play.

Now that you have the ball securely controlled in your glove and you're smoothly bringing it through the funnel to your navel, continue your body movement out of the fielding position and into the proper throwing stance by taking a quick shuffling crowhop step to line up your shoulders with first base, and complete the play with a three-quarter overhand throw and follow-through. Through the entire sequence, from your first movement out of the ready position to the follow-through after the throw, you should keep your body moving rhythmically forward. By contrast, stop-and-go, herky-jerky in-fielding leads to errors, and errors can cost runs.

THE INFIELDER'S LATERAL MOVEMENT

When a ground ball is hit some distance to your right or left, make your first movement from the ready position a crossover step. The quickest way to activate your body laterally is to throw your upper body in the direction of the

A crossover step to the right (A) requires staying low for quick, explosive muscle movement. Whether left or right, the crossover step should be comfortable (B)—neither too long nor too short.

The jab step (C) wastes time and should be avoided.

B

C

ball while simultaneously pivoting on the ball of that foot and then crossing over with the other foot toward the spot where you hope to intersect the ground ball. When moving laterally, always remember to do the following:

1. *Explode* from the ready position into your crossover step. The distance you cover with that first step may be the difference between catching the ball or missing it by an inch or two.

2. Make your crossover step a comfortable one. Step too short and you may stumble and lose your balance. Step too long and you'll drag your back foot before taking your next step.

3. Stay relatively low during subsequent strides toward the ball.

4. Think: "Get in front of the ball!" The surest way to field a ball is by practicing the funnel principle. To compromise by making a one-handed glove stab at the ball after lazily moving to the right or left is wrong.

5. Establish a slightly curved path, or "banana route," as you take your subsequent strides to the right or left. This will put you somewhat behind the ball rather than at a 90-degree angle to it, and will make it easier to bring your body under control and directly in front of the ball when actually fielding. Too, traveling a "banana route" left or right gets your body moving slightly toward first base, making your throws there easier and more accurate.

Running a "banana route" permits you to circle behind a ground ball and field it with your momentum going toward first base.

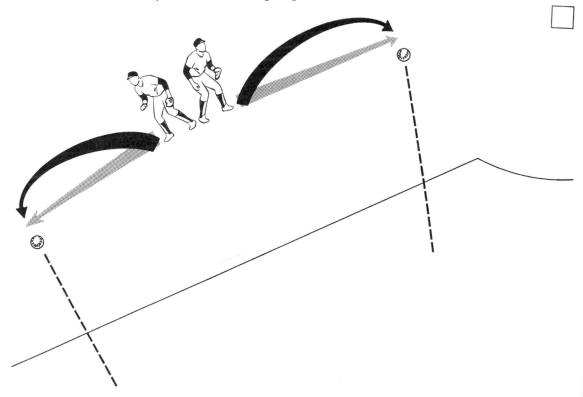

THE GLOVE-HAND-ONLY PLAY

Of course, there are times when, despite an explosive crossover step and full-speed lateral sprint, you can't get in front of the ball. In such cases, forget the banana route and instead make every attempt simply to reach the ball one-handed with your glove. Glove position is important: Open it fully to the path of the ball and turn your wrist in slightly. (The common error when making the glove-hand play is to try to flatten, or "pancake," the ball as it goes past the glove.) When you catch a grounder by stretching with the glove, your momentum generally carries you away from your throwing target. To recover quickly and get your shoulders and body lined up for an accurate throw takes unusual athletic ability and balance. This play quickly separates the men from the boys and brings two factors into consideration:

1. The importance of a proper ready position when the ground ball is hit any distance to the right or left.
2. The need for more lateral range by shortstops and second basemen, who experience this play more frequently than first and third basemen.

The Backhand Play

The backhand play is one of the most difficult you'll encounter and takes specific techniques to execute correctly. When a ground ball is hit some distance to your bare-hand side and you can't get in front of it, time your last step so

The backhand play requires that the glove be fully opened to the ball and the pivot foot braced as quickly as possible.

your right foot is forward as you reach across your body with the glove, which should be fully open with your wrist slightly turned in for firmness when the ball makes contact. With your right (pivot) foot now braced, you can throw from any of the other infield positions across to first base and retire the batter. If your left foot is forward when making the backhand play, you'll find you must take one more step to plant the pivot foot, which takes extra time.

A word of caution on the backhand play: I have a strong feeling that too many infielders resort to it when, with a better crossover step and more hustle, they could be in front of the ball and catching it using the funnel method. Certainly the backhand play has its place, and it should be taught properly; but use it *only* if you cannot get in front of a ground ball.

THE DIVE PLAY

When a ground ball is hit so hard or so far that you can't field it in one of the ways described above, you must leave your feet in a desperate last-ditch attempt to prevent it from getting through the infield. The first and third basemen can generally execute the dive play and still have time to retire a runner, and they encounter dive-play situations more frequently than their fellow infielders. A second baseman or shortstop will probably be unable to retire a runner after the dive play since the ball has traveled farther to them, but they should be able to prevent a runner from scoring or taking an extra base.

The dive play punishes the body; it hurts to throw oneself headlong to the ground while stretching virtually every muscle. The following techniques will help minimize your chances of injury and pain, but there's no way to prevent the hurt altogether.

Begin by practicing from the knees on soft grass. Without a ball, carefully extend your body and fall to the glove-hand side while bracing your fall with your bare hand in front of your chest. Extend your glove as far as possible with the pocket fully open and the wrist hooked in. Now do the same from the bare-hand side where opening the glove and hooking the wrist are a bit more difficult. After several practices, your coach can roll a ball slowly for you to dive at and catch from a kneel.

Now practice from a ready position, again on soft grass, and this time add a crossover step: First dive without going for a ball; then with your coach rolling one.

Often the dive play will result in your knocking the ball down within reach but not fielding it cleanly. In this case, scramble to your knees or feet and pick

B

A

C

Practice the dive play while kneeling on grass (A). Learn to cushion your dive with your bare hand to give you more glove control (B). Your glove must be open and your wrist turned in slightly to catch and control the ball (C,D). Once you can catch the ball, practice scrambling to your feet and making the throw.

D

up the ball with your *bare hand,* being careful to keep your chest over the ball and your eyes watching it rather than the runner. Too often, in his haste to retrieve the ball, an infielder will try to keep one eye on the runner and will fumble the ball a second time. A good rule whenever a ground ball is bobbled but remains within reach is "boot and bare hand"—in other words, keep your chest over the ball and pick it up quickly but carefully. Who knows? You may still have time to retire the runner.

CATCHING THE LINE DRIVE OR THROWN BALL

The two most important rules to remember for catching a ball hit or thrown in the air are: (1) Keep your chest in front of the ball and (2) catch it with two hands. Practicing these rules not only facilitates a clean catch but also prepares you for the next immediate responsibility: a good throw. By keeping your chest in front of every ball, your entire body is balanced and in control, and you can move efficiently from one action to another. Also, a two-handed catch minimizes the time it takes both to transfer the ball from glove to bare hand and to assume the proper grip.

Keep your chest in front of every thrown or batted ball. Catch a ball above the waist with two hands and fingers up; a ball below the waist with two hands and fingers down.

As you prepare to catch a line drive, your knees should be bent, your weight should be on the balls of your feet, and your hands should be up. To catch a ball above the waist, your hands stay up. To catch a ball below the waist, point your hands down. As you catch the ball, take a step with your pivot foot toward your throwing target and begin getting your body in position to throw. Remember: Do everything in a continuous motion; don't break the two acts, catching and throwing, into distinct, separate parts. Good infielders, whether fielding a thrown or batted ball, move fluidly through the entire action.

Throughout this chapter I've discussed the general requirements for all infielders. If you expect to excel at a particular infield position, you must have these foundations firmly in place. When you've mastered the essentials of infield play, you can move directly to the position for which you're best suited. That position will depend on your size, speed, strength of throwing arm, reaction time, range afield, courage, and other factors.

The First Baseman

The first baseman is generally underrated for his defense because his play is the culmination of the pitcher's good pitch and the infielder's successful, often spectacular, pickup and throw of a ground ball. Most of the attention and credit for infield plays are given to the pitcher and other infielders; the first baseman's contribution—unless a throw to him is high, wide, or low—is merely a foregone conclusion. The very fact that he is so often taken for granted though, is proof of how essential a first baseman is over a long season, particularly if his team expects to win a championship.

QUALIFICATIONS

Ideally, a first baseman should be tall and lanky enough to provide a good target and handle the high and wide throws. Left-handed first basemen have an advantage over righties because they're in better position to apply the tag on a pick-off throw from the pitcher and to throw to second or third base after fielding bunts or ground balls. Furthermore, with the glove on his right hand, the left-handed first baseman can cover more ground on balls hit between him and the second baseman. A

99

Steve Garvey retires the runner with a well-balanced, controlled stretch. By keeping his right foot against the bag rather than on top of it, Garvey protects against injury.

first baseman should have quick, agile feet so he can shift on the bag when throws are off-target. He should be able to handle all manner of throws, particularly those in the dirt, and must be courageous enough not to shy away. It's *not* necessary, however, for him to have as strong a throwing arm as other fielders since his longest throws seldom exceed 120 feet.

All of this is not to say that a short, right-handed player can't play first base well—Pete Rose and Steve Garvey have shown otherwise. But, all things considered, the tall left-hander has obvious advantages.

TAKING POSITION

Without a runner on first base, the first baseman should play rather deep and off the line to give greater coverage on ground balls in his direction. Most first basemen have a tendency to station themselves too close to the bag, thus adding pressure to the second baseman to cover more ground than necessary. If you're playing first base, I suggest that you stand approximately 30 feet back from the bag and 15 to 20 feet off the foul line. Of course, there are variables you should consider—such as the score, the inning, the speed of the batter, whether he's a lefty or righty, whether he's a bunt threat, etc—that can cause you to change your position. Wherever you are stationed when the pitch is made, you must know exactly where the second baseman is playing so there is no mix-up on a ground ball hit between you. A good rule to use in this case is that you, the first baseman, should break to your right if you think you can field the ground ball, but if the second baseman calls you off, allow him to make the play. If

Awaiting a throw, the first baseman must know exactly where the bag is and be prepared to stretch in any direction for the ball.

you don't hear the second baseman, then *you* should field the ground ball and throw to the pitcher, who should cover first base.

As soon as you determine that a ground ball has been hit to the pitcher or another infielder, you should sprint to the bag and establish a balanced body position facing the throw and with the heel of your throwing-side foot near or against the bag. You must know exactly where the bag is *before* you begin your stretch to receive the throw. Approximately 90 percent of all throws you receive will be with that foot against the bag, because you can stretch out farther with your glove hand to meet the throw (i.e., glove on left hand, right foot on bag; glove on right hand, left foot on bag). Never place your foot on top of the bag, because the runner may step on your foot and cause serious injury to both you and him. Instead, turn your foot so that either its inside surface or its ball is pressed against the side of the bag.

TAKING THE THROW

You've assumed the balanced position and you're facing the throw. Now, as an alert first baseman, expect . . . a bad throw. Why? Simple. If the throw is good, you'll handle it easily; if it's bad, you'll be ready for it. It's not necessary to catch the throw with two hands as other fielders should, because a first baseman's glove is much larger and constructed to catch balls in its web. Besides, you can stretch farther with one hand than with two. When taking a throw, stretch *only* when the play is close and only after you're certain of the path of the throw. Remember: Once you commit to the stretch, you don't have

A controlled stretch and sure catch are more important than the spectacular "splits" that some first basemen tend to execute.

When playing first base, remember: The ball is more important than the bag.

time to recover and correct if the throw is other than you expected. It's a common error among first basemen to stretch out spectacularly when the play is not close and put themselves in an unnecessarily vulnerable position. Use the stretch only as the final and necessary act to retire the runner.

On a low throw, try to stretch and catch it either before it hits the ground or on as short a hop as possible. In this case, two hands are best to help block the ball. Try, too, to keep your body as much as possible in front of a low throw to prevent the ball from getting by you and allowing the runner to advance to second base. If a low thrown ball hits some distance (3 feet or more) in front of your glove, draw back and catch it on a higher point of its bounce. If the ball is thrown off to one side, you might have to come off the bag to make sure you at least block it if not catch it. In all cases, the rule is "The ball is more important than the bag." Faced with the choice of ball or bag, stop the ball from getting by, even if it means the batter will be safe. That way, you at least prevent runners from getting extra bases and might even stop a run from scoring.

Incidentally, don't worry about fancy footwork if you're playing first base. It's much overrated. With good balance and body control, and keeping in mind that 90 percent of the throws you receive should be taken with your throwing-side foot against the bag, you should feel confident that you can handle any throw. Even if you're right-handed, you can stretch farther to your right by having your right foot against the base, and, if need be, crossing over with the left leg, and backhanding a ball to your right.

If either the catcher or pitcher is throwing from the home-plate area, try to give a good target. And in the event the throw is from the catcher in foul territory (as might happen on a dropped third strike), station yourself in foul territory with your right foot against the bag.

HOLDING THE RUNNER ON

The first priority in this case is to be in position to take the pitcher's pick-off throw and apply a quick tag. The second priority is to leave the bag when the pitch is made and be in the ready position described earlier. Both priorities can be met if you take a fairly wide stance facing the pitcher, with your right foot against the inside edge of the bag and in fair territory. Hold your glove up as an inviting target for the pitcher. When the pick-off throw comes, wait for the ball to get to the glove and then lower the glove straight down to a point in front of the bag where the runner's hand or foot is trying to tag. It's a mistake to reach for the ball and then sweep it to the bag; the ball will travel faster than the glove, so keep the glove over the bag and move it directly down for the tag. It's also a mistake to reach away from the bag to tag the runner; by placing the glove and ball in front of the bag, you let the runner tag himself out. Finally, try to make the tag with the *back* of the glove (rather than the pocket) to the runner's hand or foot. You're less likely to have the ball jostled loose, and there will thus be less danger of the runner's taking second base.

As soon as you're certain the pitcher is throwing to the plate (and don't assume too quickly when a left-handed pitcher is on the mound), move swiftly

With a runner on first base, the first baseman positions his right foot against the inside corner of the bag and gives the pitcher a good target (A). On a pick-off tag, rather than reaching for the runner, he places the glove in front of the bag (B).

A

B

Once the pitcher delivers to the plate, the first baseman makes a rapid
left-right shuffle into fielding position and 15 feet off the bag.

away from the bag and into proper fielding position so that you'll have good
range when the ball is hit. Start with a long stride toward second base with your
left foot, then your right, then shuffle. The shuffle hop should turn your body
toward the plate, and you should establish the ready position just as the ball
reaches the batter. This quick three-part move will carry you 12 to 15 feet out
from the bag and put you in good position to field a ball hit your way.

When the runner on first base is very slow, or your team is ahead by two
or more runs in late innings, play behind the runner and give yourself more
range. Remember, though, always to signal the pitcher of your intention, and
from time to time fake the runner back to keep him from taking a big lead.

TEAMWORK WITH THE PITCHER

On any ball hit to your pitcher's left, he must break from the mound to cover
first base in the event you field the ground ball. If, after fielding the ball, you
determine you can beat the batter to the bag, you should put the ball in your
bare hand, wave the pitcher off, and make the unassisted putout. This is the
safest approach and eliminates three possibilities of error: a bad toss from you
to the pitcher; the pitcher dropping the throw while running full-speed; and the
pitcher missing the bag. There are two reasons for putting the ball in your bare
hand rather than holding it in your glove while you sprint to the bag:

1.   You have better control. You could drop the ball out of your glove
without knowing it.

2.   You can throw to the pitcher instantly if you realize you've made the wrong decision and the batter may beat you to the bag. Also, even if you do make the unassisted putout, you may have to make a quick throw to third base or home plate to retire a lead runner.

If you elect to throw to the pitcher covering the bag, use the following techniques:

1.   Put the ball in your bare hand and take several steps toward first base, keeping your body low. Prepare to deliver the ball almost as a bowler begins his approach toward the pins. Be certain the ball is in full view of the pitcher as he sprints from the mound to first base.

2.   The throw should be of the underhand shovel type. Keep your elbow in, your palm up, and your wrist relatively stiff for accuracy.

3.   Time the throw to the pitcher so he catches the ball *chest-high* and two or three strides *before* reaching the bag. This early throw permits him to focus on the ball, catch it securely with two hands, and then focus on the bag to be sure he tags it with his foot. Usually this play is quite close, with the pitcher arriving at first base just one or two steps ahead of the batter, so it's not wise for the pitcher to be catching the ball just as he hopes his foot is tagging the bag.

4.   Continue your follow-through after releasing the ball and be prepared to alert the pitcher to throw home or to third base if another runner is attempting to advance.

If you're forced to field a ball going to your right and some distance from first base, plant your pivot foot and make a three-quarter overhand throw to the pitcher. The timing and target should be the same as on the underhand toss

On an underhand throw from the first baseman to the pitcher covering the base, timing is everything.

—that is, the pitcher should receive the ball chest-high and two or three strides before he reaches the bag. This is not easy and takes considerable practice for the timing to be effective.

THE "TOUGH PLAY"

One of the most difficult judgment plays occurs when a slow ground ball hit toward first base can be fielded either by the pitcher or first baseman. The question, requiring an instant answer, is, Who fields the ball and who covers first? Ideally, your pitcher should try to field every ball he can, and call "I have it!" when he's certain he can field it. This allows the first baseman, who has also begun moving toward the ball, to cover the bag for the throw. Sometimes, upon fielding the ball and giving the verbal signal, your pitcher may elect to outrace the batter to the bag while you veer out of the way. But if he can't reach the ground ball, he should continue on to the bag while you field the ball and toss it underhanded to him. This is the "tough play" because the pitcher must now turn his body while running and catch the ball almost over his shoulder. It's also why the pitcher is the preferred fielder in this situation and you should cover the bag. In either case, though, both you and the pitcher should move quickly toward the ground ball and coordinate with each other as soon as possible. The worst mistake is to each assume the other will do the fielding.

FIELDING BUNTS

Generally, batters try bunting toward first base because the first baseman must stay at the bag holding the runner until the pitcher delivers. Still, if they field the bunt cleanly, first basemen can throw to second or third base to force out the lead runner. The left-handed-throwing first baseman is obviously in a better position to throw upon fielding the bunt, but whether you throw left or right-handed, you should use the following techniques when moving in on the bunt:

1. Make a "banana route" and approach the ball from the first-base line so that your momentum is somewhat toward second or third base as the bunt is fielded.

2. If the bunt is still rolling, field it with two hands. The size of the first baseman's glove makes locating the ball in it difficult if you need to make the quick throw. If the bunt has stopped rolling, bare-hand it.

3. Keep your chest over the bunt with your knees well bent and your eyes

on the ball. A common mistake is to watch the runner's progress before controlling the bunt.

4.   Listen for the catcher's verbal signal telling you where to throw. He's
in a better position to judge whether you can force the lead runner or must be
content to throw to first base and retire the bunter.

On bunt plays toward first with both you and your pitcher charging the
ball, the second baseman covers first base. Too seldom do first basemen attempt
to retire the lead runner on a bunt; perhaps they're fearful of making a bad
throw or are content to "play it safe" and make the sure out at first base. But
if we consider that 95 percent of all sacrifice bunts occur with no outs and an
important runner at first or second base, it means a great deal to the defense
if the lead runner can be retired. If you move quickly, charging the bunt under
control and following a "banana route" (which gives you the right footwork
and momentum), you should get the lead runner more often. Sometimes, too,
if you practice the above techniques, you and your team might even turn an
occasional double play off a bunt by forcing the lead runner at third or second,
then throwing to first to retire the bunter.

THROWS TO SECOND BASE

With a runner on first base and fewer than two outs, a ground ball hit to you
at first base marks the beginning of one of the most difficult double plays. Your
throw to the shortstop covering second base requires a combination of quickness and accuracy, and you must be agile enough afterward to retreat to first
base for the return throw. Obviously, if you're left-handed, you can make the
throw to second with greater ease. If you're a righty, make a quick jump pivot
before you throw to get your shoulders lined up with the target, and then throw
carefully and accurately. Often the runner will be in line with you and your
shortstop and you'll have to move out of that line before releasing the ball. Your
shortstop can be helpful here by positioning himself on the inside or outside
of second base while awaiting the throw. Although a jump pivot takes an
instant longer than merely sidearming the ball toward the shortstop, it's a better
technique if you're a righty playing first, because it assures a harder and more
accurate throw.

Because so much defensive action revolves around first base, the successful
team requires a sure-handed, alert first baseman. If you hope one day to become
an all-star first baseman, you must be prepared to master the fundamentals and
techniques described in this chapter.

7

The Third Baseman

Whenever baseball talk turns to third-base play, discussion usually centers around the memorable, game-saving grabs of recent all-star third basemen. The spectacular acrobatics of Graig Nettles, Brooks Robinson, Mike Schmidt, and George Brett, among others, have set a high standard for aspiring third basemen. Nowhere on the baseball field is there more opportunity to make the great play, the astonishing catch and throw, than at the "hot corner." The frequency of difficult chances are greater at this position than any other, so to be a successful third baseman, you must possess a mix of athletic skills both inherent and acquired.

QUALIFICATIONS

Although as a third baseman you need not have the foot speed required of other players, such as the center fielder and shortstop, you must have extremely quick initial reactions, be light on your feet, and have good lateral speed for the first several strides to your right or left. Because you'll often find yourself positioned less than 90 feet away from the batter, hard-hit balls will be on you in an instant, so your first move is crucial. Brooks

109

Quick reflexes and excellent fielding ability make
George Brett an all-star third baseman.

Robinson of the Baltimore Orioles was never a quick runner when he was winning his many consecutive Gold Glove awards for being the best-fielding third baseman in the American League, but few could match his reaction speed or his initial quickness, forward or laterally.

As a third baseman, you must have a strong arm to make the long throw from deep behind the third-base bag. Your most frequent throw will be the three-quarter overhand throw (described in chapter 4), requiring distance, velocity, and accuracy. But you must also be able to throw hard from a sidearm position when fielding a slow-hit ball or bunt and when ranging far to your left to make a play.

None of these skills will serve you long, however, if you lack that intangible: courage. In a way, you must have a slightly unnatural disregard for your own safety if you're going to leave your feet for the dive play (p. 94) or block a hard smash to prevent a double down the line or a runner's scoring from second base. Sometimes the line-drive, one-hop bullet hit at you or slightly to your side cannot be caught—but by fearlessly blocking the ball and making a strong throw, you can still retire the runner. One of the most memorable for making such plays was the late "Pepper" Martin, the St. Louis Cardinals' All-Star third baseman, whose sturdy chest was blanketed with bruises by the end of the season but whose fielding statistics always appeared near the top of the National League list.

TAKING POSITION

As a third baseman, you should alter your position more than any other player as you prepare for the pitch. Not only who's hitting but virtually every circumstance dictates a different place for you to play when the pitch is thrown. Against a right-handed pull hitter with poor running speed, for instance, you

By staying in front of this hard shot, Brett prevents an extra-base hit down the line.

should normally guard the line and play deep. But if your team is three or more runs ahead in the late innings and there are no runners on base, you should shade that same hitter toward the hole and *away* from the line to prevent the more common single between you and the shortstop.

Still, these aren't the only questions you should consider in positioning yourself. Others are: Is this batter a bunt threat? Does this batter represent the tying or winning run (in which case you *must* guard the line to prevent an extra-base hit)? Do I play deeper with two outs? Where is the shortstop playing? Is the pitcher a good fielder? With a runner on second base and a base hit to the outfield, who is the cutoff man to home plate and which runner is the most important man to stop? How fast is the infield grass? Is it wet?

It's also important that your pitcher know how deep you are playing in the event the batter bunts, or hits a slow roller down the third-base line. It's your responsibility to let your pitcher know where you will be playing when the pitch is delivered. Next time you watch an outstanding third baseman play, notice how often he moves around before the pitch. Sometimes he'll even try to fool the batter into thinking he is or isn't defending against the bunt, then quickly adjust as the pitch is made. Such tactics are part of the beauty of third-base play, and come only after a significant amount of experience.

THE SLOW-HIT BALL

The most difficult play you'll encounter as a third baseman is the slow-hit ball, or bunt, that must be charged and fielded on the run and thrown sidearm to first base. Successfully making this play has distinguished players like Graig Nettles, Mike Schmidt, and Buddy Bell from their average counterparts. You can make this play in three ways, depending on what the slow-hit ball is doing as you charge it.

The Slow Bouncer

If the ball is *bouncing,* charge it straight in and field it with two hands. Why two? Simple. A bouncing ball has enough velocity to continue into the outfield if you miss it, and you could wind up with a two-base error. Also, if it has been hit hard enough to be bouncing still, the batter can't be too far down the line toward first when you field it. For these two reasons, make this play as safely as possible, with two hands, and assure maximum control of both catch and throw.

The bouncing slow-hit ball is charged straight on and fielded with two hands as the left foot comes forward.

The Slow Roller

If the ball is *rolling* toward you, take a slight "banana route" toward it from the base-line side and scoop it with your glove. As you field the ball, your left foot should be coming forward. Then, as you take your next step, quickly transfer the ball to your throwing hand, and as your right foot comes down, snap the throw sidearm to first base. Taking a "banana route" toward the rolling ball directs your momentum somewhat toward first base. If, instead, you charged straight in, as on the bouncing ball, your momentum would carry you toward foul territory behind the plate and somewhat away from first base, making your throw more difficult.

The Stopped Ball

If the ball has *stopped or almost stopped,* field it bare-handed and make the throw to first all in one motion. This is a play that either succeeds spectacularly or fails dismally—a "do-or-die play." Try to reach the ball as quickly as possible. With your left foot forward, pick up the ball and snap the throw sidearm to first base. Your right foot should be coming down as you make the throw. It's hard to throw this way with much velocity, so a clean pickup and release is essential.

By learning to "read" a slow-hit ball as quickly as possible and applying

The Slow Roller. The third baseman scoops the rolling slow-hit ball with his glove hand after establishing his momentum toward first base with a "banana route."

The Stopped Ball. The only time the third baseman fields a ball bare-handed is when it is dead or nearly dead. By fielding the ball with his left foot forward, he can throw it sidearm on his next step.

the rules above, you'll find yourself improving markedly in executing this difficult play.

Important! Reserve the bare-handed pickup for those balls that have stopped or nearly stopped. Inexperienced infielders commonly attempt show-offish bare-hand plays on bouncing or rolling balls, and the results more often than not are needless fumbles or bad throws. So avoid errors. Field each slow-hit grounder by the appropriate method.

PLAYING ALERT

As is true of every infielder, at third base you must plan ahead and be ready for any play that might occur. For instance, with two outs, runners on first and second, and a ground ball in your direction, you should plan to tag third base rather than throw across the infield to first. Consider the following dilemmas you might find yourself in at third, and note what is normally the best decision.

Runner on First Base Only

With fewer than two outs and the score close, watch for a sacrifice bunt. Recognizing the speed of both the bunter and the runner will help you decide whether to throw to second or first base. If a slow runner is on first base and the score is tied or there's a one run difference, throw to second base on the chance of forcing the runner out. If your team is ahead by two or more runs, throw to first base to get the sure out. With two outs and a ground ball hit to you, throw either to first or second base depending on the speed of both runners and how hard and where the ball was hit. With fewer than two outs and a ground ball hit to you, obviously, throw to second base to initiate a double play. Your throw should be hard and accurate and aimed directly over the bag.

Runners on First and Second Base

With no one out and the game close, expect a sacrifice bunt. Play in about 15 feet from third base and remind your pitcher to try to field the ball if it is bunted on the third-base side. Once the bunt is down, quickly decide if your pitcher *can* field the bunt and, if so, rush to the bag to receive his force throw. If you see that your pitcher can't field the bunt, then it's yours; charge it and throw to first base. By gauging in advance your pitcher's fielding ability, the speed of the runners, and the condition of the field, you're much more likely to make the right decision.

With fewer than two outs and a ground ball hit near the bag, step on third base and throw to first base to complete the double play. If the ground ball is hit at you or to your left, throw to second base to begin the double play. *Do not* attempt to tag the runner coming from second base to third base. He may delay or try to avoid the tag, and it will be too late to make the double play.

A hit-and-run or steal attempt may occur in this situation, so don't be too far from the bag when the pitch is made. If, out of the corner of your eye, you see the runner coming, hold your position as long as possible to determine whether the ball will be hit in your direction. If it isn't, rush to the bag, straddle it facing the runner, and take the throw from the catcher for the tag-out.

Bases Loaded

With nobody out and the score close, play even with the bag and close to the line. On a ground ball to you, throw for the force-out to the catcher, who should relay the ball to first base for the double play.

With one out and a ground ball hit to third near the bag, step on third and throw to first to complete the double play. If the ball is hit at you or to your left, throw to second to start the double play. *Remember:* With the bases loaded, *never* attempt to tag the runner coming from second base. With two outs, you can exercise the easiest of the three options, depending on where you field the ball: You can tag third base for the final out, or throw to second base, or to first.

Runner on Second Base Only

With fewer than two outs, look at the runner at second base after fielding the ground ball. If the runner is too far off the bag, throw to the second baseman for the pick-off. If he's not, throw to first base to retire the batter.

With two outs, ignore the runner on second and throw to first base for the final out.

Runner on Third Base Only, or Runners on Second and Third

With fewer than two outs, hold the runner close to the bag to prevent a squeeze play or a steal of home. If a ground ball is hit to you, check the runner and hold him at third before throwing to first to retire the batter. If the runner breaks home from third, by all means, throw home.

With two outs, there's still the chance the runner may attempt to steal home, so be sure to hold him fairly close. If a ground ball is hit to you, ignore the runner and throw to first base to end the inning.

GENERAL CONSIDERATIONS

When selecting a third baseman's glove, choose one somewhat larger than a second baseman's or shortstop's. A larger glove will aid you in catching or knocking down hard-hit balls to your right or left.

Pop flies near the plate or dugout are easier for a third baseman to handle than for the catcher. Take charge of that play; your glove is better designed for that catch, and pop flies normally drift toward the field (you) and away from the catcher.

Be prepared to cover second base if the shortstop and second baseman are drawn to the outfield attempting a play and there is no runner advancing toward third.

Encourage your pitcher. You're closer to the mound than any other player and can be of help and lend support to a tense pitcher.

Use the "set" and "ready" positions. They're indispensable to a third baseman since batted balls can be on him so quickly.

Any good third baseman will prevent a significant number of extra-base hits during a season. Generally a base hit past the third baseman's right and down the left-field line is a double that will score a runner from first and move a batter into scoring position. If, because of alert positioning and polished skills (in the dive play or backhand play), you can stop even half the hard-hit balls to your right, your team will be a winner. The "hot corner" is no idle phrase but highly descriptive of a key defensive position reserved for a top player.

Shortstop and Second Base: The Double Play

The phrase "two for the price of one" always attracts people's attention. Mention it to a baseball pitcher and he'll immediately think double play and begin extolling the virtues of his shortstop and second baseman, since, by far, these two middle infielders, with their double-play-making capabilities, form the foundation of a team's defense. "Besides," the pitcher might add, "who else guards the gateway to scoring and can prevent an opponent's base runners from entering? Who else roams farther afield than they do in pursuit of ground balls? And who more often gives you two outs for the price of one (in the form of double plays) than they do? Nobody!"

True. And the pitcher could also point out that the most crucial play a team can make is not the strikeout, pop-up, or throw-out of the base stealer, but the double play, wherein two-thirds of an opponent's offensive potential is wiped out on one batted ball. More rallies have been killed by a skillful double-play combination at short and second than by any other defensive ingredient. The pitcher who can boast of having a top shortstop and second baseman behind him capable of "turning two" is usually part of a winning team.

Most baseball books deal with these two posi-

Traffic gets heavy at second base, where quick footwork can save bruised and battered shins. Second baseman Bobby Grich combines courage, skill, and quick feet as he turns the double play.

tions separately, allotting a chapter to each and discussing the double play in each of the two chapters. However, since these two players must be in such harmony and have skills that so complement one another, I have chosen to consider them together.

QUALIFICATIONS

Both the shortstop and second baseman must have good range—that is, they should be able to cover a big fielding territory. More balls are hit to the middle two-thirds of the diamond than toward the foul lines, and more balls are hit sharply up the middle than toward the lines. The ability to range far to the left or right and still maintain enough balance to stay low, field a ground ball, and throw the batter out are the marks of a fine shortstop and second baseman.

Both must have sure hands and be able to field a ground ball cleanly on the first attempt. Unlike the first and third basemen, who are closer to first base when contact is made with the ball, the shortstop and second baseman cannot fumble or bobble the ball and still expect to retire the runner at first base. Use of the "funnel principle" (see pp. 90–91) will help to field a ground ball cleanly and complete the throw.

The shortstop should have the stronger arm because his throws across the infield to first base are significantly longer than those of the second baseman. But the second baseman must have a quick arm capable of snapping a hard throw to first base, particularly on the double-play pivot. Both players are required to make long and strong throws on relays to the plate and during double-steal attempts when a runner on third base breaks for home.

Both the shortstop and second baseman must have quick, agile feet and something of a ballet dancer's nimbleness to avoid the sliding runner on double-play pivots. At the same time, they need a large measure of courage to accept the inevitable collisions and injuries that occur in making the double play. Shortstop and second base are not for the faint of heart! The second baseman is particularly vulnerable to injury as he takes the pivot throw. If he regards the runner too much and the ball too little, he will be ineffective. A good second baseman is a blend of quickness, strength, and fearlessness.

Additionally, both players must be intelligent and alert. The offense will use more tricks and devices to advance runners to second base than to any other base on the diamond. Because second base becomes the focus of all this strategy, the two middle infielders must be able to predict what will happen and prevent their opponents from advancing.

Finally, the shortstop and second baseman should be leaders capable of inspiring their teammates. Because they are involved in so many key plays throughout the game, other players learn to focus on them for direction. An effective double-play combination knows the defensive responsibilities of every other player on the team and, on many occasions, will direct their teammates by instruction as well as example.

Coaches: Select your team's shortstop and second baseman with care. They will become the hub of your defensive wheel and the key to your defensive success. Quite often, the shortstop is the best all-around athlete on the team and the second baseman is the scrappy, hustling, alert leader or captain. Together with the pitcher and catcher, a strong and dependable double-play combination virtually assures a solid defense.

GENERAL RULES FOR THE DOUBLE PLAY

The following rules apply to both the shortstop and second baseman on the double play, and should be fixed in both players' minds before the ball is hit or a runner on first base breaks for second. Whether the throw that starts the double play comes from the partner, the pitcher, the catcher, the first baseman, or the third baseman, each of these rules must be obeyed to assure the double play's success.

1. *Make the first out sure.* The runner advancing to second base is entering scoring position, so concentrate first on retiring him. Don't make the grave mistake of rushing either the throw to second base or the pivot throw to first. In your haste to complete the double play, you may make an error and wind up retiring neither runner.

2. *Throw the ball chest-high over the second-base bag, using a three-quarter overhand delivery.* The only fixed target in the area is second base, and it provides your best focus as you make your throw to the pivot man. I consider it a mistake to "lead" the pivot man with a throw 3 or 4 feet inside the bag to help him avoid the runner. Before long, that lead throw becomes 5 or 6 feet from the bag, and the pivot man is stretching too far for the ball.

3. *Let the pivot man see the ball clearly.* This rule is particularly important on the ground ball fielded within 20 feet of second base. Avoid the temptation to flip the ball directly out of the glove or shovel it to the pivot man with a two-handed motion. Instead, remove the ball from your glove and shovel it clearly with your bare hand so the pivot man can see it early. This also allows

the pivot man to time his final steps to the bag and execute his footwork knowing the ball's exact trajectory.

4. *When you are the pivot man, make a fast but controlled approach to the bag and expect a bad throw.* When a ground ball is hit, you may be as far as 40 feet from the bag. You must sprint full-speed to a point approximately 5 feet from the bag and then put on the brakes and be ready to react to a bad throw in any direction. Do not come to a complete stop as you approach the bag; instead, spread your feet apart and take short, choppy steps until you see where the throw is heading, then move to the ball. Approaching the bag, you should square off in the direction of the throw to maximize body control. If you are a second baseman making the pivot, do not take a curved, or banana, route toward the bag, because even though the banana route establishes your momentum toward first base, the throw from the third baseman or shortstop may sail to the outfield side of the bag and force you off-balance as you reach for it. Going straight to the bag and keeping both shoulders squared toward your teammate will help you react faster to a bad throw.

5. *As pivot man, keep your chest directly in front of every throw, and catch the ball near the heel of the glove with two hands.* This is the single most important rule in making the pivot play at second base. Keeping your chest in front of every throw makes it easier to move your feet and shift your body correctly on a ball thrown to the right or left; and catching the ball with two hands near the heel of the glove makes the transfer from glove to throwing hand much faster and more efficient. As pivot man, if you carefully observe rules 4 and 5, you will nearly always be in proper balance as you begin your job of tagging the bag and releasing your throw to first base.

6. *Don't worry about the runner.* On the routine double play when the ball is hit fairly hard and the runner from first base has average speed, you, playing the pivot, should be able to take the throw, tag the bag, and have your throw well on its way to first base when the runner slides into second. By then, you can avoid the runner by stepping over him or jumping out of the way. You must not allow yourself to watch the runner at any time. Focus on the ball as it is thrown to you, and then on the first baseman as you relay the throw to him. Try, as the pivot man, to develop a sense of where the runner is when you take the throw at second base. With adequate planning before the ball is hit (see pp. 86–87), this instinct will become stronger and more reliable. If the runner and ball arrive together at second base, you should move across the bag and catch the ball as a first baseman would, and protect against a damaging collision. Granted, you probably won't get the batter at first, but you'll at least have retired the lead runner and spared yourself serious injury. Remember: There

is no need for foolish heroics at second base. No ball game is so important as to place any player's well-being in jeopardy.

7. *Be sure, as the pivot man, to touch the bag.* Although it is possible with practice to develop skillful footwork and catch the ball after the foot has left the base, don't do it—for several reasons. First, there is no place in baseball for cheating or for skirting the rules. Players who cheat in certain areas of the game create dilemmas for themselves and for their teammates and encourage an attitude on the team of winking at other rules and regulations. Second, and more to the point, sooner or later an umpire will catch you in the "phantom tag" and call the runner safe at second base. And you can be pretty certain that runner will score!

Practicing these seven general rules assures a careful and thorough approach to the double play. With the rules well in mind, a shortstop and second baseman can now pay full attention to their individual responsibilities in every double-play situation.

DOUBLE-PLAY DEPTH

With a runner on first base and fewer than two outs, both middle infielders must move three or four steps in toward the plate and one or two steps toward second base from their normal positions. In baseball parlance, this is called "cheating" —the only legitimate kind—and it allows the two players to act on two most likely situations: One, it allows them to get to the bag in time to make the pivot on the double play; and two, it allows them to cover second base on an attempted steal or a hit-and-run. In either case, cheating in toward the plate lets them hold their positions against the batted ball as long as possible and still cover second base if one of the several plays above occurs.

As a middle infielder, before the pitch, establish with your teammate which of you will take the throw from the pitcher on a double-play attempt, or from the catcher on a steal or hit-and-run attempt. Normally, with a right-handed hitter at the plate, the second baseman covers the bag; with a left-handed hitter, the shortstop covers. In the higher levels of baseball, where the batters are more skilled at hitting the ball through the vacated position on the hit-and-run, the shortstop and second baseman will signal one another before each pitch as to which one will cover, and thus keep the batter guessing. The middle infielders should always inform the pitcher which one of them will cover second base on a ball hit back to the pitcher. When the pitcher wheels to throw for the double play, it helps him to know which direction the pivot man is coming from.

On a ground ball hit to the third baseman or shortstop, the second baseman covers second base for the double-play pivot. On a ball hit to the first baseman or second baseman, the shortstop covers the bag.

From the "ready" position, as the pitcher releases the ball toward home plate, you, as the middle infielder responsible for covering second base on a steal attempt, must give a quick glance toward the runner on first to see if he is taking a crossover step and breaking toward second. If he is, take a quick step toward home (to protect your position if the ball is hit toward you) and then break toward second base to take the throw from the catcher. Remember: You have already cheated in a bit, so you should have no problem getting to the bag in time for the catcher's throw. It is important that you get to the bag in time to position yourself with your left foot on the base and in good balance to take the throw from the catcher and apply the tag. There is no excuse for covering late, because you have already taken a shortened position toward the plate and second base before the pitch.

If the runner on first base does not break with the pitch, and the ball is not hit, both you and your fellow middle infielder should come out of your ready positions and take several steps toward second base while watching the runner at first base. This prevents the runner from attempting a delayed steal of second base and also backs up the catcher's throw to the pitcher.

THE SHORTSTOP'S THROW TO SECOND BASE

The Normal Double-Play Throw

On a double-play ball hit slightly to your left, straight at you, or anywhere to your right, you, playing shortstop, make your first move toward the ball exactly

By dropping his right knee as he funnels the ground ball, the shortstop can open his hips and shoulders for a strong, accurate throw to second base.

as you would in fielding a normal ground ball and making the play at first base (see pp. 88–91). The crucial difference is that on the double-play ball, you must set your feet a moment sooner, funnel the ball in that position, drop your right knee, and make a quick three-quarter overhand throw to second base without straightening up. You do not have the luxury of taking time to field the ball and shuffle a step or two toward second base before releasing the throw; you must have your feet already spread and set, your seat down, and hands in front before the ball reaches you. The funnel principle is important here because it allows you to control the ball as you drop your right knee and prepare to make the quick throw to your partner at second. Remember General Rule #2 for the Double Play earlier in this chapter? By dropping your right knee almost to the ground as you funnel the ball toward your navel, you can open your hips and shoulders more easily and elevate your elbow for the three-quarter over-hand snap throw. This type of throw has more velocity and accuracy than a sidearm sling, and its flight can be easily followed by the pivot man. Don't throw sidearm here, and certainly don't throw underhanded. Both are common mistakes for a shortstop, and both are hard for your second baseman to see if you are throwing at close range. Even if you throw some distance from the bag, a sidearm throw will sink and fade by the time it reaches second base. So play it smart. Take an extra fraction of a second and get the ball off in a three-quarter overhand throw. Your time will be more than compensated by a harder, more accurate, more easily handled throw to the pivot man.

The Underhand Throw

On a ground ball hit to your left at shortstop and *within approximately 20 feet* of the bag, break from the ready position with a crossover step, take a slight banana route to get in front of the ball, funnel the ball into your glove, and, in one continuous motion with your bare hand, underhand the ball chest-high

Within 20 feet of second base, the best way to deliver the ball to the pivot man is with an underhand shovel throw. Make certain the pivot man sees the ball before you throw it.

over the bag to the second baseman. If you are fairly close to second base, you can lead with your right foot. If you field the ball out at the 18- or 20-foot distance from the bag, you may have to take an extra shuffle step as you funnel the ball into the glove and lead with your left foot to get more velocity on the toss. In either case, you must have the ball clearly in your bare hand and underhand it to your partner, keeping your palm up, your wrist stiff, and your elbow in. Following this technique will assure a firm, accurate toss. If you field the ball far to your left behind the bag, then you must toss backhanded. When this situation occurs, it is highly unlikely that there will be time also to retire the batter and complete the double play, so the second baseman should be sure to turn fully toward you (General Rule #5) and help you complete this difficult throw.

The Slow-Hit Grounder

When a ground ball is slowly hit toward you at shortstop and requires that you charge it and throw sidearm on the run, your second baseman becomes vital in helping you decide where and how to throw. This will generally be a very close play at second base, and if neither you nor your teammate exercise good judgment, both runners may be safe. To begin with, you have all you can do to field the slow ground ball cleanly and make a snap throw, so your second baseman must help with a loud "Two!" if there is a chance to get the lead runner, or "One!" if the runner at second base is likely to beat the throw. Since catching and throwing a slow-hit ground ball is never easy, your second baseman must decide if the runner coming into second base represents the tying or winning run and is worth your trying to throw out. If your team is ahead by two or more runs, your second baseman should call for the more certain of the two options. Meanwhile, your technique for executing this difficult play is the same as that for the third baseman fielding a slow bouncing ball (p. 111).

On a slow grounder, the shortstop flips the ball sidearm to second base while moving toward home plate. The second baseman can help the shortstop by calling the play.

THE SECOND BASEMAN'S THROW TO THE SHORTSTOP

If you're a second baseman, you probably already know how difficult it is to make a strong, accurate throw to the pivot man (the shortstop). Being right-handed, you must turn your body quickly into throwing position *as you field the ball* in order to unleash the proper three-quarter overhand throw. Let's look at this maneuver closely.

On a ground ball hit at you or slightly to your right or left, move toward the ball exactly as you would if playing shortstop. Everything remains the same: Your feet are spread and set an instant before the ball arrives; your seat is down; you funnel the ball toward your navel. But now, as you funnel the ball, drop your *left* knee close to the ground and open your hips and shoulders toward second base. This permits you to raise your throwing arm quickly to the proper three-quarter overhand position for a snap throw to the shortstop. If you do not drop your left knee, you will be forced into making a sidearm throw, which has less speed and accuracy.

If the ball is hit to your left, break with a crossover step in that direction, take a slight banana route to get in front of the ball, field it using the funnel principle, and make a quick jump pivot 180 degrees to your right so you can plant your right foot firmly behind you and throw in a three-quarter overhand motion to the shortstop. Anytime your momentum is going even slightly to your left when you field the ball, you should execute the quick jump pivot as you funnel the ground ball toward your navel. If the ball is so far to your left that you cannot get in front of it and must stretch and try to make a glove-hand play, you should turn the same 180 degrees to your left, plant your right foot, and gun the ball to the shortstop covering second base. In this situation, the double play is unlikely unless the batter is extremely slow.

To start the double play on a ball hit at him or slightly to either side, the second baseman drops his left knee, opens his hips and shoulders, and fires a three-quarter overhand throw to the shortstop.

On a ball hit to your right within 20 feet of the bag, make an underhand shovel toss using the same technique as the shortstop (pp. 123–124).

If you field the ball on the base line and can tag the runner going by, do so, gripping the ball firmly in your bare hand with all four fingers and thumb. If the runner stops and avoids the tag, chase him back toward first, throw to the first baseman to retire the batter, and then retire the first runner in a rundown.

On a slow-hit ground ball toward you, your shortstop takes responsibility to holler the correct play. The runner advancing to second base has to represent an important run for the shortstop to call "Two!" because throwing to second base while on the grass and charging in the direction of home plate is an extremely difficult play for any second baseman.

THE UNASSISTED DOUBLE PLAY

If, playing shortstop or second base, you field the ball within *two strides* of the bag, you should call out loudly, "I have it," tag second base for the first out, and throw the ball to first base to complete the double play. This is the easiest of the double plays and eliminates the possibility of a bad throw or dropped ball in retiring the lead runner. The coordination for this play comes when you call your partner off, but don't do so until you are sure that you are fielding the ball within two strides of the bag.

SHORTSTOP PIVOT ON THE DOUBLE PLAY

As a shortstop playing the pivot on a double play, your footwork is fairly standard and usually entails one of two basic maneuvers, depending on the position of the throw. To begin with, sprint to the area of the bag as quickly as possible, bringing your body under control 5 feet behind the bag with your hands up and in perfect line with the throw. The general rules of the double play become important here and you might be wise to review them now (see pp. 119–121). If the throw is over the bag or anywhere to your left, step across the bag and toward the ball with your left foot. As the ball hits your glove, drag your right foot over the outfield corner of the bag, take a quick shuffle crowhop to get your right foot planted and your shoulders lined up with the target, step toward first with your left foot, and fire a strong three-quarter overhand throw to first base. Performing this entire sequence as you should, in one continuous

The standard footwork for the shortstop as he makes the pivot on a throw over the bag or anywhere to his left. Note that the player keeps his chest in front of the ball.

motion, gives the visual impression that you are floating effortlessly into the ball and across the bag to complete the play. There is no need to execute different footwork from the above on a routine double play when the throw is over the bag or to your left.

If the throw is inside the base and to your right, you can still handle it with ease. Simply move your chest in front of the ball by stepping toward it with your right foot and dragging your left foot over the bag. Your right, or pivot, foot is already firmly planted when you catch the ball, so you then complete your drag step left and stride toward first base for the throw.

When the throw is inside the bag to the shortstop's right, he tags the bag with his left foot and strides toward first base.

On virtually all throws to you as the shortstop pivot, you must remember to catch the ball *at* or *slightly in front of* the bag. Don't flash across the bag and reach for the throw on the second-base side. It's too dangerous. Too often you will be out of control, and unable to keep your chest in front of the ball or get a good grip on it as you throw to first base. Remember: For efficiency and quickness in turning the double play, always approach the bag in a controlled and balanced manner. Too, when ball and runner arrive at the bag simultaneously, you, by being behind or at the bag, can move either right or left, depending on where you feel the runner will slide.

SECOND BASEMAN PIVOT ON THE DOUBLE PLAY

If you are a second baseman, there are at least seven ways for you to execute your footwork on the double play when the throw is good. You can:

1. Step on the bag with your right foot as you catch the ball, then step toward first base with your left foot and throw.

2. Straddle the bag as you catch the ball, do a shuffle crowhop toward first base dragging your right foot over the bag, step with your left toward first, and throw.

3. Step across the bag with your left foot to meet the ball, drag your right foot over the bag, shuffle-crowhop toward the mound to get your right foot down quickly, step toward first, and throw.

4. Step across the bag with your right foot to meet the good throw while dragging your left foot over the bag. (Your right foot is already down, so simply stride with your left foot toward first and throw.)

5. Step on the bag with your left foot as you catch the ball. Stride toward third base with your right foot, planting it firmly, and step toward first base with your left foot and throw.

6. Step on the bag with your left foot as you catch the ball. Step back toward right field with the right foot, then stride toward first base with the left foot and throw.

7. Straddle the bag as you catch the ball and step toward left field with your right foot while kicking the bag with the inside of your left foot. Step toward first base with your left foot and throw.

Before you scream "Enough!" let me assure you that as a second baseman you don't have to learn all of the above thoroughly to be a good pivot man. Experiment. Find the footwork with which you feel most comfortable and use that when the throw is over the bag and the runner is not a factor—in other words, on the routine double play. Methods 1, 4, 5, 6, and 7 all require a fairly strong arm because there is no shuffle crowhop to help you gather momentum toward first base. Methods 2 and 3 are good if you're a quick-footed but weak-armed second baseman, because they give you an extra shuffle step with which to gather more momentum and thrust toward your target. These two methods, though, do make you a fraction slower in getting rid of the ball because of the additional shuffle crowhop to get the right foot firmly planted to throw.

I favor methods 1, 2, and 3 on a routine double play when a throw is over the bag or slightly to your left. In method 1, you use the bag just as a pitcher uses the pitching rubber: for a strong push-off in your throw. The nicest feature of this method is that it involves the least footwork—one step to catch, one step to throw—but it does require a fairly strong arm. Method 2, with its momentum-building shuffle step, will help you if you're a second baseman with an average or weak arm; while method 3 is useful on both good and bad throws, particularly those to your left, since it allows easy lateral movement in that direction, which keeps your chest in front of the ball.

On a bad throw to the outfield side of the bag (that is, your right as the second baseman), you must have your body movement under control at the bag *before* the throw arrives. When you see the throw coming to your right, shift *your entire body*—do not merely reach with your glove—so that your chest remains in front of the throw. Plant your right foot as you catch the ball, and, tagging the bag with your striding left foot, throw.

In this pivot on a good throw to second base, the second baseman drags his right foot over the bag, then adds a crowhop to his stride, which gives his throw to first base more power.

Many throws will be off-target to the second baseman's right, but by exercising the important rule "Keep your chest in front of the ball," he can handle the bad throw and still be balanced for a strong throw to first base.

Whenever possible, throw with the three-quarter overhand motion, which gives the ball optimum velocity and accuracy and helps guarantee a successful double play. Don't bother throwing a sidearm sling to "flatten" the runner or cause him to slide early. Most of these sidearm throws sink badly into the dirt before they reach first base, and the double play is lost.

DOUBLE-PLAY DRILLS

Several drills are useful in developing the double-play combination. The first is the *underhand shovel-toss drill.* Several infielders space themselves in a circle approximately 15 to 20 feet apart. As the players shuffle clockwise with their knees bent and backs straight, they toss a ball clockwise around the circle, using the proper technique: palm up, wrist stiff, elbow in, toss firm and aimed for the teammate's chest. From this distance, each tosser needs to step with his left foot to give the throw enough velocity and accuracy. This drill also helps the first baseman practice his toss to the pitcher covering first base. After one minute, the players reverse direction and perform the drill to their right.

Perhaps the most useful drill for double-play instruction involves placing two or three players at each of the two positions, shortstop and second base, and a large screen about midway between second and first. The coach takes a position behind the pitcher's mound and in line with home plate and the shortstop, and rolls ground balls to the shortstop, who throws to the second baseman at the bag for the pivot. The second baseman throws the 45 feet toward first base into the screen. The shortstops alternate fielding the ground balls, and the second basemen alternate on the pivot throw. With a supply of fifteen or twenty balls, the coach can put his double-play combination through many repetitions in a brief time. He can roll all the different types of ground balls—to the right, to the left, straight on, slow-hit—and is close enough to the fielders to give constant instruction. After a time, the coach moves to the other side of the mound and rolls balls to the second baseman for the double play on that side. The screen frees up the first-base area for other drills: third basemen, for example, can practice their throws to first on slow-hit ground balls; and for that matter, the home-plate area is available for catchers to practice their blocks and shifts.

If your team isn't using this simultaneous-drills approach in their practices, think about incorporating it. At the University of Arizona, we practice the above drills and others simultaneously several times a week. In any case, if a shortstop and second baseman ever hope to execute "the most important play in baseball," the double play, they must do one thing and do it often: they must practice.

The underhand shovel-toss drill: particularly helpful for the shortstop, second baseman, and first baseman.

Outfield Play

I've had the privilege of seeing firsthand some of the greatest outfielders in baseball history, and all those greats—Willie Mays, Roberto Clemente, Al Kaline, Mickey Mantle, and now Dave Winfield —form a composite in my mind of the ideal outfielder. Each of them reminds us how important skilled and capable outfielders are to a winning effort. Without these players—two center fielders, two right fielders, one left fielder—none of their teams would have won the World Series or league pennants when they did. A strong outfield helps a team in so many ways that no matter how good a team's pitching or infield may be, without a capable outfield that team will flounder.

QUALIFICATIONS

Each of the three outfielders confronts different situations that demand specific skills. Determining which outfielder is best suited for each position requires a coach's careful analysis. Not only must the individual strengths and weaknesses of each outfielder be carefully weighed, but also the way all three interact and complement each other within the boundaries of each position.

133

Taking charge of any ball he feels he can reach, centerfielder Andre Dawson has priority over the infielders and other outfielders.

The Center Fielder

The center fielder is generally the fastest of the three outfielders and expected to cover the most ground. More batted balls are hit in his direction than to the left fielder and right fielder, so he must have the greater ability to field grounders and fly balls. His arm must be among the strongest on the team because of the long throws he must make to third base and home plate. He must also be able to go back well on deep fly balls, because he will have more balls hit over his head and deep to his right or left than the other two outfielders. He should be alert, decisive, have good judgment, and know the abilities of the left fielder and right fielder thoroughly. In effect, the center fielder is the captain of the outfield and should have maximum freedom to try to catch any fly ball for which he calls. A good outfield defense keys on the center fielder; wherever he moves, the left and right fielders move accordingly.

The Right Fielder

The right fielder should have the strongest arm of the three because his long and accurate throw to third base can prevent a base runner from advancing with fewer than two outs. A right fielder should have a certain amount of foot speed to cut off potential extra-base hits down the line that could otherwise roll for triples. He can play a bit deeper than the other two outfielders since, because the throw is relatively short and a long turn at first base is a risk, batters seldom try to stretch singles to right field into doubles.

The Left Fielder

The left fielder can have a lesser arm compared to his two outfield teammates since his longest throw is to home plate and his others—to second and third base—are relatively short. He must be skilled at fielding ground balls, because many ground singles hit in his field are an invitation to batters to stretch that hit to a double since they can take such long turns at first base without danger. For an aggressive batter/runner, a momentary bobble in left field means an automatic double. The left fielder should have good speed to cut off base hits down the line and hold the batter to a single or at most a double. To prevent batter/runners from getting two bases on a hit to him, the left fielder should play somewhat shallow, which means, in turn, he must be able to go back fast on a fly ball. Finally, if all else is equal and the choice is possible, the left-handed thrower should be put in left field and the right-handed thrower in right. Each, because his glove hand is closer, will have an easier time fielding balls hit down the lines.

FIELDING FLY BALLS

Proper Position

If you're an outfielder, the "set" and "ready" positions are as important for you as for your teammates in the infield. Like an infielder, you have some thinking to do before the pitch is delivered; and in preplanning your personal strategy, you should consider such variables as the score, the inning, the speed of the batter and runners, the power and hitting tendencies of the batter, the condition and pitching pattern of the pitcher, the wind, the sun, and the positioning of the other outfielders, along with any instructions from the bench. Plan your strategy while standing in the set position; then, when the pitcher delivers, take a short, quick step forward with both feet and assume the ready position—your weight forward approximately 75 percent on the balls of your feet, your heels resting lightly on the ground, your feet spread a shoulders' width apart, your back straight, and your eyes fixed intently on the batter. Don't bend your knees and lower your body as much as an infielder, because you're more likely to have to straighten up and sprint some distance to a batted ball. By watching the batter during the pitch, you can tell if he is striding and swinging in such a way as to pull the ball, hit late, push the bat, or power the bat into the pitch. All this helps in your initial break for the ball. When wooden bats were used exclusively, an experienced outfielder could tell by the crack of the bat where and how hard a ball was hit, but the advent of the aluminum bat has made it

From the ready position, the outfielder can break instantly in the direction of the batted ball.

The safest way to catch a fly ball is with two hands. Sight the ball over the upheld glove and make the catch somewhat to the throwing side of the body while moving in toward the infield. Never take your eyes off the ball.

harder to "read" the ball off the bat, so you're going to need an instant's pause before being sure whether to break in or back.

Make every effort to catch fly balls with your back to the outfield and your body moving in toward the infield as you make the catch. That way you'll establish momentum toward your target, see the ball more clearly, and have a quicker, stronger throw to the cutoff man to prevent runners from tagging up and advancing. Sight the path of the ball downward by looking over the top of your glove. Have both hands up and catch the ball with *two hands* as close to the throwing position as possible. It makes no sense at all to catch a fly ball one-handed on the glove side or over the shoulder when, with a bit more effort and technique, you can make a safer two-handed catch that is far quicker to launch from for the throw. Major-league outfielders who routinely make the flashy one-handed catch do no favor at all for young outfielders hoping to learn proper fundamentals from their idols. Even the great Willie Mays must take some responsibility for the bruised chests and sore forearms the young outfielders of the Fifties, Sixties, and Seventies suffered trying to imitate Willie's famed "basket catch."

The Shallow Pop Fly

When you determine that a fly ball is hit shallow and in front of you, break forward, keeping your eyes on the ball the entire time. If the fly ball is in your territory, shout "I have it!" as soon as you feel you can make the catch. Many outfielders lazily coast to the ball when they feel it is a routine play, and wind up making the catch out of position or running faster than they expected. This dangerous practice is known as "drifting," and the way to avoid it is to sprint to the point where the ball is descending and prepare to catch it in the manner prescribed. Try to catch every ball in as close to the ideal position as possible. If you drift, a sudden gust of wind, a slight stumble, or a ball hit harder than expected will make a difficult play out of what should have been a routine catch.

Fly Ball Hit to the Left or Right

On a fly ball hit to your right or left, the fastest way to get under way from the ready position is with a crossover step. Much like an infielder, your first move as an outfielder is an explosive lateral thrust of the upper body while pivoting on the ball of your lead foot and crossing over with your other leg. To get behind a fly ball hit to the right or left, you should run a "banana route" so that when you reach the point where you catch the ball, your body will be moving toward the infield. A banana route curving toward the outfield fence and back toward the fly ball gives you time to position your body for the two-handed catch on the throwing side and follow it with a perfect throw.

The Deep Fly Ball

When a fly ball is hit over your head, your first move should be a short drop-back step to the side of the ball. This way, you can activate your body toward the fence but still follow the ball's flight off the bat. (If your first step were a crossover and back, you would turn your head away from the ball and not see as clearly how hard it was hit.) After sensing how deep the ball will be over your head, continue back while keeping your eyes on the ball. Your first several steps are critical and must be *full-speed* back to the point where you can turn, position your body, and catch the descending ball while moving toward the infield. Again, don't drift. It's a bad habit and leads to too many over-the-shoulder catches and poor throws to the infield.

Using the banana route helps in going back for fly balls. If you're a right-handed outfielder, you'll have a harder time with balls hit over your left shoulder, because you must circle and turn back to your right to get into proper throwing position.

On a ball hit over your right shoulder, drop your right foot back, cross over with your left, and sprint back, keeping your eyes on the ball. As you move back to your right, you are already in good throwing position, providing you

On a deep fly over the outfielder's head, his first move is a drop-back step to one side of the ball, followed by a crossover step. Both help him keep sight of the ball as it leaves the infield.

get *behind* the ball and make the catch with two hands while moving in toward the infield.

When a fly ball is hit deep to the fence, your first thought should be to find exactly where the fence is while keeping your eyes on the ball. Before the ball was hit, you should already have gauged how many strides it takes to reach the fence. If there is a warning track, you should also know in advance its width in strides. With this information, you can sprint to the fence, reach out with your bare hand so you know exactly how much deeper you can go, and prepare to make the catch. If the fly ball is not going to reach the fence, you can move in to catch it in good throwing position. If the ball descends to the base of the fence, you can catch it easily. If the ball is high off the fence, you are now in a good position to gather yourself and leap straight up as high as possible. If you drift while approaching the fence, you won't know exactly where it is and will thus either jump too soon for the ball and miss, or become fearful of the fence and shy away from the ball, or crash into the fence, causing injury and missing the ball. Your outfield teammate nearest to the play can help by shouting signals as he races over to back you up.

In making deep catches, good outfielders sprint back—they never "drift"—and locate the fence immediately.

PLAYING THE SUN

Every outfielder should anticipate problems with fly balls into the sun. To begin with, you should continually glance upward between pitches to see if the sun is moving into your line of vision. If it is, practice holding your glove up at different angles as a shield against the sun's glare. Additionally, alert your teammates to the fact that you may have a problem on a fly ball so they can be in a position to back you up or take the fly ball themselves from an angle off-line from the sun. If they can't help you, another tip is to turn your head and body slightly as the ball is descending and wait for it to emerge from the sun's glare.

The best method of catching a fly ball in the sun is to wear a pair of baseball sunglasses and use them along with the glove as a shield. These sunglasses are worn under the visor of the cap and can be flipped down over your eyes with a quick tap of the fingers. Practice making this flip and generally get accustomed to wearing the sunglasses before attempting to use them in a game.

Many games, even championships, are decided because of fly balls lost in

Play the sun field using your glove and baseball sunglasses as shields.

the sun. In 1980, our Arizona team was able to battle back from behind in a key tournament game and go on to win the NCAA championship because the opponent's right fielder, with two men on base and two outs, lost a long fly ball in the sun. Embarrassingly for him, he had left his sunglasses on the bench that inning.

FIELDING GROUND BALLS

It is important to charge all ground balls and return them to the infield as quickly as possible. Keep in mind at all times that the batter or other runners may try to advance an extra base. On normal ground balls to the outfield, the same fielding principles should be used as those described for infielders in chapter 5.

If the ground ball is hit very hard, you may elect to go down on one knee. This ensures that you at least block the ball if you don't catch it, and is also a safe technique if your team is ahead and you're trying not to allow runners to advance. However, a throw cannot be made as quickly from this position.

The outfielder must also learn to field ground balls properly. On the left, the ball has been sharply hit and the defense must keep runners out of scoring position. Use the "do-or-die" technique (right) only in the late innings when the tying or winning run is trying to score.

The *only* time an outfielder is permitted to field a ground ball one-handed is during the late innings when the tying or winning run is attempting to score. Then, and only then, you must charge the ground ball, scoop it up with your glove, try to place your left foot forward as you do so, and throw quickly to the plate to retire the key runner. This hard-charging, glove-handed play is aptly called the "do-or-die." Many outfielders make the mistake of using the one-handed technique on routine ground balls when there is no runner trying to score. A slight bad hop and that routine ground ball becomes a two- or three-base error.

REMINDERS FOR THE OUTFIELDER

Watch your opponents during batting practice to get some indication as to which batters have the most power and should be played deeper. It also helps to know which are the pull hitters and which are the fastest runners who might try to stretch a base hit.

When your team is ahead, play a bit deeper to prevent an extra-base hit. You should also play deeper in the early innings and with two outs in an inning. Don't attempt a questionable catch in these circumstances either, because that "circus catch" may turn into a double or triple. The time to be daring and risky is when your team is behind, or in the late innings, when you are tied or protecting a one-run lead. In short, percentage baseball tells an outfielder to play safe when ahead or in the early innings and to gamble when behind, particularly in the late innings.

If you are ahead by two or more runs and there are fewer than two outs and a runner on third base, catch all foul balls. When one run ahead, tied, or behind and with fewer than two outs, you should *not* catch the foul fly ball if you aren't sure you can throw out the runner should he tag up and attempt to score.

Generally, throw the ball into the infield one base *ahead* of the runner closest to home plate. However, in the last two innings, if your team is ahead by two or more runs, throw to second base to keep the tying run from advancing there.

Make every effort to hit the cutoff or relay man with your throws. When an outfielder throws too high, generally a runner advances needlessly. Aim at the cutoff or relay man's chest.

Line drives hit down the foul lines will curve toward those lines. There is little chance you will overrun a line drive as you sprint toward either foul line. *However,* a high pop fly down the foul lines will drift back toward the field as it descends, and these you *can* overrun. Long line drives hit right at you in the outfield will have a tendency to rise and take off over your head.

Always check which way and how strongly the wind is blowing. Observe the flag or throw bits of grass into the air and watch their drift in the wind.

The center fielder is the captain of the outfield and has priority over the other two outfielders and all infielders. Communicate constantly with your outfield teammates. Let them know where you are playing so they can adjust. When you are not involved in the play, look for a base or throw that you can back up. When the ball is hit, even to the pitcher, there is never an occasion for an outfielder to remain standing at his position.

Your outfielder's glove should be as large as possible. A big glove with a long web can help you on a long run and last-second lunge for the ball.

Keep your arm warm between innings. Play catch with your fellow out-fielders or a teammate in the bullpen. After all, you may have to make a long, accurate throw a few minutes later.

As you play the extra-base hit off the fence, keep your chest over the ball and pick it up with your throwing hand closest to the fence and your shoulders already lined up toward the relay man.

Television's coverage of baseball in recent years has been both a blessing and a bane for outfield play. Millions of young outfielders have been able to see the spectacular plays and solid fundamentals of such leading outfielders as Willie Wilson, Fred Lynn, and Andre Dawson. But they've also been exposed to players who catch every ball one-handed, and I shudder to think of all the bad technique being emulated. Do yourself and your team a favor: Use two hands. If you pay your dues—that is, learn the right techniques and combine them with a strong arm and running speed—you might find yourself on television someday. Until then, at least you'll be a valued member of your team's outer perimeter of defense.

Pitching

There is no question that good pitching is the single most important requirement for a baseball team's success. Conservative estimates place the outcome of a baseball game as anywhere from 60 to 75 percent dependent on pitching. It is not uncommon for outstanding high-school pitchers to strike out two of every three batters they face, and the top major-league pitchers over the past twenty years—the Koufaxes, Gibsons, Seavers, Carltons, Perrys, Ryans, and Palmers—have all recorded numerous one-, two-, or three-hit shutouts in their careers when they literally dominated the game. No doubt, future records will list names like Valenzuela, Sutton, Kison, Niekro, Rogers, and Guidry: pitchers capable of doing the same.

Perhaps it's unfair to point out the disparity between pitching's importance and the amount of practice time that teams generally give their pitching staffs, but I do think that pitching should receive far more attention than most amateur teams presently give it. Unless baseball rules change drastically, the focus of a team's success or failure will remain on that raised 18-foot circle in the middle of the diamond. And the teams that develop good pitching staffs will generally be consistent winners and champions.

145

The Grand Master of Pitching, Sandy Koufax, delivers his extraordinary fastball. Note how powerfully his left leg thrusts off the rubber and how high he holds his pitching elbow during the delivery.

QUALIFICATIONS

If you're a pitcher and can throw hard, you have a good start on success, but don't despair if you're not 6'6" or built like Goose Gossage. The fact is, there is little correlation between a pitcher's size and the speed at which he can throw a baseball. Look at Ron Guidry. Some fortunate people, big and small, are simply born with an arm capable of outthrowing everyone else's on the block. Fortunately, the recent introduction of speed guns, which give an objective reading of how fast a pitcher can throw, have made even the smallest hard-throwing high-school and college players easier to spot, so don't worry: No matter what your size or weight, if you're a young pitcher who can throw 90-plus miles per hour, you're the kind of pitcher the pro scouts covet most.

But simply throwing hard is not enough. The more important quality you as a pitcher can possess is *control,* because no matter how much speed or how big a curve you may have, you are nothing if you can't get those pitches over the plate. Control is a pitcher's best ally. If you can throw two or three different pitches to a given spot at any time, you will get even the best hitters out. Baseball history is filled with stories of veteran pitchers who, despite their fastball having lost its zip or their curve ball its great spin, were still able to win games because of pinpoint control. While technique and mechanics may not improve the speed of your fastball, they can improve its control. Practice pays off. Consider the case of Sandy Koufax, who, in his first years with the Dodgers, had terrible control problems and was a mediocre pitcher despite having the hardest fastball in the majors. Sandy walked more batters than he struck out until finally he worked on his control and, with that blazing fastball and a remarkable curve, became the Hall of Fame pitcher that he is. Without the desire to work on his pitching control, Sandy Koufax would have been nobody, another baseball statistic, a loser.

The third quality you need in order to be a top pitcher is a "live arm." There is a significant difference between being able to throw hard and being able to throw so that the ball "moves." An 85-mile-per-hour fastball that sinks, slides, or rises is a much more effective pitch than the 90-mile-per-hour "hummer" that is faster but straight as a string. Here again, technique and mechanics can make the difference.

Finally, the best pitchers have an intangible quality built into their personalities. Call it "confidence," or "poise," or "coolness under pressure"—it amounts to the same thing: the pitcher's ability to overcome those negative factors outside his control and still perform at his best. Jim Kaat has it. More than any other quality listed above, Kaat's poise and self-confidence have kept him pitching successfully in the major leagues for over twenty-four years. In the 1965 American League season opener for the Minnesota Twins, Kaat had what seemed to be a complete game victory in his grasp when, with two outs in the ninth inning, a runner on second base, and the Twins ahead by one run, the opposing batter lifted an easy pop fly to the Twins' third baseman. Of the twenty-seven outs that Kaat had recorded that afternoon, this was the easiest, and the Twins' dugout began rushing out to congratulate him on a masterful performance. But the third baseman dropped the ball! The tying run scored. Most pitchers would have thrown up their hands in disgust or slammed their gloves on the ground. Not Kaat. Without changing expression, he rushed over and, with more than 30,000 fans watching, put his arm around his crestfallen teammate and told him, "Forget it. You're going to save a game for me someday." Jim then coolly returned to the mound, retired the final batter that inning, and pitched two more outstanding innings until the Twins won the game in the last of the eleventh when—you guessed it—that same third baseman drove in the winning run with a line-drive single. Oh, yes. The Twins won their only American League pennant that year, and Jim Kaat showed the way with his confidence and poise.

THE THREE BASIC PITCHES

If you're a young pitcher, don't make the mistake of trying to master five or six different pitches. When we conduct pitching tryouts at the University of Arizona, we first ask each candidate to throw the three basic pitches: fastball, curve ball (or slider), and change up. After a candidate has thrown enough of those pitches for us to grade him accurately, we ask if he has any additional pitches in which he has confidence. Most candidates will have several difficult trick pitches they want to demonstrate, but seldom will these fork balls, knuckle balls, screwballs, palm balls, or sidearm curves be any good. The unfortunate result of a young pitcher's trying to master these trick pitches is that he hasn't spent enough time on the basic three.

The Fastball

Tom Seaver has said that a good fastball is the best pitch in baseball. It is certainly thrown far more than any other pitch and has retired more hitters than all the other pitches combined. The fastball remains the most effective pitch, and the young pitcher who can throw it hard and with control has a good chance of succeeding with it 80 percent of the time.

The Rising Fastball

To throw a rising fastball, grip the ball across the long seams with your index and middle fingers spread about three-quarters of an inch apart. The ball rests on the inner bony surface of your thumb, which should be in line with your middle finger. Your third finger is curled and resting on the outside of the ball. Be sure you place the ball away from the palm of your hand and hold it with your fingertips and thumb. When the fastball is released from a normal three-quarter overhand delivery, the ball will rotate rapidly with all four long seams spinning backward toward you on a horizontal axis. The faster your arm action, the greater the pressure of your fingertips, and the harder your wrist snap on release, the more rise the pitch will have as it approaches the plate. Sandy Koufax's fastball seemed to rise 6 to 8 inches, which accounted for so many of his strikeouts. But a fastball that rises only 1 or 2 inches is highly effective and will cause batters to swing under the pitch and miss it or pop it up. If you're a young pitcher who can throw fairly hard, you'd be wise to use this grip.

The Four-Seam Fastball Grip (left). Combined with a three-quarter overhand delivery, this grip creates a rising fastball for the pitcher who can throw hard.

The Sinking-Fastball Grip Held Along the Seams (right). With less rotation than the four-seam grip, this pitch has a tendency to sink. Use it if you're not a hard-throwing pitcher; also to throw an overhand curve.

The Sinking Fastball

The sinking fastball will result in a lot of ground-ball outs. If you're not a hard-throwing pitcher, this pitch will be effective for you when kept low in the strike zone. The ball is gripped along its short, rounded seams and released in the same three-quarter overhand delivery. But now, instead of lifting the ball as in the cross-seam grip, the seams' rotation serves to drag the ball down as it approaches the plate. The danger with this fastball is that if you throw it above the batter's belt level, it will not have the sinking, fading action, and the batter will have a straight, medium-fast pitch that he can cream.

Ideally, if you can throw both the rising and the sinking fastball with control, you'll become a big winner.

The Curve Ball, or Slider

Most pitchers, it seems, are unable to throw both an effective curve and a slider —but no problem; one or the other, properly thrown, should be enough to fool the batter thinking fastball. Whereas the good fastball is designed to pass either over or under the swing of the bat, the good curve or slider breaks either away from the swing of the bat or into the hands of the batter as he swings.

The curve ball has two basic grips. Most pitchers grip the ball in the same way as for the sinking fastball, but some prefer to grip for the curve with the middle finger running along and on top of a long seam. In either case, the index and middle fingers are held a bit closer and the middle finger exerts 90 percent of the pressure during the ball's release. The idea with the curve is to create a tight, rapid rotation of the four long seams on a horizontal axis *toward* the batter, which causes the ball to drop as it approaches the plate.

Your arm action for the curve is similar to that of the fastball until your hand comes "over the top," at which point it should be closer to your head. It is extremely important that you keep your elbow up when throwing the curve, to impart as much downward snap of the wrist as possible. At the release point, your middle finger puts most of the pressure on the ball, and your wrist is snapped downward, causing the ball to roll off the middle and index fingers. Always be sure to *snap* your wrist; this gives greater spin to the ball as it reaches the plate. The looser and more flexible your wrist joint, the more effective your curve ball. The palm of your hand should be facing in toward your body as your arm completes its follow-through.

The Slider

More pitchers use the slider now because it can be thrown harder and doesn't

The Curve-Ball Release. As the hand pulls down and the wrist snaps downward, the middle finger exerts primary pressure on the ball.

require as great a wrist snap. The contrast between the two pitches can best be explained by picturing the curve ball spinning away and decidedly down from the batter anywhere from 1 to 2 feet, and the slider darting away and slightly down, 5 to 10 inches.

When holding the slider, you can use either of the two curve-ball grips, but place your two fingers off-center slightly to the outside of the ball. You throw the pitch with the normal three-quarter overhand delivery, which to the batter looks just like a fastball motion. Releasing the slider is similar to passing a football: the index and middle fingers provide a cutting or sliding motion across the outside of the ball as it leaves the hand. To put it another way, the slider has "sidespin" as it leaves the fingers, whereas the fastball has backspin and the curve ball has forward spin. Sliders literally spin like bullets.

The slider grip is held along the seams and off center, toward the outside of the ball. The release is similar to that for passing a football.

Your wrist should be loose and supple when you throw a slider but shouldn't snap downward as in the curve. Always use the three-quarter overhand motion to give the pitch its slight downward and sideward break, and *never* during your delivery drop your elbow. If you do, you will likely serve up a "hanging" slider which seems to float into the strike zone about chest-high and is the easiest pitch of all for a batter to crush.

If you're a young pitcher, try to develop only one of these two pitches. Trying to throw both puts a big strain on the arm; and besides, you're better off having a good curve or a good slider than a mediocre version of each.

The Change-Up

By far the most underrated pitch in baseball, an effective change-up not only can deceive a batter and cause a weak, off-balance swing, but can also set up the fastball. If a batter knows you have a good change-up, he must take that into account when he strides and swings, and most likely you can "sneak" more fastballs past him.

The change-up is especially needed when facing good fastball hitters. Sluggers like Reggie Jackson and Steve Garvey, who, if they got a steady diet of fastballs, would hit .400 and fifty home runs each season, can be kept off-balance at the plate with frequent change-ups. Throw the change-up with the *exact same* motion of the other pitches and, ideally, about 75 percent as fast as your fastball. Anything slower than that will allow the batter to recognize and adjust to the change-up, and still get a good swing, while anything faster becomes a mediocre fastball that most good hitters will smash. Try to keep your change-up low in the strike zone, about level with the knees. A high

One of Several Change-Up Grips. Pushing the ball deep into the palm and placing the thumb alongside the ball effectively decrease the pitch's velocity.

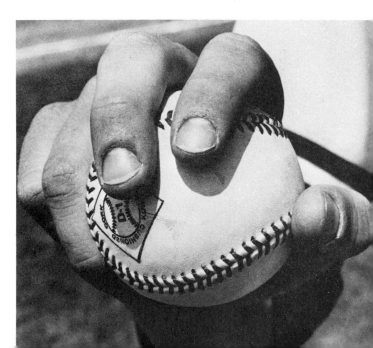

The Three-Fingered Change-Up Grip. Throw this pitch with the same pitching motion and arm speed that you would a fastball.

change-up can still be hit a long distance, even though the batter may be off-balance expecting a fastball. Some pitching coaches actually insist that their pitchers try to keep the change-up between a batter's knees and feet because so many batters swing wildly at change-ups in the dirt.

There are several good grips for the change-up. By pushing the ball back against the fleshy part of your hand and placing the soft part of your thumb along the side of the ball, you can throw as hard as you want but the pitch will be 25 percent slower than your fastball due to skin drag against the ball as it's released. You can also control the ball's speed with this grip by lifting your fingertips off the ball at release.

Another way to throw a change-up is to grip the ball with three fingers spread across the long seams and push it back in the palm. Thrown with the three-quarter overhand motion, the ball will have very little velocity upon release.

Experiment with dragging your pivot foot off the rubber when following through rather than lifting it, and turning the ball over slightly to the outside upon release to keep it low. Once you've developed an effective change-up, stick with it, and remember: Always throw with a fastball motion. It is the method of release, *not* a change in the total delivery, that slows the ball down by 25 percent.

OTHER PITCHES

There are other pitches that have been helpful in continuing certain pitchers' careers. Most are unusual, trick pitches that are difficult to control and cause more problems than benefits for most pitchers. The proponents of these exotic pitches have generally been unsuccessful with the basic, less difficult pitches and so have been forced to develop one of the following:

The Split-Fingered Fastball

The split-fingered fastball has been spotlighted since 1979 when Bruce Sutter, then of the Chicago Cubs, introduced it in his relief pitching. The "splittie" has made Sutter into the premier reliever in the National League, and when his pitch is working, he's virtually unhittable. Thrown with the same motion as the fastball, the split-fingered fastball sinks dramatically when it reaches home plate.

The Knuckle Ball

The knuckle ball is gripped with the fingernails digging into the ball. When thrown with an overhand motion, the ball flutters, barely spins if at all, and generally drops. It is a highly unpredictable pitch and only a handful of pitchers —notably Hoyt Wilhelm—have been able to use it with any success.

The Fork Ball

The fork ball is another trick pitch that takes extremely long and strong fingers

Bruce Sutter has popularized the split-fingered fastball. A difficult pitch to control, it requires long and strong fingers.

The Knuckle Ball. Actually gripped more with the fingernails than the knuckles, it's another difficult pitch to control.

The fork ball is similar to the split-fingered fastball and, when thrown hard, sinks sharply.

to throw with any speed. This pitch helped the Pittsburgh Pirates win the 1960 World Series when time and again Elroy Face marched in from the Pirate bullpen and used the fork ball to shut down the New York Yankees. When thrown hard and over the top, the fork ball has a sinking motion.

The Screwball

Former relief ace Jim Brewer of the Dodgers popularized the screwball in the 1960s and early 1970s, and Fernando Valenzuela's remarkable recent success has made the screwball famous again. The screwball is released with an outward snap of the wrist—exactly opposite from the curve ball. The left-handed Valenzuela's screwball breaks down and away from right-handed batters and usually results in batters hitting ground balls. A screwball is somewhat easier to control than other trick pitches, but is extremely hard on the arm. A pitcher would do well to have a double-jointed elbow to throw the screwball repeatedly.

Each of the trick pitches discussed above is either hard to control, hard on the arm, or both. They are better left to older, more experienced pitchers who have lost their fastball, curve, or slider and need an emergency pitch to survive. My strong recommendation is that young pitchers concentrate on throwing the three basic pitches and work on mastering each.

PREPARING TO PITCH

When taking the sign from the catcher, the rules require that the pivot foot be on the pitching rubber. In the windup position with nobody on base, it is best to keep the ball hidden in your glove or out of the batter's view as long as possible. As a pitcher, you should have the biggest glove available, for two reasons: first, to protect you from line drives and hard-hit ground balls; and second, to hide the ball and your pitching hand from the hitter and the base coaches.

In taking the sign, place your pitching hand in the glove and your pivot foot on the rubber, ideally in the middle. If, as the game progresses, you have control problems inside or outside, you can move your pivot foot in the direction to which you must adjust. Your pivot foot should extend over the front edge of the rubber and your heel should be planted on top. To begin your delivery to the plate after you have received the sign, you have two options. One, you can rock back on your left foot, pump your arms down and then up over your head, and begin turning your pivot foot to place it in front of and parallel to the rubber. This windup, or pump, delivery has the advantage of swinging the body into momentum and helping prepare both the body and the arm for their final thrust to the plate. The windup action also disturbs the concentration of the batter—as one who has batted against tall, windmilling pitchers like Don Drysdale and Don Newcombe can attest. The trouble with the full windup is that it can lead to poor balance and poor coordination as you begin the delicate process of pitching.

Your second option is to eliminate the rock-back step and overhead arm motion and go directly into turning the body and pivot foot while simply drawing the arms back into pitching position. This "no-windup delivery" has become more popular because it helps a pitcher stay in complete control and balance throughout his delivery. Whichever you use, though—full windup or no windup—keep your eyes on the target at all times. Yes, Fernando Valen-

Taking the Sign. The ball and pitching hand are well hidden from the batter.

The full windup delivery (left) gives rhythm and momentum to the start of the delivery. Too much of a windup, however, can cause loss of critical balance. The no-windup delivery (right) helps the pitcher stay in complete control of his body.

zuela throws his head and eyes skyward in the middle of his delivery, but the Valenzuelas are the exception. It's just plain bad practice to remove your visual concentration from the target for one instant.

Once you've begun your motion, use your hips and rear (pivot) leg to gather maximum force and thrust toward the target. You should raise your lead leg so that your thigh is at least parallel to the ground and bend your rear leg in a sort of coiling position. This position is called the "tuck" and it prepares every muscle in your body for the thrust home. Your shoulders and hips should be level, with your lead shoulder and lead hip turned in slightly toward your opposite side. Continue to keep the ball hidden and your eyes focused on the target as you begin to separate your hands and draw your throwing arm back. Your upper body is bent forward slightly (the tuck) to keep your weight balanced over your pivot foot, which is now in front of the rubber. Your lead, or stride, foot is pointed down slightly, rather than kicked out high in the air, so as not to tip back your upper body. The position of your hips and pivot leg is crucial here; the hips must "explode" open and the pivot leg thrust off the rubber to get maximum drive of the body and maximum speed of the pitching arm coming through. If you don't have your hips level and cocked and your pivot leg bent and coiled, such explosive movement is impossible. This is a key point at which to check your technique.

Now, from the tuck, begin your thrust home. Your stride leg comes

B **C** **D**

The Delivery: the back leg begins to bend (A) as the pitcher turns his body to begin utilizing the power in his hips. The tuck position follows (B). In practice, it is helpful for the pitcher to hold this position to test his balance before he begins driving his body toward home plate. The motion continues. The hands separate as the stride leg begins to come forward and the rear leg begins to power the entire body toward home plate (C). The stride foot lands to the left of the imaginary straight line between the rubber and home plate (D), thus opening the hips more powerfully, which in turn generates more arm speed. All parts of the body, acting in perfect sync (E,F), maximize the arm's speed as, elbow up, it throws. The pitcher follows through in good fielding position (G).

forward as your hips begin to open, powered by your pivot leg driving hard off the rubber. You should keep your lead, or glove, arm fairly close to your body to help your shoulders open, and let your pitching arm draw back into the three-quarter overhand position.

Your stride should be comfortably long so that your entire foot hits the ground firmly with your toes pointing straight ahead. If you overstride, your

F **G**

heel will land decidedly sooner than the rest of your foot and jar your delicate balance. Your stride should be 4 to 6 inches to the left of an imaginary line running from the pivot foot to home plate. As with any throw, this permits your hips to open fully and frees the upper body to provide maximum arm speed. Let the elbow of your glove arm move in its natural downward arc. This helps your shoulders stay level and keeps you on top of the ball.

The point of release is when you maximize the use of your entire body. The rotating motion of your hips, along with your stride, have added to your upper body's momentum as it powers open to bring your pitching arm through.

Your stride foot should land in the same place every time, and your follow-through should be free and complete. Let your arm continue across your body and down after release and let your pivot foot be carried forward by your body's momentum so that it lands nearly parallel to your stride foot. A good stride and follow-through increase both control and velocity of the pitch and put you in good fielding position.

Three Pitching Styles: Tom Seaver's flawless delivery (left) minimizes arm strain and maximizes efficiency.

By stepping to the right of the straight line home and delivering with a sidearm motion, Kent Tekulve (below left) throws an effective sinking fastball.

Bob Gibson's awesome pitching featured a full body thrust toward home (below), but look at the resulting follow-through!

The set position is used to hold base runners close and also quicken the pitcher's delivery to the plate.

PITCHING FROM THE SET POSITION

When it is important to hold runners on base, you take your sign, go into your stretch, come to the set, and either pitch home or throw to a base for a pick-off. The rule book clearly states that when taking the sign from the set position, you must have your pivot foot on or touching the rubber; your free, or stride, foot in front of the rubber; and your pitching hand hanging loosely at your side. When your hands come together in front of your body, you have assumed the set position and may, from that position, either pitch to the plate, attempt a pick-off at one of three bases, or step back from the rubber and thereby become an infielder.

If you're a righty pitching to the plate from the set, you must be careful to deliver the ball as quickly as possible to prevent a runner at first or second

If the pitcher lifts his stride leg higher than the hip or kicks his foot out toward third base, he loses valuable time in his delivery while the base runner steals a base.

base from getting a big jump and possibly stealing. Raise your lead leg quickly and only as high as necessary to cock your hips well, bend your back leg, and unload to the plate. Any high kick or pause after you have begun your delivery will allow the runner several more steps in his break if he steals.

Pitcher Pick-Offs at First Base

Holding runners close at first base can be the difference between winning and losing. Although you will actually retire a runner only a small percentage of the time with a pick-off at first base, you must still throw there frequently to warn the runner that you may get him the next time. Each near-miss profits the defense because the runner will shorten his lead.

The Right-Handed Pitcher Pick-Off at First Base

If you're a right-handed pitcher, you must turn your head and note the runner from the corner of your eye. You may open your left shoulder a bit to aid in turning your head; the important thing is to have the runner in clear view.

When you throw to first base, take a quick, short step toward the bag with your lead foot and pivot your rear foot on the rubber toward the throw to provide proper push. Shorten the arc of your arm to allow a quick overhand snap throw. The throw needs to be hard and accurate, so it is crucial to throw overhanded and stride toward the bag. Indeed, poor footwork and sidearm flips are the most common cause of wild pick-off throws to first base.

Some right-handed pitchers use a quick jump pivot on their pick-off

By rule, the right-handed pitcher must step toward first base when attempting a pick-off there (left). His snap throw as the hips open (right) gives the ball needed velocity.

throws to first base. In this technique, you leave the ground momentarily as you quickly turn your upper body to throw. Whether you pivot your right foot or do a jump pivot, *your left foot must step toward first base* or you will be charged with a balk—and the runner will be awarded second base.

The Left-Handed Pitcher Pick-Off at First Base

If you're a left-handed pitcher, you have a big advantage over a righty on a pick-off move to first base, because your stride leg is raised in that direction during your normal delivery. Thus, with a runner on first, you can choose more

A B C

The left-handed pitcher should keep his eyes on home plate when he begins his pick-off move (A). Thereupon, he can either pitch to the plate or throw to first base for the pick-off (B). With his eyes still on home plate, he begins his stride toward first base (C), then picks up his target there (D) and makes a quick three-quarter overhand throw (E).

D E

easily to either pitch to the plate or throw to first base. Too, a runner must hold at this stage of your delivery for fear of getting picked off, and if you do go to the plate, you will, as often as not, have moved him back toward the bag. As a lefty, you have no excuse for giving up long leads and stolen bases.

When attempting a pick-off at first base, as a left-handed pitcher you should keep your eyes toward home plate as long as possible to deceive the runner. When you do move your right foot toward first base, then you must turn your head to your target and complete your throw with a short, snapping, three-quarter overhand motion. The rules state that a left-handed pitcher, like a righty, must step toward first base to avoid a balk; but in fact umpires are more lenient with left-handers' moves to first base, and most left-handed pitchers step toward a point on the base line 30 feet before the bag.

The Left-Hander's "Flip Move"

A more recent weapon for keeping the runner close to first base is the left-hander's "flip move." From the set position, take a quick backward step with your left foot. As your foot leaves the rubber, separate your hands and snap a quick throw to first base. If you're a pitcher with a strong wrist, you'll be surprised how fast you can get this throw off, and if the runner is looking for your right foot to be lifted first, he is going to be picked off. The flip move is an effective counter to the long "one-way" lead where a runner goes out 18 to 20 feet and starts *back* to first base when the pitcher makes his first move, regardless of whether the pitcher goes to the plate or to first base. After six or seven one-way moves back to first base, the runner will break for second base

The "flip move" has become an increasingly effective pick-off move for the left-handed pitcher. To initiate the move, the rear foot takes a quick step back off the rubber and the hands separate. Since the throw allows only a short arm arc, a pitcher needs a strong arm to execute this move.

on the pitcher's first move. If the pitcher delivers to the plate, the runner will steal second easily. If the pitcher throws to first base, a fast runner may still beat the first baseman's throw to second base because his lead was out so far to begin with. The one-way lead is a good offensive device against a left-handed pitcher *unless* that pitcher can execute the flip move. An accurate flip move will get the runner nearly every time if his lead is 18 to 20 feet.

Whether you're right- or left-handed, there are three basic times when you can effectively throw to first base for a pick-off.

1. *On the way up in the stretch.* This time is particularly good because many runners are increasing their lead at that moment and a quick pick-off throw will catch them with their weight unbalanced.

2. *On the way down in the stretch.* Also good for the same reason.

3. *From the set position after the stretch has been completed.* At this point, the runner has established his lead and you may pick him off if he is leaning toward second base and anxious to begin his steal attempt.

Pitcher Pick-Offs at Second Base

In chapter 12 on defensive strategy, the several pick-off plays with the second baseman and shortstop are described in detail. Because the runner at second base is in scoring position, he must be held as close as possible to the bag. Given the chance to increase their lead, good base runners can steal third base easily unless the alert pitcher "looks" them back or attempts to pick them off.

From the set position, the right-handed pitcher executes a quick 180-degree jump pivot for a pick-off at second base. He plants his right foot firmly for a solid throw to the bag.

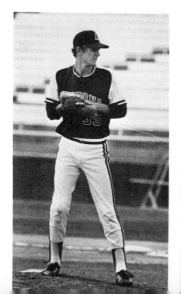

At Arizona, we teach a different technique from the counterclockwise turn that most right-handers make when throwing to second base. We prefer that a pitcher turn to his *right* with a quick 180-degree jump pivot followed by a short, crisp snap throw. This move is just as fast and accurate as the customary turn to the left and provides two additional advantages: (1) The pitcher is facing the runner in the event the runner breaks for third base; and (2) the move to the right is more similar to the start of his normal delivery than turning to his left, and may deceive the runner into making one more move toward third base.

This jump pivot to the right is unnatural for most pitchers and will require serious practice. The key is a complete 180-degree jump that leaves the right foot firmly down for the push toward second base and permits a strong, accurate throw. Turning only partway in the jump pivot forces a pitcher to throw sidearm and off-balance.

The left-handed pitcher's pick-off move is also turned toward third base so that the runner remains in full view of the pitcher. By turning to his right, or glove-hand, side, the pitcher need only whirl on his pivot foot and stride toward second base, ready to throw.

Holding the Runner on Third Base

As a pitcher, you should never allow a runner to take a big lead at third base. He's too close to scoring! If you elect to pitch from the windup, look at the runner. Make sure he has stopped his lead before beginning your pump, because once you begin your windup, you are committed to completing the pitch without pause or interruption, and if the runner gets a big lead and breaks on your windup, he could steal home. If, before starting your windup, you see the runner too far off the bag, step off the rubber and fake a throw to your third baseman. (Remember, an incomplete throw to second or third base is not a balk. You do not have to complete your throw.)

Of course, the best way to hold a runner close to third base is to pitch from the set position. Now the same pick-off moves are available to third base as were available to first, and if you're a right-handed pitcher, you even have the "flip move" at your disposal.

Pick-off moves at all bases are a matter of technique and practice. Quick footwork, a short arm arc, and accurate throws will not only anchor runners to the bases but retire a good many as well.

I mentioned Jim Kaat earlier as a pitcher with poise and composure. Another quality Jim is famous for is his fielding excellence. The mantel over Jim's fireplace is literally crowded with Gold Glove fielding trophies. He is truly a fifth infielder and has won many of his own games with outstanding defensive performances.

With practice and concentration, you, too, as a pitcher, can excel at fielding ground balls and bunts. Some helpful tips:

1.　When throwing to a base after fielding a ball, be sure to step and throw. Don't throw flat-footed even if the throw is short and easy. Take care to throw straight and hard rather than get panicky, rush, and risk a wild throw. Never ease a throw to a base.

2.　Keep your shoulders lined up with the expected target when fielding a bunt or slow-hit ground ball. Circle the ball slightly so when you do field it, all you have to do is step in that direction and throw.

3.　Keep your chest over a bunt or a ball that you have knocked down and are rushing to pick up. Keep your eyes on the ball and not the runner.

4.　A right-handed pitcher fielding a bunt down the third-base line and throwing to third base for the force-out, should turn to his left after fielding the ball, and throw.

5.　When covering home plate on a wild pitch or passed ball, help your catcher locate the ball by hollering "Left," "Right," or "Straight back," and

When fielding a bunt or slow-hit ball, keep your chest over the ball and your shoulders lined up with the base to which you will throw.

The pitcher backing up third base or home plate should stand as far back as the field permits.

get to the plate as fast as possible. Position yourself facing the throw and on the first-base side of the plate, but never risk injury by blocking the plate. Take the catcher's throw on one knee and tag the runner with the back of your glove.

6.   A pitcher must back up throws to third base and home plate by being as deep as the field will permit. Hustle to the dugout, backstop, or retaining wall as fast as possible and be in line with the throw from the outfield. Remember: it's easy to come forward to field a wild throw, but very hard to retrieve a ball that sails over your head or past you on the side. Back up as deep as possible.

7.   Covering first base for a throw from the first baseman, second baseman, or shortstop is a key play for the pitcher. On anything hit to your left, you should break hard to first base in the event the first baseman can't get there or has to field the ball. On a ground ball hit at or to the left of the first baseman, you should sprint to a point on the first-base line about 20 feet from the bag and come up to the bag running parallel with the line about a foot inside fair territory. Have both hands up to catch the ball, which the first baseman should toss to you two or three strides before you reach the base. First catch the ball, *then* look for the bag on the next step and tag the inside edge to avoid being stepped on by the runner. If the ball is hit to your first baseman's right or will be relayed from the shortstop on a double play, go directly to the base, put your right foot on the bag, turn, and be ready for the throw.

Always hustle to the bag! Better to be too early than too late and watching the ball disappear into the first-base dugout.

CONCLUSION

As a pitcher, you carry a heavy responsibility when you take the mound. You have more control over the outcome of a game than anyone else on the field. But don't let this cause you to feel that you must strike out every batter! In fact, the more strikeouts you try to get, the more bases on balls you'll give up. Likewise, the bigger the break you try to put on your curve ball, the more it will hang; and the harder you *try* to throw, the more tired and erratic you'll become. If you have several or all of the qualities mentioned earlier, you now must rely on your preparation and simply relax and do your best. By your example, you can put confidence in your catcher to call a good game, in your fielders to make the plays, and in your hitters to get some runs. The best pitchers in baseball are team players. Sure, the pitcher initiates play on every pitch, and of course the other fielders key their action to his moves, but the pitchers who emerge to become stars of their leagues are dependent on the rest of the team for their success. There is no room in baseball for prima donnas. A pitcher's greatest success comes when he recognizes and appreciates the contributions of his teammates.

Catching

The catcher is the quarterback of a baseball team, the on-field strategist who determines the best means for keeping opponents off the bases. He has the clearest vantage point for adjusting the defense; and if he is any good, he is thinking before his teammates are about how to retire the next batter. More than any other player on the field, he can inspire and encourage his teammates, particularly his pitcher. He is the backbone of a team, the glue, the fiber, the fulcrum.

Catching is a punishing position. When high-school or Little League teams announce tryouts, you can count on there being lots of candidates for pitcher, shortstop, first base, and center field, but not so many for catcher. Top catchers are a special breed of person. But when a team wins a championship, it's a callow player or fan who doesn't look back and say, "We couldn't have won without the fine, consistent performance of . . . our catcher!"

Catcher Tony Pena prepares to discard his mask after sighting a foul pop in Wrigley Field.

QUALIFICATIONS

A good catcher must be a leader. He should have the self-confidence that will permit him to lead and direct from behind the plate. He must be decisive and firm when handling pitchers, so that he gives them the feeling that his judgment is best. Part of a catcher's leadership is vocal, and any shyness must be left behind when he puts on his equipment.

A catcher must be aggressive. The hustling, determined catcher will stand out early in a game and be a threat to the opposition and an inspiration to his ball club.

With the increasing emphasis on the running game, catchers are faced more and more with runners attempting to steal second and third bases, so the good catcher must have a strong, accurate arm. Along with that, he had better have quick feet to shift properly and throw accurately when base runners take off, and also to move his body in front of wide or low pitches. He must be durable enough to withstand collisions at home plate along with the constant squatting and standing the position requires.

EQUIPMENT

If you are a catcher, you should guard your equipment with the same care that a hitter watches his bat and an infielder his glove. Your shin guards and chest protector should fit snugly and give maximum protection. Your chest protector should be cinched up enough to cover the throat and clavicle. Your mask can be either a bar- or wire-front type, depending on your preference, though the wire mask seems more popular these days because it allows better sight lines on the high pitch and pop fly. If you don't own a protective cup for your groin area, buy one, and you should strongly consider wearing two optional protective items—the throat guard and the catcher's helmet. The throat guard gives you added protection against foul tips in that vulnerable area, and the helmet will protect you against a batter's wild backswing or a thrown bat.

You have several choices of catcher's gloves. Up until around 1975, most major-league catchers used the inflexible, pan-shaped "no-break" model that required two hands to control. It was felt that a catcher's glove wasn't meant to "catch" the ball but rather to stop it while the bare hand folded over and controlled it. In fact, one-handed catching was discouraged because of the belief that catchers could not get the ball out of the glove fast enough when runners tried to steal.

Very few catchers still use the no-break model. Instead, most now use the single-break, hinged glove seen throughout this chapter. The glove is somewhat like a first baseman's in that the ball can be trapped near the web. Its most important feature, though, is that now the bare hand need not be used and can be held out of the way of foul tips. In using this glove, then, when there is no one on base, hold your bare hand behind your back. When runners are on base and there is a steal threat, of course, you must have your throwing hand ready so you can swiftly remove the ball from the glove. In that instance, place your bare hand behind the glove and near the web with your thumb lightly curled inside your fingers for added protection.

There are some double-break catcher's gloves on the market, but stay away from them because the ball tends to get buried in the web and becomes difficult to remove quickly.

SIGN-GIVING POSITION

As a catcher, you must be careful that your signs can be seen only by the pitcher and the middle infielders. The position that permits flashing signals to the pitcher without being seen by the coaches at first and third base is a comfortable crouchlike squat. The knees are bent and the weight is resting on the balls of the feet. The feet are parallel and approximately 12 to 15 inches apart. The back is straight, the head up, the elbows fairly close to the body, and the glove arm is resting on the left leg with the glove itself in front of the knee as a shield against the third-base coach's or runner's view. The right hand is placed over the thigh and back deep against the crotch to prevent the first-base coach from seeing the sign.

The catcher's signs must be well hidden from runners and base coaches.

Giving Signs

There are many systems of sign giving. Guard against making signs so complicated that your pitchers get confused and lose the needed confidence in you. A missed sign, or "cross-up pitch," particularly with a runner on base, is a needless penalty against your team. Without a runner on second base, most catchers flash single signs with their fingers. One finger means a fastball, two fingers a curve, three a slider, four a change-up, and the fist a pitchout. These signs are pretty universal, so when a runner reaches second base, another system must be used to prevent the runner from reading the sign and relaying the information to the batter. A relatively easy system is to flash a series of four or five signs and have it prearranged as to which is the actual pitch. For example, first sign for the first three innings, third sign for the middle three, and fourth sign for the last three innings. Some catchers prefer "pumps" rather than finger signs. Instead of counting the number of fingers put down, the pitcher counts the number of times signs are flashed or pumped. Three pumps is a fastball, four a curve, and so on.

Whichever system is used, it must be consistent throughout the pitching staff so that when a relief pitcher enters the game, a new system does not have to be devised while everyone waits. The shortstop and second baseman should also be able to read the signs to help determine who covers second base and to anticipate where the ball is likely to be hit.

As your level of competition increases and the pitcher's control gets better, you can signal location of the pitch, either before or after you give the sign(s), by using your hand to motion slightly up, down, in, or out.

You should give your signs as close to the hitter as possible without interfering with his practice or actual swing. This will allow you to see any runners on base as they begin their leads, and will also enable you to keep your movements to a minimum as you go from the sign-giving to the receiving position.

THE RECEIVING POSITION

There is a distinct difference between your position for giving signs and your stance for catching the pitch. Once the sign is given and acknowledged by the pitcher, you elevate yourself to the receiving position. Your feet are spread more than a shoulders' width apart for stability and balance, and your right foot is dropped back slightly with the toes of both feet opened. Your weight is

With no one on base, this catcher's receiving position protects his bare hand from foul tips.

forward about 60 percent on the balls of your feet with your heels lightly touching the ground. Your thighs are parallel to the ground, and your upper body bent forward so that your weight is over your feet and not back on the haunches. Your head is up, your eyes perfectly level. Hold the glove comfortably away from your body with the pocket up and give the pitcher a steady target. Your wrist should be loose and relaxed and your elbow bent and also relaxed. Don't hold the glove too far from your body lest you lock your elbow. In this position, you should be able to sway from side to side, rise quickly for a high pitch, or drop to your knees to block pitches in the dirt. Crouching low invites your pitcher to keep his pitches low, but once he begins his delivery, you must remain motionless in the receiving position and offer him a good, low target.

With runners on base, the catcher keeps his bare hand close to and behind the glove in case the runner attempts to steal. The thumb is tucked lightly inside the fingers for added protection.

As mentioned before, if there are runners on base, you must bring your bare hand up to the glove to be ready to throw instantly if the runners go. There are several ways to hold the bare hand to prevent injury from the catcher's biggest enemy: foul tips. The most common way is to clench the fist and keep the bare hand near the glove. The recommended way is to place the hand behind the glove with the thumb tucked into the lightly clenched fingers.

RECEIVING THE PITCH

Some skilled catchers give the impression that catching is so easy they could do it in a rocking chair. Other catchers are so stiff and awkward they seem to fight the ball. Your glove and arms should give with the pitch in a smooth, fluid motion toward the strike zone. In a way, the catching motion is similar to the funnel principle an infielder uses to control a ground ball.

Framing

A high pitch should be caught with the glove fingers up; the low pitch with the fingers down; the pitch on the outside corners of the plate with fingers curling in. With your body in the proper position, you can sway in any direction and thus keep your body in front of the pitch and your glove under maximum control. By catching each pitch with the proper glove angle and easing the ball down, up, or sideways into the strike zone as the glove gives smoothly with the force of the pitch, you increase the likelihood of close pitches being called strikes. This practice, used by the best major-leaguers, is called "framing."

Framing the high strike down into the strike zone (A), the low strike up (B), the pitch on the corner into the strike zone (C).

A

B

C

Framing is not pulling bad pitches into the strike zone and hoping to fool the umpire; that practice rarely works and serves only to alienate the umpire. Framing is used to ensure that pitches on the edge of the strike zone will indeed be called strikes. The high strike is framed down, the low strike framed up, and the corner strike framed in to the strike zone.

If your glove angle is bad, the force of the close pitches will carry the glove out of the strike zone and the pitch will be called a ball. One helpful suggestion for developing the "soft hands" characteristic of a good catcher is to let the pitch come to the glove, not reach the glove out at the pitch. Good body balance will help you control your hands and glove, but if you find you are dropping pitches frequently, or not getting the close strikes from the umpire, you should alter your receiving position until you feel more comfortable. Try not to crouch so low that your hips get locked, or raise yourself so high that you tend to tip forward when the pitch arrives.

Catching the Low Pitch

The low pitch in the dirt is the most difficult of all for a catcher. With runners on base, you must do all you can to keep the ball in front of you and prevent the runners from advancing. The key in handling the low pitch is *not* to try to *catch* the ball in the dirt but rather to concentrate on *blocking* the ball and keeping it within reach in front of the plate, so that if the runner goes, you can pounce on it and still throw the runner out. If the low pitch comes directly in front of you, drop to both knees and keep your glove on the ground, your arms close to your body, your chin down, and your shoulders hunched over the ball —in short, try to block every opening where the ball may get through. In this fashion, you will actually catch some low pitches on the short hop, and certainly will block all of them.

If the low pitch is to either side, immediately drop the knee and shoulder over and down, dragging your other leg down and across. Try to curl your lead shoulder in, so that if the ball bounces up, it will rebound off your upper body and back in front of the plate. Your glove and arms go down to the ground just as they did for the low pitch in front of you. Remember: The main objective in handling the pitch in the dirt is to block it out in front of the plate. If you get into the bad habit of trying to scoop the low pitch like a first baseman fielding a low throw, most pitches in the dirt will get by.

Practice is essential in handling low pitches. Dress in your full gear with additional padding on your wrists and arms and have your coach throw low pitches at you from 30 feet away. Some bruises will result, but soon you'll be a catcher who can prevent runners from advancing on pitches in the dirt.

On the pitch in the dirt, the catcher's priority is to block the ball and keep it in front of him.

THROWING OUT RUNNERS

A good catcher is never surprised when a runner tries to steal. In fact, on every pitch as the pitcher begins his delivery, you should glance toward first to see if the runner is breaking. And when the runner does break, you must activate your body and get your feet moving before the pitch reaches your glove. Of course, your throwing hand has been ready, positioned beside or behind the glove.

On a good pitch received over the plate or about a foot either inside or immediate position to throw: the *jab step,* the *rock-and-throw,* and the *jump pivot.* Whichever of the three you use, you must first be in the proper receiving position with men on base.

The Jab Step

The jab step with the right foot is a good way to gain some momentum with your body and add force to your throw. As you're about to catch the pitch, jab your right foot forward about 6 to 8 inches, planting it perpendicular to second base. As the right foot plants, the pitch hits your glove. Now you have a pivot foot firmly set so you can cock the ball quickly back as you stride with the left foot and throw. This shifting method can help you if you're a catcher with quick feet but a mediocre arm.

The Rock-and-Throw

If you're an unusually strong-armed catcher, you should consider the rock-and-throw method. This is how Johnny Bench, for instance, used to gun down

Catchers with average arms should use the jab-step technique.

runners when he was the premier catcher in baseball. When the ball hits the glove, keep your right foot stationary, rock your weight back over your pivot foot, draw back to the throwing position, and fire to second base. The obvious value of the rock-and-throw is its efficiency and quickness: You receive the pitch and make the throw with very little footwork. The drawback to this method is that there is no forward momentum established as you catch the ball, so your arm must do all the work. For rifle-armed catchers, though, this is a good choice.

The Jump Pivot

The third basic method of shifting to make the throw to second is the jump pivot. In order to make a fast, accurate throw 127 feet to second base, your

The Rock-and-Throw Technique. While the quickest and most efficient method for throwing to second base, the rock-and-throw requires a strong arm because there is no preliminary movement to activate the body forward.

Most catchers prefer the jump-pivot technique. As he catches the ball, the catcher jumps quickly to the side and plants his right foot where the left foot had been while simultaneously striding toward second base for the throw.

pivot foot must be firmly planted and your shoulders lined up with the target. As the ball hits your glove, you instantly lift both feet and make a quick, clockwise, 90-degree jump so your right foot lands perpendicular to second base and your shoulders are aimed toward second base as you begin your stride and throw. Most catchers use the jump pivot because it gives the body both quickness and forward momentum for the throw.

Other Considerations

With the runner stealing and an outside pitch to your right, the jab step is the only reasonable shift that will give your upper body lateral movement and keep your chest in front of the ball for control. When the pitch is far to your left, use a jab step left to stay in front of the ball, and follow it with a quick jump pivot to make the throw.

No matter what method you use for shifting your feet and body, remember:

1.   Keep your upper body in front of the pitch as much as possible. Use footwork. Don't fall into the bad habit of reaching out one-handed to spear the pitch while keeping your feet stuck in one place.

2.   Make the throw with the proper grip across the long seams of the ball.

The percentages for catchers throwing out base runners are dropping every year. In the 1982 major-league season, only one team in twenty-six threw out more than half the runners who attempted to steal against them! Paying more attention to their footwork and technique behind the plate may help catchers at all levels of baseball win more battles against base runners.

CATCHER TAGS

The catcher's glove is the least well constructed of any for making tags. Infielder's gloves are all designed so the ball can be secured in the pocket or web and the tag made with the glove itself. Not so for the catcher. Because of his glove's bulky construction, he must use a different technique to make sure the ball is not kicked or jarred out of his control by the sliding runner.

If you're a catcher, by the rules, you cannot block home plate without the ball. When taking the throw from the outfield or cutoff man, you should stand facing the play with your left foot on the plate and your feet spread for good balance. As you receive the throw with two hands, drop to your right knee and turn to tag the runner, leaving your left foot on or in front of the plate and your shin guard exposed to the runner's slide. As you bring the glove down for the tag, place the ball in your bare hand and clutch it tightly with all four fingers and your thumb, but keeping the bare hand in the pocket of the glove. Tag the runner's foot with the back of the glove and, as contact is made, separate the hands and pull the bare hand away, clutching the ball. Do not hold the ball in the glove alone since it is so difficult to close the glove around the ball and keep it secure.

Although there will be collisions and frequent contact at home plate, as a catcher you should not belligerently invite the runner to try to run you over to prove your manhood and courage. If the throw beats the runner to the plate

Once the catcher has the ball, he can block home plate from the runner with his left leg (A). Note how the glove and the hand holding the ball separate as they apply the tag (B).

A

B

and the runner's only hope of scoring is to bowl you over and knock the ball loose, you should stand facing the oncoming runner 3 or 4 feet in front of the plate and crouched slightly with your hands together and the ball held firmly in your bare hand. As the runner makes his lunge to knock you over, tag him at the hips with both hands and simultaneously spin away to your left to roll away from the runner's impact. I recall an outstanding college catcher who was scheduled to sign a large bonus contract with a major-league team the day after his college season ended. In the last game of the year, with the head scout from that team in the stands, this catcher decided to prove his toughness and take a scoring runner head on for the tag play. There was a vicious collision at the plate and both players went down stunned and injured. Although the catcher held on to the ball and the runner was out, he sustained a badly broken collarbone and was out of action the rest of the summer. The major-league team subsequently withdrew its bonus offer.

After all tag plays at the plate, you must be alert to stop other runners from advancing. Holding the ball firmly in your bare hand when making the tag not only protects from having the ball knocked loose but also allows you to make a quick throw to second or third base following the play at the plate.

For a force play at home and subsequent throw to first base for the double-play attempt, discard your mask, straddle the plate, and face the throw with your hands up. If the throw is over the plate or anywhere to your left, step to the ball with your left foot and keep your chest in front of the ball while dragging your right foot over the plate. With a quick jump pivot to your right, your shoulders and right foot are lined up for a strong throw to first base.

If the force throw is to your right, step to the ball with your right foot and drag the left foot over the plate. This way, your right foot is already planted as you catch the ball, and you simply stride toward first base with your left foot

The Force Play at Home. The catcher discards his mask and faces the throw while straddling the plate (A). As he catches the throw, he drags his right foot over the plate (B) and executes a quick jump pivot to line his shoulders up with first base for the throw (C).

A   B   C

The catcher reaches a bunt via the "banana route." He keeps his feet spread, his chest over the ball, and scoops the ball into his bare hand with the glove.

after dragging it over the plate, and throw. Shortstops pivot similarly when the throw is to the inside of second base (see pp. 127–128).

In all force plays at home plate, you must attempt to keep your chest in front of the throw and catch the ball with two hands. On the wild throws left, right, or over your head, consider the ball more important than the plate. Of course, if you can stretch, catch the ball, and still keep your foot on the plate, fine, do so. But you cannot permit the throw to get past you and allow yet another runner to score or advance.

FIELDING BUNTS

Whenever a bunt is expected, be prepared to field it. Never automatically depend on the first baseman, third baseman, or pitcher to make the play. Anticipating the bunt, you should assume your receiving position with your body a bit higher than normal and your right foot dropped back a bit more to allow you a faster break from behind the plate.

If the bunt is laid down the third-base line and the throw is going to either first or second base, discard your mask immediately and move quickly to the ball, taking a slight banana route to the ball's left. By doing so, your chest will be directly over the ball when you field it and your shoulders lined up with the throw. If the throw is going to third base, no banana route is necessary and you approach the ball from the left.

If the bunt is in front of the plate and the throw is to second base, go straight to the ball and pick it up on the left side. If the throw is going to first base, you'll need to take a slight banana route.

Three important rules to remember if you're a catcher fielding a bunt:

1. Be certain your shoulders are lined up with your target. Sometimes

you need to make a banana route to bring you into line with the base you're throwing to.

2. When fielding the bunt, keep your eyes on the ball and not the runner, and keep your chest directly over the ball.

3. Field the bunt by placing the glove in front of the ball with your fingers pointed down, and scoop the ball into your bare hand by bringing the hands together on the ground. Trying to pick the bunt up with just your bare hand is a very risky proposition.

CATCHING POP FLIES

The first and third basemen have priority over you, the catcher, on all pop flies. You should try for all pop-ups you think you can reach but give way to the first or third baseman if they holler for the ball. (See "Pop-Fly Priorities," pp. 220–222.)

As soon as the pop fly occurs, you must remove your mask and locate the ball. The best way to remove the mask is to grab it by the bottom with the thumb underneath the chin and the fingers grasping in front and pull up and out from your face. You should hold the mask until you know which way the ball is descending and then toss it well out of the way, ideally in the opposite direction from the ball.

Pop flies behind the plate, down the foul lines, and in fair ground between first and third bases will drift back toward the infield as they descend. This is known as the "infield drift" and you must take it into account as you break after the ball. It is important, too, that you position yourself with your *back* to the infield so that the ball will break *toward* you as you prepare to catch it. By doing this, you can backstep with the ball rather than chasing toward it as it curves away. A good rule of thumb to allow for infield drift: If the ball is fouled to your left, run to the right of the ball; if the ball is fouled to your right, run to the left of the ball, which Tony Pena is doing in the picture on page 168. If the ball is fouled straight back, turn, discard your mask, move toward the screen, and allow the ball to come back to you. Of course, a strong breeze will affect the infield drift and require that you make further adjustments.

The best way to catch the pop fly is to sight the ball over the top of your glove as it descends and catch it with two hands with your fingers pointing up and the glove held at head or shoulder height. This way, you will see the ball right into the glove and be able to gauge the infield drift and the ball's spin most accurately.

Johnny Bench sights a pop foul over his upraised glove and compensates for "infield drift" by keeping his back to the infield.

On a foul pop fly near a wall, screen, or dugout, the catcher protects against collision by sliding feetfirst as he catches the ball.

There will be times when, sprinting, you will arrive at the screen, retaining wall, or dugout just as the foul pop fly descends. If you were to remain on your feet and crash into the screen, you would very likely drop or miss the ball and injure yourself besides. Anticipating this close and dangerous play, you can protect yourself and still keep your eye on the ball by sliding feetfirst into the barrier while keeping your head and hands up and ready to catch the pop fly. Don't worry—your shin guards will protect your legs from the impact against the barrier, and the more vulnerable head, throat, and upper body are free from danger.

CONCLUSION

The catcher, besides needing all the qualities mentioned earlier, is also the busiest player on the field. He backs up first base on all ground balls to second base, shortstop, and third base when there are no runners on second or third. He covers third or first base when those positions are vacated and there is no play at the plate. He has studied and should know all the particular characteristics and idiosyncrasies of the entire pitching staff, and he must also remember the strengths and weaknesses of every opposing batter as they come to the plate. Before games, he warms up the starting pitcher, and—oh, yes—he must look after three times more equipment than any other player!

So you want to be a catcher? Good for you! You will be one of the smartest, hardest-working, and most important players on your team.

12

Defensive Strategy

Those readers familiar with the game of chess can appreciate the intricacies of defensive baseball. A master chess player looks several moves ahead and tries to predict what his opponent will do before he himself makes even the simplest move. Chess players become great by taking a thoughtful, analytical, and predictive approach to their game. Good baseball coaches approach the deployment of their defense in the same way and try to stay one move ahead of their opponents. An impulsive coach who pays little attention to detail will seldom make the right defensive moves and rarely will prevent a team at bat from advancing runners and scoring important runs. On the other hand, a coach who recognizes his opponents' pattern of run-scoring strategies and who plays the percentages according to his players' abilities will generally be able to stop an opposition's multiple-run attack and thus keep a game in his grasp.

Certain managers in the major leagues would make excellent chess players. Always a treat for me, and a valuable learning opportunity, too, is watching American League managers Gene Mauch, Sparky Anderson, Billy Martin, Dick Howser, and Earl Weaver match defensive wits with one another. In the National League, Dick

185

The meeting on the mound, repeated hundreds of times in a baseball season, generally plans crucial defensive strategy.

Williams, Tom Lasorda, Whitey Herzog, and Chuck Tanner have all proven themselves extremely capable defensive strategists, too. A coach whose team is in the field has a harder time making a strategic choice than does his opponent, since the latter has the advantage of *knowing* what strategy he will employ, whereas the defensive coach can prepare his defense for only one of numerous possibilities. The defensive coach, then, must try to predict his opponent's *most likely next move* and set his defense for that.

Of course, a large part of making a correct prediction comes from experience. But it also helps to know a given strategy's percentage of success. For example, a sacrifice bunt with one out is poor percentage offensive baseball. Why? Because in advancing a runner to second or third base, the team at bat gives up a third of its offensive potential that inning, leaving itself with only one more out to score the runner. Unquestionably, the chances of scoring a runner from first base with one out are better than those of scoring a runner from second base with two outs. So, with one out, the alert defensive coach would not bring his third baseman and first baseman in close, expecting a bunt, as that would make them more vulnerable to a ground ball getting past for a base hit. In the same fashion, a smart coach whose team is ahead by two or more runs would not bring his infield in with a runner on third and fewer than two outs. The important man to retire in this case is the hitter, so the smart coach keeps his infielders back to allow them more range for fielding a grounder or pop fly.

I advocate percentage baseball *providing* a team has proven it can successfully execute the routine defensive plays. If I can teach my team to avoid errors, both physically *and mentally,* then I know we can employ our defense for the most likely move a team at bat will attempt, and retire the key batter or runner most of the time. If a team at bat consistently ignores the best percentage offensive choice and tries to beat our defense by surprise, they will fail most of the time because the percentages are against them.

The defensive strategies outlined in this chapter are designed to meet virtually any maneuver a team at bat is likely to try in a given situation. In many ways, a sound defense in baseball resembles a zone defense in basketball: Wherever a possible shot (play) could occur, a defensive player must be stationed; and if that defender is caught out of position for some reason, a teammate must be prepared to help out.

GENERAL PRINCIPLES FOR TEAM DEFENSE

Certain principles should prevail when you, as coach, begin planning your defensive strategies. Put these principles, or rules, if you please, into the form of questions. Ask yourself:

1.   Which player on offense represents the priority out? Is it a base runner, the batter, a player on deck or in the dugout?

2.   Will every base be covered where a possible play may occur?

3.   Will this defense maximize our particular strengths and minimize our weaknesses? (For example, in defensing a double steal, it would be unwise to choose a defense that requires a sore-armed catcher to throw through to second base.)

4.   Does this defense assure that we will get at least one out if we execute properly?

Using these four general principles will give you a consistent system from game to game as you approach each challenge your opponents hurl at you. Call these principles the solid foundation for sound defense. They never vary, no matter what level of baseball is being played.

THE VARIABLES OF TEAM DEFENSE

You must also consider a host of variables before signaling a particular defense to your team. Situations vary from game to game—indeed, from inning to inning, and even pitch to pitch. Consider the many ways a defensive situation can change, depending upon the following factors:

1.   *The score.* If your team is ahead by two or more runs, it is best to play your defense to retire the batter. If you're one run ahead, tied, or behind, it is best to play your defense to retire the lead runner on base.

2.   *The stage of the game.* In the early innings, try to prevent your opponent from having a "big inning." In the late innings, if the score is close, play to prevent single runs from scoring.

3.   *Home or visitor.* When home, choose your defensive deployment with the knowledge that your team has the last at-bat if you fall behind. When your team is the visitor, your defensive choices become more critical. If the wrong choice is made, the game could be over before you know it.

4.   *Your pitcher.* His fatigue level, his pitch control, his fielding ability, his effectiveness holding runners on base, his maturity, his right- or left-handedness, the readiness of a relief pitcher and *his* strengths and weaknesses against the batters he might face—these are just a few pitcher-related matters that you must consider before making a defensive move.

5. *Your catcher and double-play combination.* If your catcher has an outstanding arm, it will influence both defensive *and* offensive strategy choices. The same is true for the defensive abilities of your shortstop and second baseman.

6. *The hitter(s).* If the man at the plate is an outstanding power hitter, he probably won't bunt. If he is a poor hitter, he probably will sacrifice-bunt. If he is extremely fast and not likely to hit into a double play, chances are he will not bunt. If he is a pull hitter, or an opposite-field hitter, you must set your defense appropriately. Is the on-deck hitter more or less of a threat than the hitter at the plate? What about possible pinch hitters?

7. *The runner(s).* If a runner on first base is an excellent base stealer, the sacrifice bunt is less likely. Is there an open base for a possible intentional walk?

8. *The field.* Before setting your defense, consider whether the grass is wet, whether the wind is blowing out, whether the sun is a factor to either the hitter or the fielders, and whether the fences are close.

The above are just some of the variables to consider before making a particular defensive choice. Once you've weighed all the variables, it's time to signal which defense you want deployed to prevent what you think your opponent will attempt.

TEAM DEFENSIVE POSITIONING

In effective team defense, seven men move as a unit into position for each hitter, sometimes even repositioning themselves after each pitch. With the exception of the pitcher and catcher, whose positions are fixed, all fielders should move to protect the area in which the batter is most likely to hit the ball. Each fielder must also know where his teammates are when the ball is hit. As coach, you are responsible for positioning the defense for a pull hitter, an opposite-field hitter, a bunt threat, a double-steal attempt, an extremely fast batter, an extremely slow batter, and most of the other situations mentioned earlier. But each player should also remind his closest teammates if he is playing somewhat out of position, so they can adjust accordingly.

It is no accident that perennially strong teams in the major leagues—such as the Los Angeles Dodgers, Kansas City Royals, Baltimore Orioles, and St. Louis Cardinals—have alert, communicating fielders who operate and shift as a unit and help cover each other's position as well as their own. If a batter is a pull hitter, all fielders shade him to pull. If a batter is very fast, all fielders play a few steps in. If there are two outs, all fielders play to prevent an extra-base hit. If a teammate is making a play, all fielders move into position to back up the play in case of an error or bad throw. In a winning baseball season, team defense indeed becomes *teamwork*.

INFIELD POSITIONING WITH A RUNNER ON THIRD BASE

With a runner on third base, there are four basic ways to position the infielders, including the pitcher. Your choice will depend upon who the priority out is.

Infield Back

In the infield-back position, the defensive priority is to retire the batter. With a runner on third base, the infield should still play back, providing that this runner does not represent the tying run, winning run, or a run that would put the offense further ahead. By assuming rather deep positions, each infielder allows himself more range for reaching balls hit to his right or left. Once a ground ball is fielded, the infielders (with the exception of the pitcher) ignore the runner scoring from third base and throw to first base to retire the hitter. Remember: The priority is preestablished by the position in which the coach puts the infielders before the pitch.

Infield In

With a runner on third base and fewer than two outs, the infield-in position can

Infield In, Infield Back

be used. The priority is to stop the runner from scoring, so any ball fielded results in either a throw home if the runner attempts to advance, or a look to third to hold the runner, followed by a throw to first to retire the batter. The obvious risk with this defense is that it significantly reduces the infielders' range on balls hit to their right or left and could lead to scratch hits and a big inning for the offense. Thus, the runner on third base *must* represent the tying, winning, or go-ahead run before you order your infield into this vulnerable position. It is *not* good defensive strategy to play your infield in when your team is ahead by two or more runs.

Halfway In

The third way of infield positioning is halfway. Now the infielders have a choice of where to throw depending upon (a) what the runner on third base does when the ball is hit, and (b) the speed of the ground ball. If the runner breaks from third base, obviously the infielder throws home; otherwise he throws to first base to retire the batter. There is a better chance to get the runner attempting to score if the ball is hit hard. If the ball is hit slowly, the infielder should try to get the batter. Although the infielders have increased their range by moving back 20 to 25 feet from the infield-in position, this is still a risky and vulnerable defense. While the ground ball is approaching the infielder, he may be tempted to lift his eyes to check the runner on third before controlling the ball, and thus make an error. Even if he does field the ball cleanly, he still faces a very close play at the plate if the runner at third base has average or better-than-average speed. Whereas in the first two infield positions the priority was preestablished, the halfway position confronts an infielder with a difficult split-second decision.

Cornermen In and Middlemen Back

The cornermen-in-and-middlemen-back position normally is assumed with fewer than two outs and runners on first and third, or the bases loaded. Recognizing that most ground balls are hit up the middle, you as coach order the shortstop and second baseman back for the double-play attempt. However, the runner on third base is still very significant, so the first baseman, third baseman, and pitcher play in and stop him from scoring. This is a calculated defense based on careful consideration of the variables mentioned earlier.

The first requirement in preparing several bunt defenses and choosing the correct one in a particular game situation is recognizing when the offense is likely to utilize the sacrifice bunt. A bunt situation has several or all of the following characteristics:

1. Nobody out, runner on first base or runners on first and second.
2. Close game where runner(s) on base represents tying, winning or lead-increasing run(s).
3. Middle to late innings.
4. Weak batter at the plate *or* very strong batters coming up next.
5. Poor fielding pitcher.
6. Wet grass in the infield.
7. Effective pitcher on the mound for either team, increasing likelihood of low-scoring game.

An alert defensive team is never surprised by a sacrifice bunt. Knowing the bunt is likely, choosing the right defense, and building your players' confidence in executing the play will most times, believe it or not, result in your team's forcing out the lead runner as he tries to move into scoring position. It is imperative, though, that *your defense get at least one out on the sacrifice,* so every base must be covered where a possible play may occur.

Runner on First Base (Standard)

In the standard method of defensing the sacrifice bunt, the third baseman positions himself 15 to 20 feet in toward the batter, the shortstop and second baseman begin at double-play depth, and the first baseman holds the runner close at first base. It's best to have your pitcher attempt several pick-off moves to first to hold the runner as close as possible, and also to see if the batter begins assuming his bunting stance. As soon as the batter shows his intention to bunt (by moving his feet, upper body, or hands on the bat), the third baseman, shortstop, and second baseman all begin moving quickly *toward the plate.* Each infielder must be aware that the batter may fake a bunt and swing away, so he must not give away too much lateral range. The first baseman must be certain the pitcher delivers the pitch to the plate before he charges. Once the defense is certain the ball is being bunted, everyone quickly moves to his responsibility: the third baseman on the line, the pitcher in the middle, the first baseman on his line, the second baseman to first base, the shortstop to second. The catcher, unless he fields the bunt, hollers "Two" or "One" depending on where he thinks the throw should go.

The catcher is the "captain" of this play because he can see its whole development and is closest to the player fielding the bunt. Additionally, the catcher is responsible for covering third base if the pitcher or third baseman forget and the runner tries to go from first to third on the play. Ideally, if one of the four players near the bunt can field it and force the runner at second base, the shortstop could execute a double play by relaying the ball to the second baseman covering first.

In this defense it is important that the pitcher throw strikes (preferably fastballs up in the strike zone, which are the most difficult to bunt). The good defensive team *wants* the batter to bunt, because they have confidence, built through many hours of practice and execution, that they will retire the lead runner. If the pitcher falls behind the batter 2 and 0, or 3 and 1, this defense becomes more tentative and uncertain. If the batter lays down a good bunt and the catcher hollers "One," it is often possible for the second baseman, after taking the throw and retiring the batter at first base, to quickly throw to the shortstop covering second base and get the lead runner, who has taken a wide turn at second base and is attempting to return. All three outfielders should be moving into backup positions in the event of an overthrow at first or second base.

It is not uncommon for the batter to pop up the bunt attempt. If the pop-up is in fair ground, the alert pitcher, third baseman, or first baseman will appear to attempt catching the ball in the air (thus freezing the runner at first base), but at the last instant trap the ball and throw to the second baseman covering

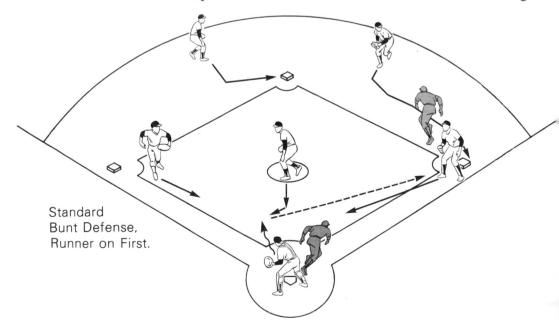

Standard
Bunt Defense,
Runner on First.

first base, retiring the batter. The runner must attempt to advance when the ball hits the ground, but it's too late for him to reach second base by the time the second baseman throws to the shortstop. Remember, the force was removed when the batter was retired first, so now the runner must be tagged between first and second bases. Also remember, if the popped-up bunt is in foul ground, catch it!

Runner on First Base (Special First Baseman Early Break)

In this defense, the initial positioning is the same as in the standard defense, but the first baseman can flash a prearranged signal to the pitcher *before* the pitcher gets set on the rubber, indicating he will break for home plate early, before the pitcher delivers to the batter. This brings the first baseman closer to the ball when it is bunted and in better position to force the lead runner at second base. The pitcher must acknowledge the early-break signal to prevent two possible mistakes: (1) The pitcher must not unwittingly attempt a pick-off at first base while the first baseman is charging the plate, and (2) the pitcher must not hold his set position longer than two seconds while the first baseman is breaking for the plate lest the runner on first get far too big a lead with no one holding him on the bag. The first baseman in the early break is much closer to the plate as the batter bunts, and thus counters the batter's normal inclination to bunt the ball down the first-base line when he sees the third baseman begin moving in.

This defense is used only when the first baseman feels certain the batter will attempt a bunt. It is unwise to use this defense too many times on successive pitches because it allows the runner to get a longer lead once he sees the first

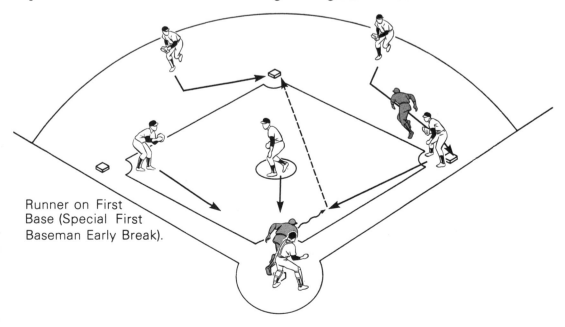

Runner on First
Base (Special First
Baseman Early Break).

baseman begin his break toward the plate. To counter this possibility, the pitcher and first baseman could have a prearranged signal that would call for the first baseman to break in two hard strides, stop, and return to the bag for the pick-off throw. (I painfully remember the effectiveness of this fake break and pick-off. In 1956, first baseman Stan Musial and pitcher Lindy McDaniel of the St. Louis Cardinals combined to work this play on a startled Chicago Cub rookie base runner named Kindall!)

The other possible pick-off play is with the catcher throwing to the second baseman, who covers first base. This is also prearranged and must be preceded by a pitchout at the plate to create the necessary timing for the second baseman to break in behind the unsuspecting runner who increases his lead as the first baseman, becoming a decoy, breaks early toward the plate.

Pick-off plays notwithstanding, the catcher remains the captain of this and all bunt plays once the ball is on the ground. His quick and accurate judgment as to where the throw should go—to "one" or to "two"—is the final factor in the success of the bunt defense.

Runners on First and Second Bases (Standard Defense)

When the necessary characteristics of a bunt situation appear with runners on first and second base, the defense can react by positioning itself in the following way:

The third baseman locates himself about 15 feet in from the bag and about 10 feet off the line *facing* the pitcher. In this way he can see both the bunter at the plate *and* the runner leading off second base in case he breaks for third in a steal or in a hit-and-run attempt.

The second baseman has moved in and is ready to cover first base when the ball is bunted.

The first baseman is quite far in toward the plate, ready to pounce on any ball bunted in his direction and force the lead runner at third base.

The shortstop is the key to this defense and it is his responsibility to hold the runner as close as possible to second base *and* to signal the pitcher when to deliver the pitch. Obviously, the later the start and the farther the runner must go, the greater the opportunity for the pitcher, catcher, or first baseman to field the bunt and throw to the third baseman for the force-out at third. So the shortstop very early takes a position right behind the runner at second base and makes sure the runner knows he is there, thus making the runner cautious about taking too large a lead.

As the pitcher comes to his set and looks back at second base, the shortstop takes a quick step toward second, slaps his glove in the runner's left ear, hollers

"Back!" and then breaks hard to his normal position in case the batter swings away. These three simultaneous, abrupt actions serve to startle the runner, and may even cause him to take a step or two backward toward the bag. When the pitcher sees the shortstop slap his glove, he delivers the pitch to the plate and tries to throw a strike so the batter will attempt to bunt. If the bunt is to the first-base side, the third baseman spins to his right, rushes back to the bag, turns with his right foot on the bag, and takes the force throw from the first baseman. If the ball is bunted toward the third-base line, the pitcher must make every effort to field the bunt and throw to the third baseman, who has retreated to cover the bag. This is the tricky part of the defense. The third baseman must hold momentarily to make sure the pitcher *can* field the bunt before he spins to his right and covers third. If the bunt gets past the pitcher, then the third baseman must field it and throw to the second baseman covering first to retire the batter. Once again, the catcher hollers where the throw should be directed, but if there is a mix-up and the pitcher and third baseman each think the other will field the bunt, all runners are safe and the defense is faced with bases loaded and nobody out.

The success of this bunt defense is built upon the shortstop's ability to hold the runner close at second base. If, when the pitcher in his set looks back at second base, the shortstop feels the runner is too far off the bag, he merely breaks all the way to the bag with no slap of the glove and the pitcher has a good chance to pick the runner off. The other key to this play is the coordination and timing between the pitcher and third baseman as to which one fields the bunt. The defense *wants* the pitcher to field the bunt and retire the lead runner. Pitchers and third basemen should prepare and practice this play together carefully.

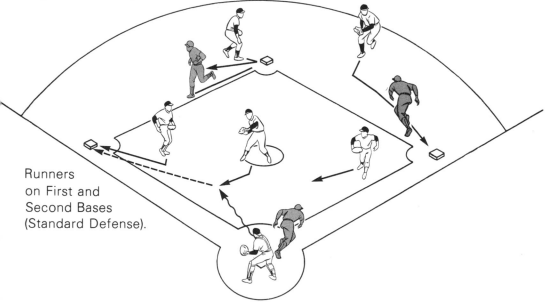

Runners
on First and
Second Bases
(Standard Defense).

Runners on First and Second Bases (Special Defense)

If the defense is quite certain the batter will bunt, a special defense can be signaled from the bench which will, if properly executed, provide a 50-percent better chance of forcing the important lead runner at third base. The defense sets up exactly as they did for the standard defense, but when the shortstop slaps his glove in the runner's left ear, takes a quick step toward second base, and hollers "Back," he immediately sprints to third base. The pitcher watches the shortstop take two strides toward third base, then pitches, and charges straight in toward the plate to field the bunt up the middle. As the pitcher delivers, the third baseman, instead of holding to see where the bunt goes as he did in the standard defense, charges in on the third-base line. (He must hold an instant to make sure the runner at second base does not try to steal third base. If the runner does try to steal, the third baseman retreats to the bag for the catcher's throw.) The first baseman takes any bunt in his direction from his already shortened position toward the plate. Now any bunt is well covered by one of the three charging players, and the catcher calls "Three!" or "One!" The shortstop should arrive at third base in ample time to position himself and take the force throw. This special defense should result in retiring the lead runner at third base nine times out of ten.

The obvious problem in using this defense too often is that the runner at second base will become so familiar with the shortstop's breaking toward third that he will greatly increase his lead or even attempt to beat the shortstop in a footrace to third base while the pitcher is delivering the pitch to home plate. This problem can be countered by having a prearranged pick-off with the second baseman covering the bag while the shortstop acts as a decoy running toward third base.

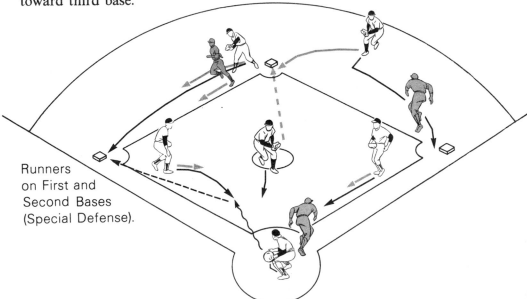

Runners
on First and
Second Bases
(Special Defense).

There are other defenses against the sacrifice bunt that could be mentioned here, but they fall into the category of trick defenses and can easily backfire on a defensive team. They include such risky moves as having the second baseman charge the plate while the first baseman holds the runner on first base; or bringing in an outfielder to cover a base, which increases the coverage of the bunt by one more infielder. The bunt defenses explained and diagramed in this chapter are altogether sufficient, provided they are understood and practiced diligently by your entire team. An effective way to practice these bunt defenses is to have the extra outfielders simulate the runners, the coach at home plate rolling the ball to simulate a bunt while the infielders, catcher, and pitcher react as they would in a game situation.

Runner on Third Base—Squeeze-Play Defense

A well-executed suicide squeeze is perhaps the most difficult of all bunts to defend. If the runner at third breaks home at the correct time and the batter disguises his intention until the last instant and then puts the bunt down in fair ground, it is virtually impossible to prevent the run from scoring. But the offense will often make a mistake on the squeeze attempt, and then the defense, if prepared, can record a key out.

The squeeze play is a possibility when there are fewer than two outs. (Remember, a good defensive team is not surprised by any offensive maneuver.) Obviously, if the offense elects to squeeze the runner home, it must be an important run. Thus, the infield will be playing in to cut off the run at the plate. Furthermore, the pitcher must be in the stretch position and the third baseman holding the runner close to prevent a big lead. As soon as the squeeze is apparent—by either the runner's breaking home or the batter's turning to bunt —the third baseman, pitcher, and first baseman charge hard toward the plate. The second baseman and shortstop start in toward home plate in case the batter bunts the ball hard past the three charging players, and then break to cover the corners. The second baseman breaks to cover first base to retire the batter on a successful squeeze bunt, and the shortstop covers third base in the event the batter misses the bunt and the runner is trapped in a rundown. It is possible that one of the three hard-charging players—the third baseman, pitcher, or first baseman—could field the bunt and underhand it home to catch the runner at the plate. That is why they must charge hard. The other possibilities are a popped-up or missed bunt attempt, in which case this defense has every base covered where a possible play may occur. If the runner or batter reveal the squeeze play prematurely, before the pitcher delivers the ball, the pitcher automatically throws a fastball high and away from the batter to prevent the bunt. The infielders react as described above, however, in the event the batter still gets the bunt down.

DOUBLE-STEAL DEFENSES: RUNNERS ON FIRST BASE AND THIRD BASE

At every level of baseball competition below the major leagues, one of the best offensive strategies for advancing runners, pressuring the defense, and scoring runs is the double steal. (Chapter 13, "Offensive Strategy," describes five double-steal variations.) There are a number of reasons why the offense often wins this battle of strategies: weak and inaccurate catchers' throws, pitchers unable to hold runners on effectively, nervous and inexperienced infielders who become easily rattled are only a few. But the most common and disturbing reason for the double steal's success is lack of preparation and planning on the part of the defense. Far too often I see high-school, college, amateur, and even professional teams stand helpless and confused while a runner either scores or advances into scoring position as part of a double steal. I submit that no matter what double-steal variation they face, the defense can have a play ready that *can* stop the runner who represents the priority out. For a catcher to hold the ball and concede the runner's stealing second base without a play is very poor defensive strategy. In fact, it's not strategy at all, but defensive cowardice.

The six double-steal defenses explained in the following pages are not guaranteed to retire a runner every time, but they will often result in getting the priority runner and, at the very least, will prevent the offense from running wild. Perhaps just as important, these defenses will give your team the confidence that they are prepared and ready for any contingency, thus making them a stronger team and a more likely winner.

As a coach choosing the best defense for a given situation, you must consider the following variables:

1.   Which is the most important runner to retire: the runner on first base or the runner on third?
2.   What are the strengths and weaknesses of my infield, pitcher, and catcher?
3.   Which of the two runners is the faster? The slower?
4.   What are the strengths and weaknesses of the hitter at the plate?
5.   What is the score?

The Throw-Through Double-Steal Defense

This defense provides for getting either runner. There are occasions when both runners are important and the advance of either would be very damaging to the defense. For instance, if the runner on third base is the tying run and the runner on first the winning run, then the throw-through defense is a good selection. It requires that both the catcher and middle infielders have strong, accurate arms, and will prove effective if the following techniques are executed:

1. The pitcher must hold the runner as close as possible to first base.

2. When the runner at first base takes off, the first baseman hollers "Going!" to alert the catcher and middle infielders.

3. The catcher must look the runner back at third base and, if he thinks the runner can be picked off, feel free to fire the ball to the third baseman. Also, if the third baseman feels the runner is far enough off third base to be picked, he can throw up both arms as a visual signal to the catcher to fire to third base. If, at a quick glance, the catcher sees neither of the above, he throws through to second base.

4. The pitcher fakes catching the ball by slapping his glove above his head as the ball travels over the mound. This will freeze the runner at third base into thinking the pitcher has cut off the ball. Then the pitcher sprints in to back up home plate.

5. If the batter is right-handed, generally the second baseman covers second base. When the runner at first base breaks for second and the first baseman hollers "Going," the second baseman in the ready position also sees

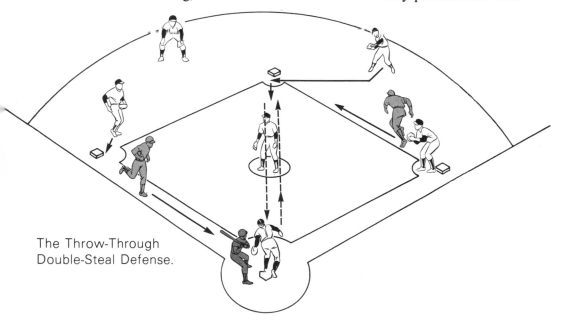

The Throw-Through
Double-Steal Defense.

the runner out of the corner of *his* eye. His first move is two steps toward the plate, in the event the batter hits the ball in his direction. He then sprints to a point *3 feet* in front of second base and facing third. If the runner at third base breaks home as the ball is coming to the second baseman, he can see this because he is facing that way. He simply takes a few more steps toward the plate, catches the ball, and throws home. (The third baseman should also holler "Going!" to further alert the second baseman.)

6.   If the runner at third base does not break home, the second baseman catches the ball, drops his left foot back, and tags the runner sliding into second base.

If the batter at the plate is left-handed and the second baseman is playing to his left, the shortstop will cover second base. It is a bit more difficult for the shortstop to get to the position 3 feet in front of the bag and facing third base, because it requires that he change direction.

Pitcher-Cut Double-Steal Defense

In this case, the runner at third base is the priority out and the defense hopes to decoy him off the bag by making him think the throw has gone through to second base. The important techniques in this defense are the following:

1.   When the runner at first base breaks for second, the catcher does *not* look the runner at third base back, but fires toward second base using the pitcher's cap as his target.

2.   The pitcher cuts the throw off and quickly wheels toward third base to see if the runner is trapped. If so, he either throws to the third baseman

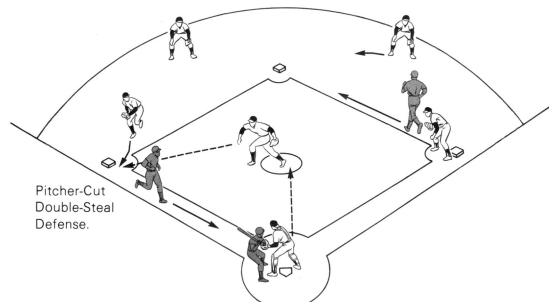

Pitcher-Cut Double-Steal Defense.

coming to the bag or runs directly at the runner and forces him into a rundown toward third base.

3. The second baseman or shortstop, depending on who has coverage responsibility, holds his position to make sure the ball is not hit in his direction, and then moves toward second base in the event of an overthrow by the catcher.

The pitcher-cut double-steal defense is fairly common but can still be effective if properly executed. It should be selected over the other double-steal defenses when the runner at third is eager and venturesome and likely to fall for the trap, or if the second baseman or shortstop has a sore or weak arm that would preclude using the throw-through defense.

Catcher Fake Throw to Second Base, Throw to Third Base Double-Steal Defense

In this defense, the runner on third base is the critical concern for the defensive team. When the runner at first base breaks for second, the catcher makes as realistic a fake throw as possible toward second base with full body and arm action, even to the point where the pitcher fakes seeing the throw go over his head. Hopefully, the fake will draw the runner off third base, enough so the catcher can regain his balance and fire to the third baseman. The other infielders hold their positions against a possible batted ball; then the third baseman breaks to the bag, and the shortstop and left fielder back up a possible overthrow. The catcher's throw should be aimed 2 feet inside the line to avoid hitting the runner diving back to the bag.

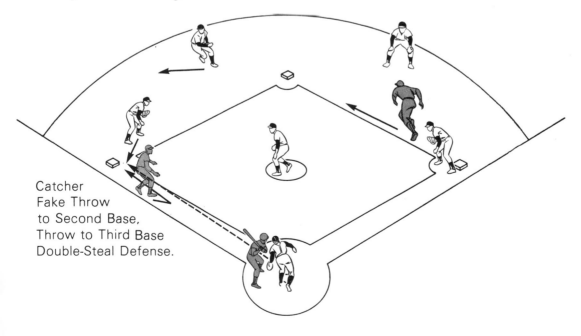

Catcher Fake Throw to Second Base, Throw to Third Base Double-Steal Defense.

Fake-and-Cut Double-Steal Defense

Generally, the runner at third base makes the decision to break for home when he sees the ball clear the mound area on its way to second base. The percentage for the offense is that the ball must be accurately thrown 127 feet from home to second base and another 127 feet back again, and a runner must be tagged who himself need run less than 75 feet. This fake-and-cut defense is designed to lead the runner into thinking the throw is going all the way to second base when actually it is cut off about 90 feet from the plate. Once again, the priority runner is at third base and must be stopped from scoring. The techniques are fairly simple but must be executed properly to assure success.

1. The runner from first base breaks toward second base with the pitch, and the first baseman hollers "Going!"

2. The second baseman takes two steps (left, right) toward second base as if he is going all the way to cover (this is the "fake" move in the defense), but then pivots on his right foot and comes hard, but under control, toward the plate.

3. The catcher does not look the runner back to third base (the defense *wants* this runner to break home), but instead throws directly to the second baseman coming toward him. From his angle at third base, the runner can't see that the throw has not in fact gone 127 feet to second base, so he breaks for home. The second baseman cuts off the throw only 90 feet from home and relays the ball there well ahead of the runner. Two reasonably accurate throws will retire the fastest runner from third base even if he breaks upon the catcher's release. The shortstop executes the fake-and-cut when a left-handed batter is at the plate, and the only difference is that the shortstop takes a right-left

Fake-and-Cut
Double-Steal
Defense.

two-step fake toward second base so that his outside foot provides a good push as he veers toward the plate.

The fake-and-cut defense has worked well for us at Arizona over the years. Several years ago we were playing the Cuban National team in an international tournament held in Holland. The Cuban team is well known for its aggressive and skillful baserunning, but the fake-and-cut defense retired their fastest base runner at the plate by 20 feet!

Catcher-Pop Double-Steal Defense

This defense is designed to catch the runner at third base who takes a longer, more aggressive lead than normal. When the runner at first base breaks for second, the catcher simply fires the ball to third base. A quick catcher with a good arm will surprise many runners at third base who are expecting some sort of play, or at least fake play, on the runner advancing from first to second.

Double-Cut Double-Steal Defense

When the defense is quite certain the runner is going on the next pitch, the double cut is an excellent defense to use because it offers an opportunity to get either runner, and perhaps *both*. The coach must be sure his team sees him when he signals the double cut because the play involves both a pitchout *and* moving the shortstop and second baseman out of position. The techniques are these:

1. A pitchout is essential because the middle infielders both vacate their positions when the runner on first breaks for second, and a batted ball could easily get through the infield if the batter were allowed to swing.

Catcher-Pop Double-Steal Defense.

2.   As soon as the runner on first base breaks, the second baseman sprints to a position approximately 25 feet in front of second base and facing third. The shortstop goes to second base for the possible tag there.

3.   The catcher looks the runner back to third base and is free now to exercise the same options as in the throw-through defense. If he chooses *not* to throw to third, he throws through all the way to second base. If the runner on third base breaks home as the ball clears the mound, the third baseman hollers "Going!" The second baseman also sees the runner breaking, and cuts the throw off and returns it home to the catcher for the tag. If the runner on third base does *not* break home, the second baseman allows the throw to go through to the shortstop for the tag at second base.

It has happened in the double-cut defense that the runner on third is so effectively frozen by the possibility the second baseman may cut the catcher's throw that when he sees the ball go through to the shortstop, he finally breaks home much too late. The shortstop tags the runner at second base and still has time to get the runner at home. Instead of the offense having a double steal, the defense has a double play!

Practice the six double-steal defenses a great deal early in the season and review them often throughout. Not only will your team be well prepared to retire a key runner, but the reputation it soon gets for being well prepared makes opponents reluctant even to contemplate double steals. This keeps more opposition runners out of scoring position, keeps the double play a greater weapon, and allows your infield to play back more often.

An excellent way to practice double-steal defenses is to simulate game

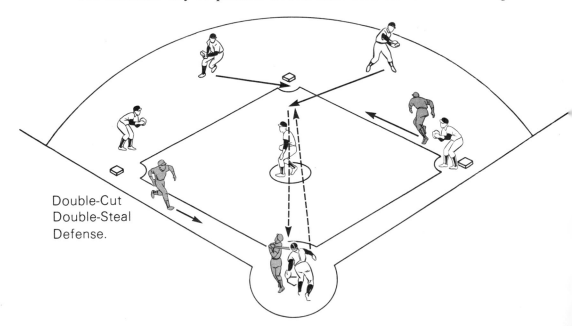

Double-Cut
Double-Steal
Defense.

conditions with runners and a batter. You, as coach, stay in the dugout and flash signals to your defense indicating which of the six defenses you want executed. Once the six defenses are learned, fifteen minutes a day is sufficient to keep all the fielders brushed up on the techniques.

RUNNERS ON FIRST AND THIRD BASES, FOUL FLY BALL OR POP FLY

An alert offensive team may try to advance one or both runners from first and third bases on a caught foul fly ball. When the ball is caught, both runners tag up and the runner on first breaks hard for second base. If the fielder throws to second base, the runner on third breaks home and scores, while the runner on first retreats or gets into a rundown. If the fielder throws home after he catches the ball, the runner on first base easily makes it to second base and into scoring position. This play can be effectively defensed if either the third baseman, first baseman, or pitcher rush to a cutoff position approximately 60 to 70 feet from home, and in line with the fielder catching the foul fly or pop-up. If the first or third baseman is involved in chasing down the foul fly in his

Runners on First and Third Bases,
Foul Fly Ball or Pop Fly.

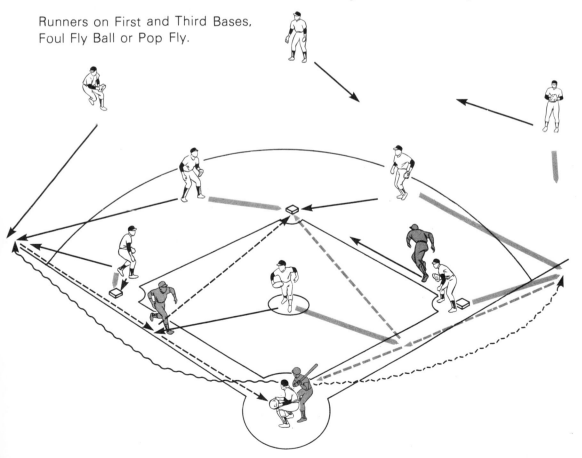

territory, then the pitcher must react and be the cutoff man. When the fielder catches the foul fly, he immediately throws to the cutoff man at the plate. If the runner on third base attempts to score, the cutoff man (in the diagram, the pitcher) relays the ball home or lets it go if on target. If the runner on third base does not attempt to score, the pitcher cuts off the throw and retires the runner going from first to second base.

RUNNER ON SECOND BASE, BALL FOUR, WILD PITCH TO THE BATTER

This situation seldom occurs, but when it does, it gives the base runners an excellent opportunity to "steal" a run, or at least get the batter/runner to second base if the defense fails to react quickly. If ball four is a wild pitch, the runner on second base advances easily to third and rounds the bag while the batter/runner hustles to first base as the catcher retrieves the wild pitch against the screen. When the batter/runner reaches first base, he keeps going full-speed to second base. If the catcher throws all the way to second base—perhaps as far as 180 feet—the runner on third scores easily. If the catcher does not throw toward second base, the batter/runner easily coasts into scoring position.

The diagram shows how the alert, well-prepared defense can solve this dilemma. The pitcher must, of course, cover home; the third and first basemen remain at their bags for a possible play; and the second baseman covers his base

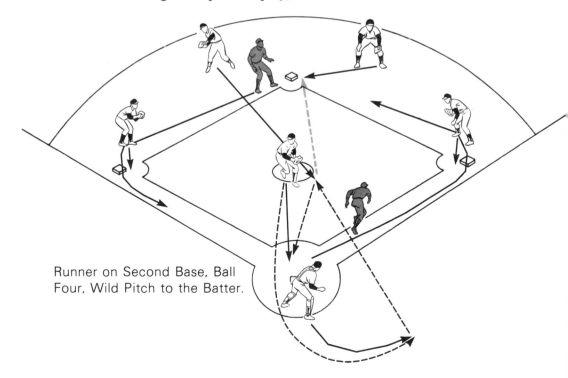

Runner on Second Base, Ball Four, Wild Pitch to the Batter.

for the approaching runner. The shortstop becomes the key to this play by instantly sprinting to the mound area when the wild pitch occurs and hollering for the catcher to throw him the ball as soon as he retrieves the wild pitch. When the shortstop gets the ball, he can either relay it to second base or throw home to the pitcher, depending on which runner is attempting to advance.

CUTOFFS AND RELAYS: TEAM DEFENSE

In a recent game I saw at Yankee Stadium, the New York Yankees won an important victory over the California Angels due to a key defensive play involving four Yankee players. With an Angel runner on first base, two outs in the seventh inning, and the Yankees protecting a slim lead, an Angel batter drove a long extra-base hit to left center field. Because this is an unusually deep area in Yankee Stadium, almost everyone, player and fan alike, assumed that the runner on first would score easily. But Dave Winfield, the Yankee left fielder, recovered the ball against the fence and threw perfectly to shortstop Roy Smalley, who was sprinting out to left center to meet the throw. Smalley, in turn, quickly threw a long strike toward home plate, where first baseman Bob Watson was perfectly lined up about 60 feet from catcher Butch Wynegar. All in one motion, Watson cut off Smalley's throw and threw to Wynegar, who made the tag on the sliding runner attempting to score from first. The inning was over and the Yankees went on to win the game.

This was team defense performed at its best and illustrates the important roles the relay man (Smalley) and the cutoff man (Watson) play in preventing runners from advancing extra bases. The defensive team with a well-planned system of cutoffs and relays, that practices hard to assure that all nine players go to their proper places when a base hit occurs, that insists the throws be accurate, and that works hard to save split seconds in their catches and throws through proper footwork and body control, over a long season, will prevent a significant number of runs from scoring. And that team will win games!

To be certain the terms are consistent in describing team defense, let it be understood that *the relay man is the shortstop or second baseman,* who will go out into the outfield and receive a throw from the outfielder on an extra-base hit, and then "relay" that throw toward home plate, third base, or second base. *The cutoff man is normally the first baseman, third baseman, or shortstop,* who positions himself 60 or 70 feet from the base where the play will occur and in line with the throw from the outfield. He will "cut off" the throw if it is off-target, weak, or too late to get the runner, and either complete the throw to the intended base or throw to another base where a second runner may be attempting to advance. It is imperative that every defensive player recognize his role in stopping the offense from taking extra bases and scoring easy runs. When a base hit occurs, each of the nine players on the field moves quickly into a position where he will either handle the ball or back up a teammate or base.

When I was a young infielder with the Chicago Cubs in 1957, I was thrust into playing third base, an unfamiliar position. I can remember my feeling of panic when, with a runner on second base in a game at Wrigley Field, I realized I did not know if I was the cutoff man at the plate on a single to center field. As I frantically tried to get the attention of the Cub first baseman and ask through sign language if it was he or I in such an event, the batter grounded a single up the middle to center field and the runner on second base stormed around third base on his way to the plate. I rushed to the mound area to be the cutoff man and nearly collided with the first baseman coming to do the same. As the center fielder's throw bounced too late into the plate and the batter/runner continued on to second base, I realized with embarrassment I did not know the system!

The following system of team defense, with emphasis on cutoffs and relays, is built on the four general principles mentioned earlier in this chapter. It is very similar to a zone defense in basketball: the ball's location, as well as the runner's, determines the defensive role of each player.

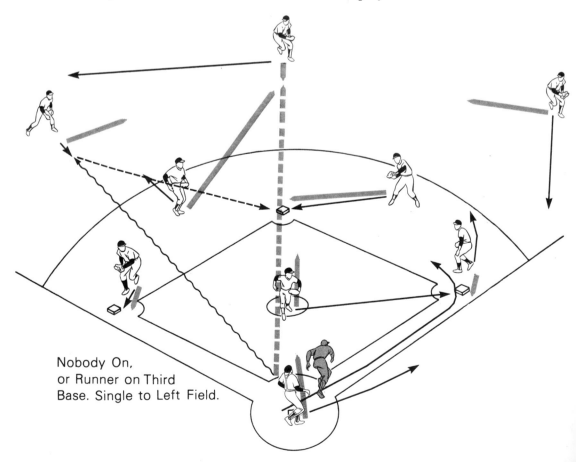

Nobody On,
or Runner on Third
Base. Single to Left Field.

Nobody On, or Runner on Third Base. Single to Left Field.

In this play, the shortstop moves out to the edge of the infield approximately 60 feet from second base and in line with the left fielder's throw to the second baseman. In the event the ball gets past the left fielder, the shortstop keeps moving out to become the relay man and prevent the batter from reaching third base. The first baseman and right fielder back up the throw to second base, and the pitcher moves over to cover first base in case the batter/runner rounds the bag too far. The catcher moves down the line to back up first base. It is crucial that the left fielder not be nonchalant and lob the ball to the shortstop, thereby giving the batter opportunity to reach second base. Rather, he should field the ball and throw hard to the shortstop. If the batter attempts to stretch the single to a double, the left fielder throws all the way to second base.

Nobody On, or Runner on Third Base. Single to Center Field.

The shortstop or second baseman moves out to the cutoff position while the other covers second base. The pitcher backs up the throw while the first baseman remains at first base, observing if the batter/runner touches the bag and preparing for a possible pick-off throw from the second baseman if the batter/runner rounds too far. Note that both the left fielder and right fielder back up the center fielder in the event he misses the ball.

Nobody On, or Runner on Third Base. Single to Right Field.

This situation creates a special play for the defense that can trap the batter/runner into a wide turn at first base and a possible pick-off. The right fielder throws the ball in to the second baseman while the shortstop covers second base and prepares to signal the second baseman if the surprise pick-off play develops. The first baseman drifts out toward right field, fooling the batter/runner into thinking that nobody is covering first base and that he can continue a wide turn at the bag. The catcher follows the batter/runner down the line but swings out in an arc to avoid being seen by the first-base coach, who is watching the ball. Once the batter is well on his way toward first base, the pitcher sprints to the area of the first-base dugout to back up the pick-off throw. When the right fielder's throw reaches the second baseman, whose back is toward first base, the shortstop hollers "Yes!" if the batter/runner is taking a wide turn, and the second baseman spins to his left and fires the ball to the catcher, who arrives

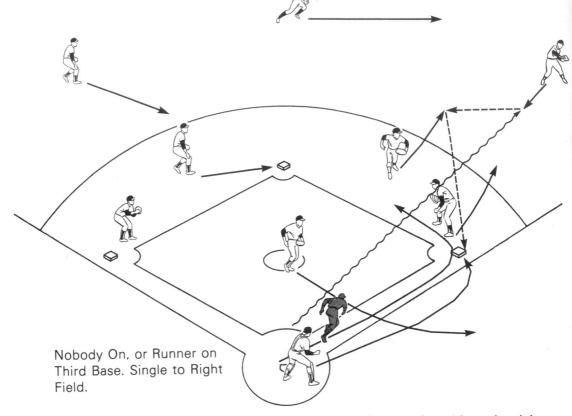

Nobody On, or Runner on Third Base. Single to Right Field.

at first base behind the runner. If the batter/runner is not vulnerable to the pick off, the shortstop shouts "No," thus saving a possible bad throw.

Runner on First Base, or Runners on First Base and Third Base. Single to the Outfield.

The runner who must be prevented from taking an extra base in this case is the one on first base. If the outfielder were to throw the ball all the way to third and was slightly off-target or too late to get the runner advancing from first to third, the batter/runner could move to second base and thus also be in scoring position. The shortstop is the key defensive man to prevent these runners from advancing; he goes directly to a cutoff position approximately 60 feet from third base and in line with the outfielder's throw. By having the outfielder throw to the shortstop, a wide or low throw can be cut off and relayed to third base, or cut off and thrown to second to stop the batter/runner from advancing. The pitcher is also important in backing up third base in case of an overthrow.

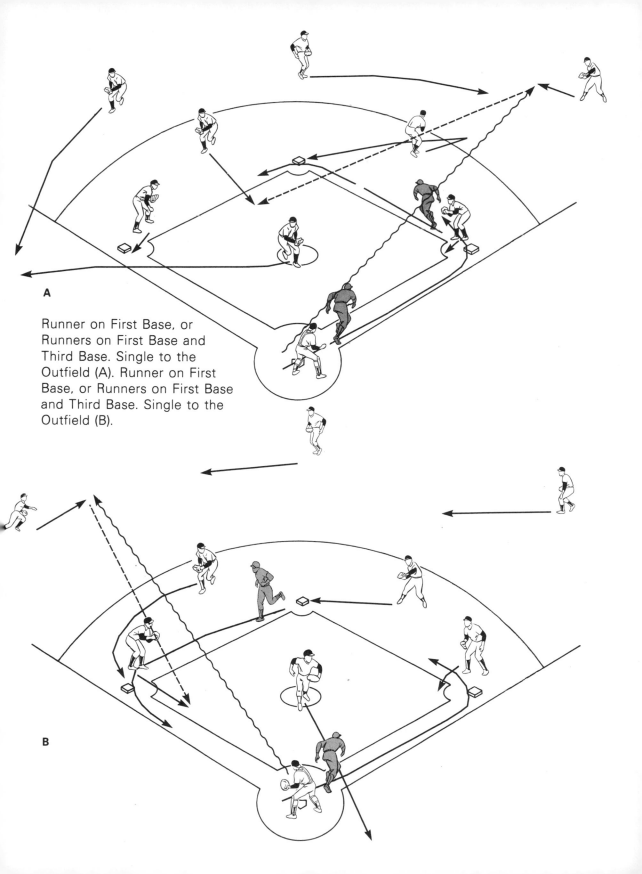

A

Runner on First Base, or
Runners on First Base and
Third Base. Single to the
Outfield (A). Runner on First
Base, or Runners on First Base
and Third Base. Single to the
Outfield (B).

B

Runner on Second Base, or Runners on Second Base and Third Base, or Runners on First Base and Second Base, or Bases Loaded. Single to Left Field.

In this situation, since the obvious play is to try to stop the runner at second base from scoring, the outfielder's throw goes to the plate. But it is also important to prevent the trail runner or batter/runner from advancing extra bases. So the need for a cutoff man at the plate is crucial. Who shall it be? In this case, because the single has passed the infield to the shortstop's *right* and gone into left field, the entire four-man infield defense rotates *counterclockwise* and *the third baseman* becomes the cutoff. The shortstop covers third base, the second baseman covers second, and the first baseman makes sure the batter/runner touches first base and then covers there. The pitcher backs up home plate and the catcher remains at home awaiting the throw from the left fielder. In this way, every base is covered where a possible play may occur. (See General Principle #2 for Team Defense, p. 187.)

Same Situation as Above. Single to Center or Right Field.

Remember my dilemma in Wrigley Field as a rookie third baseman? The problem is solved by applying the following rule for cutoff responsibility: With a runner on second base, on any single that leaves the infield to the shortstop's left, the infielders rotate in a *clockwise* fashion and *the first baseman becomes the cutoff man.* The second baseman, if possible, covers first base, the shortstop covers second, and the third baseman remains at third. Of course, the pitcher backs up home plate.

In the several situations above, with a runner on second base and a single to the outfield, every infielder and outfielder must move instantly to a prearranged position to keep base runners from advancing more than one base. By setting up the shortstop as an obvious reference point in relation to where the ball leaves the infield, each player immediately knows his responsibility and that of his teammates. This rule on cutoffs at the plate also applies on a fly ball hit to the outfield with less than two outs and a runner on third base, or runners on second and third, first or third, or bases loaded.

Nobody On, or Runner at Third Base, or Runners on Second Base and Third Base. Extra-Base Hit to Left Field, Left Center, or Center Field.

In this situation, the defense is concerned with the batter/runner and preventing a triple or inside-the-park home run. The lead runners have scored easily on the cinch double. The key player is the shortstop as he moves out quickly toward the outfielder retrieving the ball and becomes the *relay* man in line with third base and the ball. Because there was *no runner on first base* when the ball was hit, the second baseman can move out to a backup position about 30 to 35 feet behind the shortstop in the event a bad throw from the outfielder gets by the shortstop. It is crucial that this first throw from the outfielder be one the relay man can handle. By having the second baseman in a backup or double-relay position, a bad throw can still be handled and the batter/runner held to second base. The first baseman, after making sure the batter/runner touches first, trails him into second base to prevent him from taking a wide turn and hollers instructions to the relay man on where to throw the ball. If the runner tries for a triple, the first baseman hollers "Cut three!" If the runner

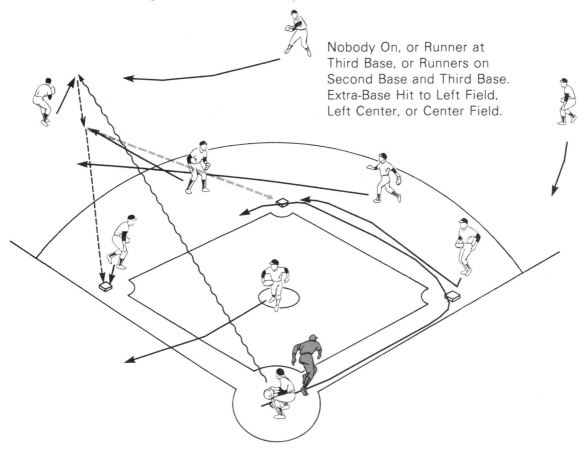

Nobody On, or Runner at Third Base, or Runners on Second Base and Third Base. Extra-Base Hit to Left Field, Left Center, or Center Field.

makes too wide a turn at second base, the first baseman hollers "Cut two!" and takes the throw at second from the shortstop. In that case, the right fielder backs up second base, the pitcher backs up third. It may happen that the batter/runner will try for an inside-the-park home run, in which case the first baseman hustles from his trailer responsibility into the cutoff position at home plate, and the pitcher moves to back up the catcher.

Same Situation. Extra-Base Hit to Right Center or Right Field.

Now the second baseman becomes the primary relay man with the shortstop backing him up as the double relay. The other players' responsibilities remain the same *except* in the rare event that the ball is hit very deep into the right-field corner and the second baseman's relay throw to third is an extremely long one. Then the first baseman, after initially trailing the batter/runner into second base and seeing the runner going for a triple, sprints to a cutoff position for the throw to third base.

In both the above extra-base-hit situations, there was no runner on first base when the ball was hit. This allowed the double-relay system, or safety valve, of the backup man. It also freed the first baseman to trail the batter/runner into second base, since there was little likelihood of a play at home plate —any runners at second or third scored easily on the extra-base hit. Once again, every base was covered where a possible play might occur.

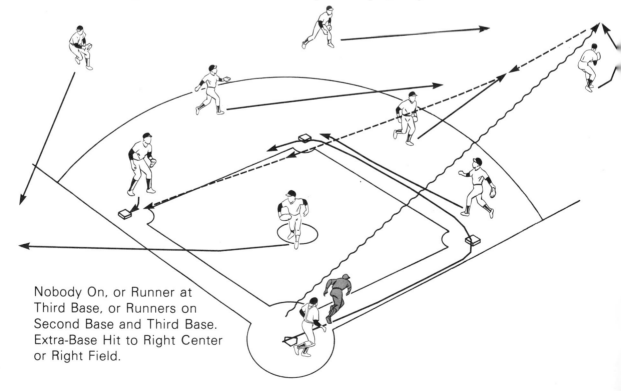

Nobody On, or Runner at Third Base, or Runners on Second Base and Third Base. Extra-Base Hit to Right Center or Right Field.

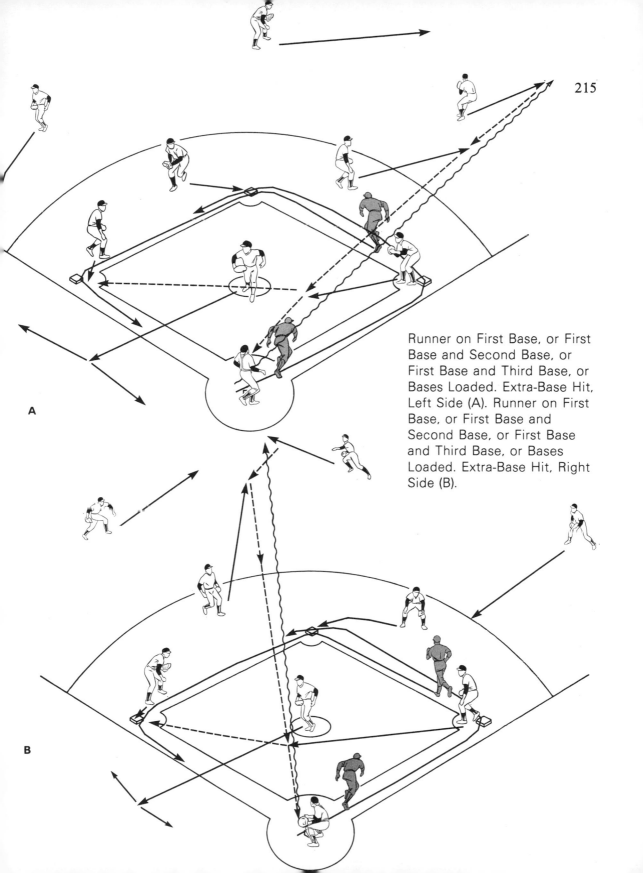

Runner on First Base, or First Base and Second Base, or First Base and Third Base, or Bases Loaded. Extra-Base Hit, Left Side (A). Runner on First Base, or First Base and Second Base, or First Base and Third Base, or Bases Loaded. Extra-Base Hit, Right Side (B).

A

B

215

Runner on First Base, or First and Second Bases, or First Base and Third Base, or Bases Loaded. Extra-Base Hit.

Now the concern of the defensive team is stopping the runner at first base from scoring, and also preventing the batter/runner from going to third base. A cutoff man will be needed at the plate. He is *always* the first baseman, no matter where the extra-base hit has gone. The reason is that there is obviously no play at first base, so the first baseman is the only player free to become the cutoff. A play *is* likely to occur at second or third base, so both those bags must be covered. On an extra-base hit to left center field, the shortstop goes out for the relay and the second baseman covers second base. This applies on extra-base hits between the left-field line and deep center field. On an extra-base hit to right center or right field, the second baseman is the relay man and the shortstop covers second base. The pitcher has backup responsibility at either third base or home plate, depending on where the relay man's throw is directed. He should take a position in foul territory halfway between third base and home plate, see where the throw is going, and then sprint to back up.

RELAY AND CUTOFF FUNDAMENTALS AND TECHNIQUES

The difference between a runner's being safe or out on a cutoff or relay play is the split second the defensive man either gains or loses as he catches the ball,

The shortstop and second baseman act as relay men on extra-base hits. Here, the shortstop has positioned himself for the centerfielder's throw and his subsequent relay to third base.

The Relay Man. By waving his arms and yelling "Hit me! Hit me!" the relay man offers a clear target for the outfielder's throw. As the throw approaches, the relay man begins moving toward the infield. He catches the ball with two hands as his right foot plants for the throw. Poor foot or hand action and the runner will be safe.

transfers it to his throwing hand, and makes a hard, accurate throw. When we consider that for every second the cutoff or relay man has the ball in his possession, the runner at full speed is covering 12 to 15 feet, then the following techniques become quite important:

The Relay Man

1   On an extra-base hit, the relay man (shortstop or second baseman) should keep sprinting toward the outfielder retrieving the extra-base hit until

The relay drill includes all the techniques of effective relay throws.

the latter stops and begins picking up the ball. The shorter of the two throws in a relay-cutoff play should be the outfielder's to the relay man because, to initiate an effective relay, the first throw must be accurate.

2. When the outfielder stops and begins picking up the ball against the fence, the relay man should stop and turn the glove-hand side of his body partially toward the base to which he will throw. He should frantically wave his arms and holler at the top of his voice, "Hit me! Hit me! Hit me!" The outfielder, picking up the ball with his back toward the relay man, needs both the visible clue (waving arms) and the audible clue ("Hit me!") to locate the relay man for the crucial first throw.

3. The relay man's throw to third base or home plate will be a long one and must be unloaded quickly and with velocity and accuracy. As the outfielder's throw approaches the relay man, he should be already turned toward his target with his knees bent, hands up, and weight on the balls of his feet. When the ball is nearly to him, he starts moving his body toward the infield, keeping his chest in front of the ball and catching it near the heel of the glove with both hands. As he removes the ball from his glove, he takes a quick shuffle hop with his right foot, then plants it firmly for the long throw to the base where the runner is advancing.

An effective drill for relays is to place a four- or five-man line of infielders about 75 feet apart and have them perform all the techniques mentioned above while throwing the ball back and forth from one end of the line to the other. The priorities in this drill are footwork, body control, and glove-ball action, so in the beginning the distance between the players is short. As their skill increases, widen the distance to more realistic game distances, up to 150 feet.

Proper body positioning, footwork, and body control will permit relay men to catch and throw the ball in one continuous, split-second motion.

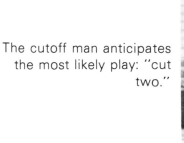

The cutoff man anticipates the most likely play: "cut two."

The most likely play in this case is "relay" home.

The Cutoff Man

The cutoff man is the final link in the two or three throws to retire the runner. His throw to the plate, third base, second base, or perhaps even first base, must be extremely quick and accurate. The following techniques are important for a successful cutoff man:

1. As quickly as possible, he should take a position in line with the throw, approximately 60 feet from home plate. A reasonably strong throw from the outfield, if it is aimed at the cutoff man's chest, will, if allowed to continue, bounce once en route to the catcher. The outfielder should throw the ball to the cutoff man using the latter's chest as the target.

2. When at his position, the cutoff man should wave his arms and holler "Hit me! hit me! hit me!" to give the outfielder or relay man every indication where the throw should go. Remember, the outfielder or relay man is on the move and focusing on catching the ball before turning to throw to the cutoff.

3. The cutoff man should position himself to prepare for the most likely play. If, for example, the third baseman playing cutoff anticipates throwing to second base, he turns his body in such a way that he can catch and throw in that direction with a minimum of body adjustment.

4. If the cutoff man is to catch and throw home, his footwork and preparatory movements are the same as the relay man's described earlier.

5. If the throw from the outfielder or relay man is strong and accurate and will reach the catcher without the need for a cutoff in time to make the tag on the runner, the cutoff man should slap his glove and fake catching the ball as it goes past. This may freeze the batter/runner and prevent him from going to second base.

All outfielders can profit from the box drill, which emphasizes quick hands and feet.

A good drill to help the cutoff man develop quick feet, body control, and quick throws is the box drill. Stationed approximately 50 feet from one another, the infielders throw the ball hard and fast around the square. The cutoff throw is quite realistically simulated by keeping the chest in front of the throw, catching with two hands near the heel of the glove, having the pivot foot planted as the ball is caught, and throwing quickly to the next man. Then, to simulate the quick adjustment necessary when anticipating one play and having to execute another, they reverse the direction of the ball. Such an adjustment occurs when the cutoff man is set to cut and throw home and then is ordered by the catcher to "cut two."

Verbal Cutoff Signals

The defensive player covering the base where the play will occur is solely responsible for instructing the cutoff man what to do. As the throw approaches the cutoff man and the runner is bearing down on the base, the common calls that a catcher, third baseman, shortstop, or second baseman make are "Cut home," "Cut three," "Cut two," "Cut one," or "Cut, hold." If the catcher, or whoever is covering the base where the play is occurring, says nothing, the cutoff man fakes catching the ball by slapping his glove, and lets the throw go through to the base.

Poor communication between fielders results in dropped fly balls and/or injuries to the fielders.

POP-FLY PRIORITIES

A common and needless error in defensive play is the easy pop fly that falls untouched between two or three players, or a pop fly that is dropped when one player crashes into another. There are priority areas within which each fielder is allowed to catch the pop fly once he has signaled for the ball, and it is a mistake for any other player to attempt a catch out of his area so long as the first player has clearly signaled he can catch it.

As a fielder, you must determine that you can catch a pop fly before you signal. If there is any doubt in your mind, do not holler but continue to pursue the ball until you hear a teammate call for it. Because the involved players must keep their eyes fully focused on the ball in the air, your best signal when you decide you can catch the pop fly is a loud "I have it"* at least once, preferably three times. The teammate closest to you should veer out of your way and indicate he has heard your call by saying, "All yours, take it." Whenever a pop fly is hit that either one, two, or three players could catch, the following priorities should prevail:

The THIRD BASEMAN has PRIORITY over the pitcher and catcher.
The SHORTSTOP has PRIORITY over the third baseman, second baseman, and pitcher.
The SECOND BASEMAN has PRIORITY over the first baseman and pitcher.
The FIRST BASEMAN has PRIORITY over the pitcher and catcher.
The CATCHER has PRIORITY over the pitcher.
All OUTFIELDERS have PRIORITY over all infielders.
The CENTER FIELDER has PRIORITY over the left fielder and right fielder.

*English grammar not withstanding, it is acceptable to holler "I got it" on the baseball field.

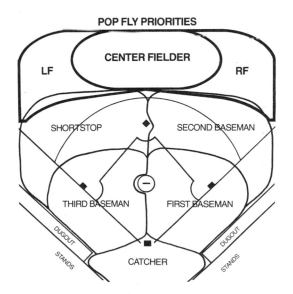

Pop-Fly Priorities.

After recognizing who has priority on a particular fly ball, the player closest to the fielder making the catch should shout, "Take it! Take it!"

When every fielder recognizes the boundaries of his priority area and signals *loudly and clearly* when he can make the catch, pop flies should not be a defensive problem. The priority areas and principles are constructed on these facts:

1.   It is easier for the third baseman and first baseman to catch a foul pop fly than for the catcher. Their gloves are better designed than a catcher's mitt to catch flies, and the foul pop is drifting toward them and away from the catcher.

2.   It is easier for the shortstop and second baseman to catch a pop fly behind third base and first base than it is for the third baseman and first baseman. Their path to the ball is at an angle, while the third baseman and first baseman must turn their backs on the ball and look over their shoulders.

3.   It is easier for an outfielder to catch a pop fly coming in than for an infielder going back.

RUNDOWNS

When the offensive team commits a baserunning error that results in a runner being caught between bases, the defensive team should welcome this "gift" with gleeful shouts and open arms. Thirty-three percent of that inning's offensive potential has essentially been handed over to the defense with the challenge merely to tag the runner out. Sound simple? It should be, but in fact it is one of the most messed-up plays in baseball. From the Little League to the Major League, runners commonly escape rundowns because the defense is poorly prepared to deal with the gift of a runner "hung out to dry."

As in other areas of baseball defense, rundowns are truly a *team defense,* requiring that the players involved know not merely what is expected of them alone but of all teammates as well. There are several systems of rundowns, and variations of each; but no matter which system a team uses, it is essential that certain rules be made clear to all defensive players and the system be the same no matter which bases the runner is caught between.

The rules for the system I prefer are the following:

1.   After the rundown is initiated, one throw should be sufficient to retire the runner. Two throws may be required, but any more dramatically increase the margin of error, and the other runners ahead or behind the runner caught in the rundown are probably advancing.

2.   The runner must be forced to run *hard* and commit himself immediately. The longer the runner is allowed to dance around between the infielders, the less likely the defense is to retire him. Except between third base and home plate, it makes no difference toward which base the defense forces the runner. When the rundown occurs between third base and home plate, every effort must be made to have the runner retreating toward third base when the tag is made.

3.   The defensive player with the ball at the start of the rundown must put the ball in his bare hand and have his arm in a three-quarter-overhand-snap position. Then he must run full-speed at the runner on the inside of the base line.

4.   The player toward whom the runner is being forced at full speed takes a "short" position approximately 18 feet in front of the base and also on the *inside* of the base line. This player becomes the "receiver" in the rundown. (All defensive players must remain on the inside of the base line to avoid throwing across the path of the runner and obscuring the vision of the receiver or hitting the runner.)

5.   When the receiver feels that the runner is close enough and moving fast enough so that he cannot stop, retreat, and avoid the tag, the receiver signals for the ball to be thrown to him. Common signals at this point are verbal ("Throw," "Now," "Yes," etc.), visual (slap the glove, wave the hands, step forward, etc.), or a combination of both. Whatever signal is chosen, it must be clear and decisive so there is no mistake when the snap three-quarter throw is released to the receiver. If the receiver judges accurately and the throw is good, the runner is tagged out as he stops and begins retreating.

6.   The tag-out should be made with the ball firmly in the bare hand and

The rundown play needs a well-understood system of rules and guidelines to assure success.

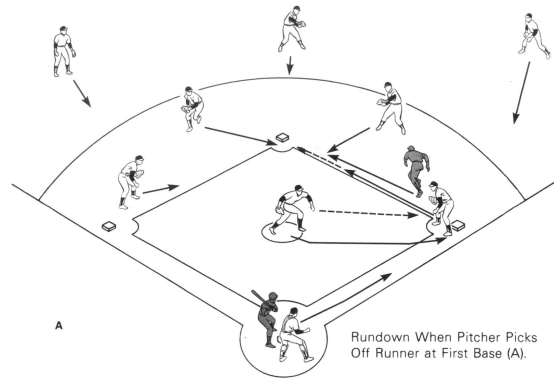

A

Rundown When Pitcher Picks
Off Runner at First Base (A).

Rundown When Pitcher Picks
Off Runner at Second Base (B).

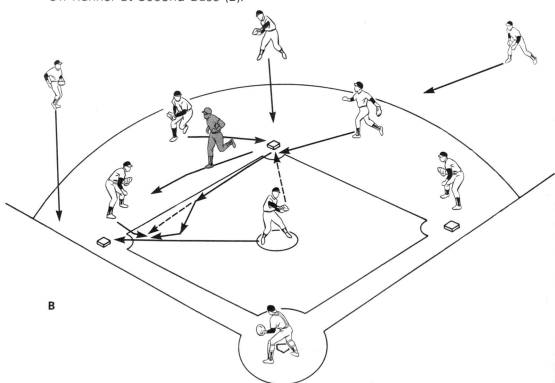

B

applied low to the runner's body. Agile runners, when certain of being tagged, may drop to their hands and knees and try to scramble under the tag.

7. When the ball is released to the receiver, the thrower should veer sharply toward the infield to avoid obstructing and interfering with the retreating runner. The thrower should then follow his throw to the base for backup if necessary.

8. There should be backup men at each base in case the receiver's signal is either too early and the runner starts back toward where he came, or too late and the runner dashes by the receiver.

9. When the rundown is initiated, by a pick-off throw or some other means, and the defensive player sees the runner already halfway toward the next base and moving away, he should throw immediately ahead of the runner without waiting for the signal. He then takes the short position 18 feet in front of his base in the likelihood the runner will be coming back toward him.

As shown in the two diagrams illustrating rundowns, every player has a role in this play, but its success is built on two main factors: (1) the judgment of the receiver as to when the ball should be thrown to him, and (2) the accuracy of the throw(s). Rundowns should be executed hundreds of times in practice to assure a team's being able to accept this "gift" under game conditions.

CATCHER PICK-OFFS

It is quite common for pitchers to attempt pick-offs during the course of a game, and they'd better; with the proven effectiveness of aggressive baserunning, more runners are taking daring leads off the bases and causing increasing anxiety for the defense. A second way to counter long leads at the bases is for the catcher

Catcher pick-off plays require prearranged signals and precise timing. A well-executed catcher pick-off can bail a team out of a serious predicament.

to prearrange pick-off plays with the infielders. After all, the catcher has one of the strongest arms on the field and this asset should be utilized as often as possible. All-star catcher Gary Carter of the Montreal Expos is known for his willingness to try frequent pick-off throws—many of them successful—and National League runners are reluctant to stray too far off base when they play the Expos.

In executing a pick-off throw to first, second, or third base, the catcher first alerts the infielder that he has a pick-off in mind by stepping in front of home plate. It is important that the infielder acknowledge in some way (perhaps by touching his cap or belt) that he has received the sign from the catcher, so no mix-up will occur and no throwing error result. I advocate a pitchout at the plate for most catcher pick-offs to guarantee that a batted ball does not go through an infielder's vacated position. Too, pitchouts are easy for the catcher to handle and thereupon set himself for a strong, accurate throw to the baseman breaking to the bag.

Besides holding runners close at all three bases, catcher pick-offs strengthen an infield defensively by making each infielder more alert as he watches the catcher's signals for a possible pick-off. Even the outfielders should know and watch for the catcher's pick-off signals so they can position themselves quickly to back up a bad throw.

PITCHER PICK-OFFS

The particular pick-off techniques for both right- and left-handed pitchers were covered earlier in the chapter on pitching. Now let's fit those techniques into the larger pattern of defensive strategy. I hope you'll see that a team profits if its pitching staff makes frequent pick-off attempts.

Rickey Henderson of the Oakland A's is quite blunt about the failure of most American League pitchers to hold him close to the bag. After he set the major-league record for stolen bases in a single season, Henderson maintained that most pitcher pick-off moves were quite predictable and easy to spot. His stolen-base record was largely attributable to the pitchers rather than the catchers.

Pitchers must understand the variables involved in keeping runners from stealing too many bases or getting long leads on bunt or force plays. Consider the following:

1. With a 15-foot lead at first base, a fast base runner can get to second base in 3.5 seconds.

2. The best catchers in baseball can deliver the ball to second base in 1.9 seconds from the time the ball hits the catcher's glove until it hits the second baseman's or shortstop's glove. Most catchers are in the 2.0-to-2.1-second range.

3. Most right-handed pitchers deliver the ball to the catcher in about 1.5 seconds from the time they begin their pitch from the set position until the ball hits the catcher's glove.

Thus, the time taken from the start of the pitcher's delivery until the ball hits the second baseman's glove is approximately 3.5 seconds, or *the same time it takes a fast runner to steal second base from a 15-foot lead!* It takes a *perfect throw* and tag even to *create a tie* between the runner and the ball! So the percentage of success is clearly with the runner, *unless* the pitcher can either prevent the runner from taking that long a lead or cut down his delivery time. Both are possible, particularly keeping the runner closer to the bag, and the most effective means is the pick-off attempt.

Pitcher Pick-Offs at First Base

The first baseman must always be ready for, and indeed encourage, the pitcher to throw over to first base. A verbal or visual signal to the pitcher is helpful whenever the runner is edging too far off the bag. Remember, the pitcher is concentrating intensely on how to get the batter out and may overlook the runner's long lead at first base. Both the pitcher and first baseman must recognize when a runner's lead has become too long and too threatening, and demands an immediate pick-off.

An excellent time to signal a prearranged pick-off at first is when the first baseman is playing behind the runner with bases loaded, or with runners on first and second. Either the pitcher or first baseman can initiate this play by a signal to the other: a tip of the hat, a pull of the ear, a wiggle of the glove, or some similar sign. The *sign must be acknowledged* and the pick-off play confirmed; otherwise, the possibility of a balk, bad throw, or ball hit through the first baseman's vacated position is too great. With a right-handed pitcher on the mound, this pick-off is executed when he looks toward second base in his set position, ostensibly to check the runner there. Out of the corner of his right eye, he sees the first baseman break behind the runner toward first base. When the pitcher sees that first movement, he wheels toward first and throws over the bag. The first baseman arrives there an instant before the ball, catches it, and applies the tag. With a left-handed pitcher on the mound, the time for the first baseman to break toward the bag is when the pitcher lifts his right foot.

Pitcher Pick-Offs at Second Base

There are several excellent methods designed to hold runners close to second base and one hopes, to pick them off. One is the *count play,* where either the shortstop or second baseman flashes a prearranged signal to the pitcher, which he must acknowledge. The acknowledgment is vital to prevent a mix-up that could lead to an error, balk, or scratch hit through an open position. The pitcher comes to his set position and begins counting, "One thousand one, one thousand two," then turns and throws to the second baseman or shortstop, who began breaking toward the bag when the pitcher came to his set.

Another effective method is for the catcher to signal the pitcher when to turn and throw to second base for the pick-off. The advantage of this play is that the runner is lured farther off the bag because the pitcher never looks at second base. The disadvantage is that the play involves three players, which makes the coordination of signal, acknowledgment, and execution more difficult.

The method I prefer is simpler and involves only the shortstop and pitcher. I favor this system because it relieves the pitcher of the distraction of having to check first with the second baseman, then the shortstop, then the catcher (and then perhaps even the dugout!) before he begins concentrating on his primary objective—getting the batter out. As the runner leads off second base, the pitcher takes his sign for the pitch from the catcher, stretches and comes to his set position, and then looks back at the shortstop. The shortstop is now responsible for determining whether the runner is a threat to steal third base or vulnerable to a pick-off. If he's either, the shortstop takes two hard steps toward second base (right, left) and flashes a prearranged signal—an open glove, a glove wiggle, a raised glove, a clenched fist, etc.—to the pitcher at the end of the second step. When he sees the sign after the second step, the pitcher turns back to the plate, counts "One thousand one, one thousand two," wheels, and throws to the *second baseman,* who also was watching the shortstop, saw his sign, and broke to the bag immediately.

If the shortstop chooses to cover the bag, he takes two hard steps toward second base and continues all the way. When the pitcher sees daylight between the runner and the shortstop, he wheels immediately and throws to the shortstop covering the bag. It isn't necessary for the pitcher to turn back to the plate or count, because the shortstop is already near the bag and moving fast.

If the runner at second base is neither too far off the bag nor a threat to steal, the shortstop can take two steps toward second base, not give a signal (or give a fake signal), and return to his position. He is thus telling the pitcher, "Go ahead and pitch—the runner is no problem." Or the shortstop can simply remain in his ready position when the pitcher looks back, which means the same thing.

Making the shortstop responsible for pick-offs at second base has two advantages: He is in the best position to guess the runner's intentions, and he frees the pitcher's mind as much as possible to focus on the batter.

One other pitcher pick-off play at second base that has become more popular in recent years is the *swing move*. I first saw this move in 1961 when veteran pitcher Tom Morgan of the California Angels used it to pick me off second base in a spring-training exhibition game. The swing move began surfacing again in college and pro baseball several years ago and has proven a good defensive strategy to counter aggressive base runners at second base. It requires a prearranged signal between the pitcher and second baseman or shortstop, whoever will cover. As the pitcher lifts his lead leg to begin his delivery, instead of striding toward the plate he swings his leg toward second base while keeping his eyes toward home plate. He then completes a 180-degree turn and throws to second base, where the second baseman or shortstop began breaking when the pitcher first lifted his leg. Most runners will increase their lead when the pitcher begins his motion toward home plate, and the swing move will often catch them. Another situation ideally suited to the swing move is with runners on first and second or the bases loaded; two outs; a count of three balls and two strikes on the hitter; and the runners moving with the pitch.

Pitcher Pick-Offs at Third Base

A runner at third base is only 90 feet from scoring and has made it three quarters of the way around the bases. Furthermore, a pitcher cannot balk toward third base. Given these facts, we encourage the pitchers at Arizona to try frequent pick-offs at third base, and we give them several basic methods.

Either the third baseman or pitcher can flash a prearranged signal to the other, but it *must* be acknowledged! Once a sign has been flashed, the pitcher assumes the windup position (facing the hitter, pivot foot on the rubber, ball in his bare hand) and watches from the corner of his right eye for the third baseman to begin breaking toward the bag. When he sees movement, the pitcher swiftly backs off the rubber and fires low and hard toward the bag. If the timing is right, the third baseman will arrive at the bag an instant before the ball, just in time to set himself, catch the ball, and tag the runner out.

With the right-handed pitcher in the set position, the third baseman delays his break until the pitcher lifts his left foot to begin what the runner thinks is the stride toward home plate for the pitch. Instead, keeping his eyes on home plate until the last second, the pitcher steps toward third base and fires hard and low to the bag. With a left-handed pitcher in the set position and his back toward third base, a pick-off attempt at third base is questionable because the pitcher's vision is badly obscured and he may make a bad throw.

Pick-Off Practice

Successful pitcher pick-offs depend on timing and accurate throws. Coordinated movement between pitchers and infielders does not develop overnight. Literally hours of concentrated practice are required before everyone understands the techniques and has the confidence to try pick-offs in key game situations. A useful drill is letting three pitchers practice pick-offs to each base simultaneously, with a runner on each base taking a lead, infielders flashing signals to the pitchers, and the pitchers acknowledging them. Each pitcher makes five consecutive pick-offs at one base and then rotates on the mound to the next base for five more pick-off attempts. Intense practice like this has made the University of Arizona the national collegiate leader in pitcher pick-offs in recent years.

True, most pick-off attempts do not succeed. But the very attempt reminds a runner that the defense is alert and ready for any tricks. The runner thus becomes reluctant to risk a big lead or early jump, and the defense gains a foot or two in its effort to keep the offense from scoring.

Multiple-Pitcher Pick-Off Practice. Simulating game conditions in this drill improves the confidence and timing of pitchers and fielders alike.

With the ball securely in the glove, the fielder holds the glove within a 6-inch radius of the bag and the sliding runner tags himself out.

TAG PLAYS

On a nationally televised baseball game I watched recently, Bill Buckner of the Chicago Cubs evaded a tag and successfully stole second base. The slow-motion video replay showed that the catcher's throw had clearly beaten Buckner and that the second baseman had the ball in his glove awaiting the slide. But Buckner's expert hook slide away from the bag lured the second baseman into reaching for Buckner's foot while his hand was slipping in under the tag.

The proper way to apply a tag and avoid such embarrassment is *to wait for the runner to tag himself out.* When the throw has clearly beaten the runner, you should have the ball securely in your glove, the back of the glove exposed to the slide, and the glove *on the ground* within a 6-inch radius of the bag. The runner's foot or hand must eventually reach for the bag, and the glove and ball will be waiting there for the tag. Don't reach for the runner!

On an extremely close tag play when the runner's foot or hand reaches the bag at the same time as the glove, flash the tag down and lift it straight back up again. If you leave the glove down by the bag after a close play, chances are the umpire's call will be "safe" because he'll see the runner's leg or arm on the bag and the glove on the runner's hip or shoulders. Down-and-up tags deny umpires this luxury of "waiting until the dust clears."

13

Offensive Strategy

The first principle, if you're a coach putting together an offensive system designed to score runs, is to know your players' abilities. It makes little sense to try all manner of complicated, surprise maneuvers if your players can't execute them. That's why you'll seldom see Johnny Bench stealing a base or Reggie Jackson swinging for the hit-and-run. Each player's strengths and weaknesses must be carefully assessed and analyzed before any coach or manager can put offensive strategy into motion.

Second, baseball is essentially a game of percentages that have been proven over thousands of repetitions of the same game situation. In his 1964 book *Percentage Baseball,* Earnshaw Cook drew some revealing conclusions concerning the relative success or failure of offensive strategies, and those conclusions still have relevance today. Cook proves, for instance, that there's a greater likelihood of scoring a runner from first base with nobody out than of scoring a runner from second base with one out. That's a revealing statistic, and one that has a direct bearing on whether or not to order a sacrifice bunt with a runner on first base and nobody out.

Each game situation, though, presents a host

233

An effective bunt attack—the "short game"—can often turn things around for the offense.

of variables that cause such percentages to waver and change, so you as coach must know which is the best offensive move at any moment. Help in deciding comes from applying the two principles above. Never, when you're coaching, let your hunches, impulses, whims, or fancies dictate your offensive strategy. You may win a game or two with a surprise offensive move, but over the long season you'll be wrong more often than right.

I advocate percentage baseball. Providing that our players at the University of Arizona have a competitive degree of skill and are carefully coached in what is expected of them in every situation, I believe we can win three out of every four games using the principles of offensive strategy outlined in this chapter. You'll seldom see the Arizona Wildcats pull an "off-the-wall" offensive surprise. We try to execute the fundamentals and take a percentage approach into each game. This isn't to say we aren't aggressive. In fact, we're more aggressive than ever in moving and scoring runners. But we carefully calculate each move as to its percentage of success or failure, and consider all the variables surrounding a given situation.

OFFENSIVE VARIABLES

Most of the same variables mentioned in chapter 12, "Defensive Strategy," must also be weighed in choosing the right offensive move. Such important considerations as the score, the stage of the game, whether a team is home or visiting, the fatigue level of the pitcher, the strengths and weaknesses of particular defensive players, the hitter (both at the plate and coming up later that inning), the runner(s), the weather, and the field should all influence a coach's decision to use a particular strategy.

OFFENSIVE CHOICES

After you've assessed the players' abilities and calculated the percentages of a situation, you, as coach or manager, can choose from the following offensive weapons: the take or the hit, the sacrifice bunt, the base-hit bunt, the suicide squeeze, the safety squeeze, the hit-and-run, the single steal, the delayed steal, the double steals, the hit behind the runner, the fake bunt and slash, the scoring base runner, and the stretched base hits.

Each of these offensive weapons has great value and can tip the scales from loss to win when executed correctly and used at the right time. When used at the wrong time, or with the wrong players, these same weapons can backfire and blow up in your face.

Take or Hit

Far more games are won by swinging the bat than by taking pitches. Sure, there's a time and place for the "take" sign, but, by and large, batters will produce far better if you show confidence in their ability to hit. Frequent "take" signs are self-defeating because the batter finds himself behind in the count and forced to become a defensive batter. I would much rather see an aggressive batter at the plate with confidence—in himself and his ability to hit, and in his coach for allowing him to hit. Instruct your batters to swing if the pitch is a good strike unless you flash a sign otherwise. At Arizona, we've mounted very good individual and team batting statistics year after year because we encourage our hitters to be aggressive and positive at the plate. When my two sons, Doug and Bruce, were playing Little League baseball, they were fortunate, generally, to have excellent volunteer coaches. But one coach had the wrong idea. He instructed all his players to take the first two strikes "because pretty soon the pitcher will walk four batters and we'll have a run." At that level, his strategy sometimes worked, but it created in the youngsters a negative approach to hitting.

There are, of course, situations when the "take" sign is in order. Let's say your team is two or more runs behind in the late innings, or the opposing pitcher is having control problems, or the ball is wet—that's when a batter should take a strike. If the count goes to 3 and 0, the batter should take two strikes. In these situations, your team needs base runners to mount a rally, and the opposing pitcher may be bothered or tired enough to walk some on for you.

When your team is ahead, tied, or behind by one run, hit away. Counts of 2 and 0 and 3 and 1 are ideal ones for a batter to look for his pitch and drive it hard for a base hit. The better hitters on your team should even be allowed to hit on 3-and-0 counts. It's simple: Aggressive hitters will score more runs and win more games for you than those who frequently take pitches.

The Bunt Offense

The Sacrifice Bunt

The sacrifice bunt is a questionable and overused offensive weapon. Although necessary in certain key situations in close games with certain batters and runners, the sacrifice bunt gives away one-third of a team's offensive potential, and thus should be carefully considered before being used. The alternatives to the bunt in advancing the runner(s)—the steal, the hit-and-run, the fake bunt and slash, the base-hit bunt—may well be better choices, and those strategies don't sacrifice outs.

Use the sacrifice bunt with nobody out and a runner representing the tying, winning, or lead-increasing run on first or second base. Seldom should you call for a sacrifice bunt with one out, because that would leave your offense with only one remaining out to score the run. Bunts should be placed down either line, depending on the mobility, arm strength, and positioning of the pitcher, first baseman, and third baseman. "Sacrifice" is a good and descriptive term for this bunt because the batter turns early enough to make sure he bunts the ball properly before thinking of running to first base. He literally sacrifices his turn at bat to advance the runner.

With runners on first and second bases and nobody out, the ball should be bunted down the third-base line to force the third baseman to leave the bag and field the bunt.

The Base-Hit Bunt

The base-hit bunt utilizes both the element of surprise and the batter's speed. It can be executed with nobody on or with runners on base, but the base-hit bunt's primary purpose is to *get the batter on base.* The best times for the base-hit bunt are when the third baseman or first baseman is playing deep; if either of them or the pitcher is a slow and poor fielder; if the grass is wet; or if the batter is in a slump and having difficulty getting base hits. Base-hit-bunt attempts can have a devastating effect on mediocre infielders since they force an infielder to field and throw off-balance. (See pp. 44–45 for a discussion of the fundamentals and techniques of base-hit bunting.)

The Safety and Suicide Squeeze Bunts

These bunts are something of a last-ditch measure to score a runner from third base. Use them in the late innings of a close game with one out and a weak hitter or excellent bunter at the plate. It's bad strategy to attempt a squeeze bunt with nobody out, because the chances of the runner scoring on a base hit, error, wild pitch, or passed ball are excellent and can keep the threat of a big inning alive. With one out, your chances for a big inning have diminished and your priority now becomes scoring the runner from third base even if it means giving up a second out.

The "safety" squeeze gives the batter the option of getting a good pitch to bunt, and the runner on third attempts to score only if he is sure he can make it. The batter hides his intention as long as possible before turning to bunt, and if the pitch is a ball, he lets it go. The runner, meanwhile, takes a safe lead at third base and, before breaking home, makes sure the bunt is safely on the ground and that he can score. To score on a safety squeeze bunt, the runner on third must be fast and able to judge whether or not he can make it home.

The "suicide" squeeze bunt is aptly named. If the batter misses the bunt attempt or pops it up, or the runner alerts the defense by leaving third base too soon, it's suicide! Yet it's often worth the risk since a well-executed suicide squeeze is virtually impossible to defend and nearly always results in the run scoring. Signal the suicide squeeze when the count requires that the pitcher throw a strike on the next pitch; 1 and 0, 1 and 1, and 2 and 1 are good counts to try the squeeze. The batter stays in his normal hitting stance and, disguising his intention until the last instant, turns to bunt when the pitcher's lead foot hits the mound in his delivery. The batter *must* bunt the ball! If he gets it down safely virtually anywhere toward the infield, the runner will score. The runner takes a safe and normal lead at third base and, as the pitcher begins his delivery to the plate, shuffles further down the line. When the pitcher's front foot hits the mound, the runner breaks full-speed toward home. (See "Baserunning," p. 64.)

The Fake Bunt and Slash

The fake bunt and slash can be effective when the defense is expecting a sacrifice bunt and the infielders are either charging in or charging toward the bases, thus opening lots of room for a batted ball to get through safely. The batter turns to bunt a bit earlier than he would for the sacrifice, but at the last instant draws back with the bat and slashes at the pitch, attempting to drive a hard ground ball past the charging infielders. He doesn't take a full swing; instead, he brings his hands together in a choked-up position on the bat, draws back about three-quarters of the way into his normal stance, and slashes hard. He must get a good strike to execute the slash. If it's a ball, he lets it go. The fake bunt and slash neutralizes the hard-charging third baseman and first baseman from fielding the bunt and forcing the lead runner. You can also give your batter a choice in this situation: If the infielders charge hard, slash; if they lie back, bunt.

The Hit-and-Run

The best time to try the hit-and-run is with one out, a runner on first base who has average or poor speed and would not be a steal threat, a batter at the plate who makes consistent contact with the ball, and the batter ahead in the count. The runner breaks with the pitch, and the batter *must swing* at the pitch and attempt to hit the ball on the ground. Some coaches insist the batter try to hit the ground ball through the vacated position of either the second baseman or shortstop, whichever moved to cover second base. My own feeling is that few hitters are skillful enough in handling the bat to do that consistently, and most will pop up or miss the pitch in their attempt. The important thing is that the batter *hit the ball somewhere on the ground* and protect the runner.

The value of the hit-and-run is that the double play is averted and, even though the batter may be thrown out, the runner has moved into scoring position. Too, the ground ball may get through the infield, enabling the runner to move all the way to third base.

In executing the hit-and-run, remember these key points:

1. Your runner on first base *must go* on the pitch. You, as coach, have chosen that particular pitch for the play, and your batter *must swing* no matter where it is, except for a pitch clearly in the dirt.

2. Your runner must glance to home plate after two or three strides to know what is happening to the ball. If the ball is a grounder, he must watch to see if it gets through the infield or not. If it's a pop fly, he should stop and retreat to first base. If it's a low line drive, he keeps going because if it's caught by an infielder he'll be doubled off anyway. If it's a high line drive or fly ball, he stops to see if an outfielder will catch it. If it's swung at and missed, he tries to complete his steal of second base. If it's a wild pitch or passed ball, the runner may be able to go all the way to third base.

3. Your runner must never be picked off first base on a hit-and-run. This is not a steal attempt, so he must take a safe lead and make sure the pitcher delivers before breaking toward second base.

4. Use the hit-and-run when your team is ahead, tied, or down one run. If your team is down by two or more runs, your batter needs to get on base and it's poor strategy to make him swing in the event the pitch is a ball. For the same reason, it's poor strategy to attempt the hit-and-run with nobody out; your team has a chance for a big inning and you don't want to force your batter to swing at what might be a bad pitch.

The hit-and-run is also a good offensive strategy with runners on first and third, or first and second, because it averts the double-play possibility. Also, your team picks up an advantage whenever runners are put in motion, since their movement forces infielders to leave their positions, thus creating more opportunity for a ground ball to get through into the outfield.

The Single Steal

An alert, aggressive, fast runner on first base causes the defense to become anxious and to alter their pattern significantly. The pitcher is distracted and his concentration shifts from the batter to the runner. The catcher is tense and reluctant to call for off-speed pitches that will give the runner more of a jump on his steal attempt. The shortstop and second baseman move in and closer to second base for coverage on the expected steal and yield more space for a batter to hit a ground ball through the holes. The outfielders move back several steps to cut off extra-base hits that would allow the fast runner on first base to score. The steal threat alone keeps a defense nervous and on edge. A team known for stealing bases is a tough one to defense!

The percentage of successful stolen bases is high at every level of baseball. Even most big-league catchers throw out fewer than half the stealing runners they face. The running teams in the major leagues are generally the teams leading, or near the top of, their divisions. Every season, division leaders usually rank either first or second in stolen bases. The continuing year-to-year success of the Los Angeles Dodgers, the Kansas City Royals, the Montreal Expos, and the Philadelphia Phillies gives striking evidence of their effective running games.

As the pitcher's ability to hold runners close and the catcher's ability to throw runners out diminish, the base-stealing success ratio increases. Base stealing at the high-school and college levels can have a devastating effect on the defense. It is not uncommon for teams at these levels to have an 80-percent success rate in stealing second and third.

The best time to steal second base is with two outs and a left-handed hitter at the plate. The best time to steal third base is with one out and a right-handed hitter at the plate. Of course, an extremely fast runner skilled at getting good jumps can steal virtually anytime during a game. In either case, a good lead is essential and will be the difference between success and failure. A good lead at first base with a right-handed pitcher on the mound is 15 feet. As a runner, practice getting consistent leads so your right foot is positioned 15 feet from first base. The defense must now regard you as a definite steal threat. A 10- or even a 12-foot lead is not a threat—it's difficult to steal from that short a distance. Consider the many times a runner is safe or out at second base by less than a foot and you'll see that the length of the lead at first base becomes quite crucial. A good rule for the single steal is to have a good lead *and* a good jump before breaking for second base.

As far as the score is concerned, the best time to steal a base is when your team is ahead, tied, or down by one run. When down by two or more runs, be positive you can steal the base before you go, because the batter or on-deck batter represents the tying run and his getting on base takes priority in the offense. For this reason, too, it's wise for a coach to decide when runners should attempt a steal. You can run your team right out of a game through foolish steal attempts. A coach should generally not permit players to run on their own.

Double Steals

Runners on first base and third base present an offense with splendid opportunities for severely pressuring the defense. If the runner on first base breaks with the pitch, the catcher faces this dilemma: "If I throw to second base, the runner on third may score. If I don't throw to second base, another key runner goes into scoring position. What shall I do?"

Double steals are generally tried with two outs in hopes of causing a bad throw or some mistake that will score the runner from third base. The double steal is also in order with one out and a slow batter at the plate who may hit into a double play. I don't recommend double-steal attempts with no one out, because the chance of a big inning looms large for the team at bat, and to risk having a runner thrown out at the plate is self-defeating.

Following are five offensive strategies with runners on first and third base, all of which are designed either to score the runner from third base or to move the runner on first out of the double-play situation and into scoring position. Which of the five methods to use is up to the coach after he has carefully considered each variable mentioned earlier in this chapter. One of the two runners must be considered priority and an effort must be made to advance him. The important prevailing rule on double steals is: WITH TWO OUTS, THE RUNNER ON FIRST BASE MUST NOT GET TAGGED OUT BEFORE THE RUNNER

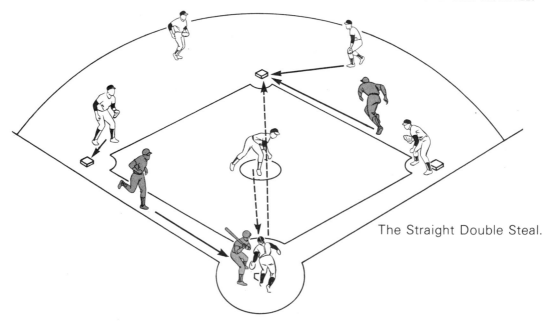

The Straight Double Steal.

ON THIRD BASE CROSSES HOME PLATE! If the throw beats the runner to second base, he must stop and get himself in a rundown to give his teammate at third base time to score before the third out is recorded. With fewer than two outs, the runner on first base should try to steal second base and go in sliding hard.

The Straight Double Steal

The straight double steal is designed to score the runner from third base. The runner on first base breaks with the pitch, challenging the catcher to try to throw him out. When the runner at third base sees the catcher release the ball toward second base, he breaks home. The runner on third base must have a good lead, but not so far that the catcher could pick him off with a quick throw. The keys to this play are the two long and accurate throws required to retire the runner attempting to score. The straight double steal is a good offensive choice if the runner on third base is fast and the runner on first is slow. Use it, too, if either the catcher's or second baseman's arm is weak or inaccurate.

The Long-Lead Double Steal

The long-lead double steal is also used to score the runner on third base. The runner on first takes an unusually long lead and *deliberately* invites a pick-off from the pitcher. When the pitcher falls for the ploy and throws to the first baseman, the runner takes off *full-speed* for second base and the runner on the third increases his lead significantly. The instant the first baseman releases his throw to second base to stop the first runner, the runner on third base breaks for home.

The key to this play is for the runner on first to put immediate pressure on the first baseman to throw to second base, thus allowing his teammate to break for home plate. If the first baseman is allowed time to gather his wits,

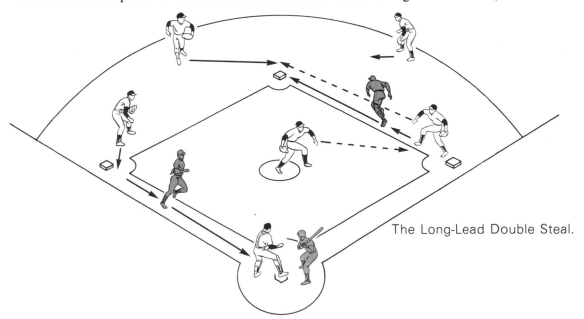

The Long-Lead Double Steal.

he can fake the runner back to third base and still have time to retire the first runner with a throw to the shortstop. With two outs, the first-base runner has a tough responsibility executing this play. He must break for second base at full speed and try to draw the first baseman's throw, but still be able to stop and get himself caught in a rundown long enough for the runner at third base to score. This is a good choice of double steal if the first baseman is inexperienced or has a weak arm, or if there's a left-handed pull hitter at the plate to force the shortstop to take the throw from the first baseman on the run. Under such circumstances, it's difficult for the shortstop to recover and throw home.

If the pitcher does not fall for the long lead and delivers to the plate, the long-lead double steal immediately reverts to the straight double steal.

The Delayed Double Steal

The delayed double steal is primarily used to move a slower runner at first base into scoring position while simultaneously creating the strong possibility of a bad throw to second. When the pitcher delivers to the plate, the runner on first takes two long shuffles in his secondary lead toward second base. Whoever is covering second base, either the shortstop or second baseman, glances toward first base to see if the runner has broken toward second base in a steal attempt; not seeing that, he turns his attention toward the batter. When the ball hits the catcher's glove, the runner on first base breaks toward second base. The catcher begins his throw to second base, but chances are no one is there to cover, or they will be late covering. The runner on third base breaks for home when he sees the catcher release the ball toward second. The delayed double steal takes advantage of both the shortstop's and second baseman's inattention.

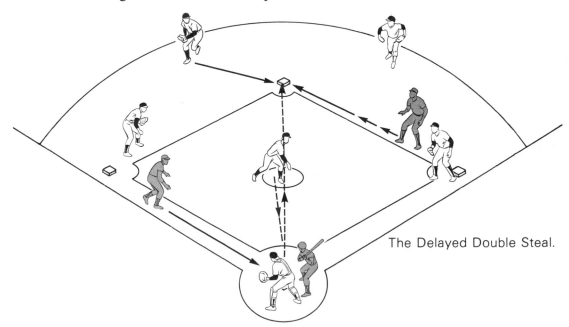

The Delayed Double Steal.

The Early-Break Double Steal.

The Early-Break Double Steal

The early-break double steal is a last desperate attempt to score a runner from third base with two outs and the hitter behind in the count. It can only be attempted with a left-handed pitcher on the mound, who, it is hoped, is also young and inexperienced. With the left-handed pitcher's back toward him, the runner on third base takes his lead as far as possible without alarming the defense. When the pitcher raises his arms from his sides to begin his stretch, the runner on third base breaks full-speed all the way home. At the instant the first step toward home is taken, the runner on first base breaks full-speed toward second base, drawing the attention of the pitcher. The runner on third base should score if (a) the pitcher balks; (b) the pitcher completes his stretch, steps off the rubber, and throws to second base; or (c) the pitcher pauses a second or two after completing his stretch, wondering what is happening. If the pitcher completes his stretch and looks quickly toward the runner at third base . . . well, that's why this is a last-ditch effort to score.

This early-break double steal was first introduced to me one morning in the 1963 Cleveland Indian spring training camp when manager Birdie Tebbetts spent over an hour showing us this offense for use against a young, left-handed rookie pitcher that the San Francisco Giants were throwing against us that afternoon. Fortunately, or unfortunately, we knocked the rookie out of the game in the second inning and didn't have a chance to use the play that day. Nor did we use the play that season! But it has worked a number of times for us at Arizona and is worth practicing.

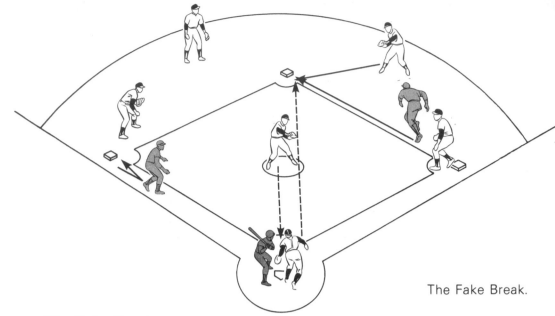

The Fake Break.

The Fake Break

There are times with runners on first and third when the offense is primarily interested in advancing the runner at first base. In this case, regardless of how many outs, the runner at first tries to steal second base while the runner at third base serves as a decoy. The runner at first breaks with the pitch, making every effort to steal second base. The runner at third base takes a *very short lead,* and when the catcher's throw clears the mound on its way to second base, the runner fakes a two- or three-step break toward home plate. The second baseman sees the runner at third breaking and begins relaying the ball back toward home plate. By the time he realizes it's a fake break, the runner from first is sliding safely into second base.

THE POWER OFFENSE

Most of this chapter thus far has dealt with offensive strategy behind what, in baseball parlance, is called the "short game"—that is, scoring one run at a time, with offensive choices based largely on speed and surprise. Another, vastly different offensive philosophy that has also proven successful and brought winning baseball over the years is the power game.

Beginning with the Babe Ruth–led New York Yankees in the 1920s and continuing with such outstanding teams as the Brooklyn Dodgers in the mid-1950s, the Yankees again in the early 1960s (featuring Mickey Mantle and Roger Maris), the "Big Red Machine" in Cincinnati during the 1970s, and more recently the Pennant winning "Bronx Bombers" in 1981, the keynote to this offensive attack has been the home run. The power game is characterized by long-ball, extra-base, muscle-laden teams that feature strength rather than speed, bash rather than bunt, slug rather than slash. In the older, more confined ball parks—such as Crosley Field, Ebbets Field, Connie Mack Stadium, the Polo Grounds, Wrigley Field, and Fenway Park—the power game was a good choice. A manager could load his lineup with home-run hitters who'd aim for those short fences and win games regularly by lopsided scores. In the power offense, the premium is on waiting for the big inning, when, with one swing of the bat, several runs will cross the plate. In this type of attack, the coach will seldom order a sacrifice bunt, a hit-and-run, a squeeze play, or a stolen base.

The determining factor in choosing whether a team plays the short game or the power game is the personnel. The short game makes no sense if most of the players are slow, powerful home-run hitters who strike out frequently. Likewise, the power offense is useless if most of the players are like Pete Rose and Tim Raines.

The ideal would be a combination of speed and power that gives the coach or manager opportunity to utilize the many ways to score runs. My caution is to make certain the strengths and weaknesses of each player are well considered before establishing your offense. Tailor your offensive philosophy to the players, not vice versa.

ADVANCING BASE RUNNERS

Chapter 3 deals with the fundamentals and techniques of baserunning. The larger question of when to run and attempt an extra base belongs in this discussion of offensive strategy. Many teams penalize themselves with indiscriminate, shortsighted attempts to advance runners who are needlessly thrown out, thus killing rallies or short-circuiting big innings. For those who coach, the following guidelines reflect percentage baseball and, applied to a knowledge of your team's personnel, will help score runs and keep rallies alive.

When Behind by Two or More Runs

Play it safe on the bases. The important runner is the one representing the tying run, and any runner in front of him mustn't get thrown out trying to advance. The best time to take calculated chances with your runners is when your team is tied or has the lead.

With Nobody Out

Do not take chances trying to advance into scoring position. The big inning is a good possibility now, so be careful not to let your players get thrown out and kill the opportunity to score multiple runs.

When to Stretch a Hit, or Steal

The best time to try to stretch a single to a double is with two outs. The best time to steal second base is with two outs. The best time to advance to third base is with one out. A good rule to remember whether your team is ahead *or* behind is, Never make the first or third out at third base.

When to Score on a Base Hit or Error

The best time to try to score on a base hit or error is with two outs. Only one more out remains at that point in the inning, so your runner should try to score if he has only a 30-percent chance. If he remains at third base, there is only a 30-percent chance the next batter will drive him in with a base hit.

With nobody out, a runner trying to score should do so only if he has a 100-percent chance to be safe at home; but with one out, he need have only a 75-percent chance to be safe at home.

When to Tag Up

With nobody out, a runner on second base should *tag up* on a questionable catch deep in the outfield. If the ball is caught, the runner can advance to third base. If the ball falls safely or is dropped by the outfielder, the runner will probably score anyway.

With one out, the runner should be halfway to third base on a questionable catch in the outfield. If the ball is caught, he retreats to second base and there are two outs. But if the ball drops in, the runner is assured of scoring.

Runners on First and Third and Fewer Than Two Outs

The runner on third should try to score on any ground ball to the infield. If the infield misses the double play, the run scores. If the infielder throws home and the ball beats the runner, he should stop and get caught in a rundown long enough to allow the runner on first base to reach third and the batter to reach second.

The runner should try to score on any ground ball with his team ahead, tied, or one run behind. His correct technique is to concentrate intensely on the path of the ball off the bat at contact. By taking a moving lead off third base as described in chapter 3, and seeing the ball go *down* off the bat, he can break home instantly. If the ball is a slow grounder or one hit to the right or left of the infielder, the runner will score. Although a ball hit medium-hard or hard directly at the pitcher or infielder will probably retire the runner at the plate, more often the ground ball is a difficult chance that permits the runner to score. If the runner holds at third base on ground balls with one out and the batter is thrown out at first base for the second out, the subsequent batter has a 30-percent chance or less to score the runner with a base hit. The percentages thus favor sending the runner at third with one out.

With nobody out and the infield in, the runner should hold on a ground ball until he is sure it goes through. With fewer than two outs, the runner at third should freeze if the ball shoots off the bat on a line. With fewer than two outs, the runner at third should hustle back to the bag to tag up on any ball leaving the bat at an "up angle."

THE BATTING ORDER

Throughout this chapter, I have urged the coach or manager to measure his players' strengths and weaknesses carefully, to best utilize them in a winning effort. In a way, players are like pieces in a jigsaw puzzle: no two players are alike, and each has a special place where he can best fit and help form the completed picture. Constructing a batting order takes the same thoughtful approach as completing a complicated jigsaw puzzle.

The Lead-Off Man

He should have good speed, a good eye at the plate to work the pitcher for walks, good ability to protect the plate and make consistent contact with the ball, and a good on-base average. He needn't be a power hitter.

The Second Batter

He, too, should have good speed, to stay out of the double play. He must also be a good contact hitter, an excellent bunter, and adept at hitting behind a runner at first base and moving him to third. He must be unselfish and willing to take strikes while the lead-off man, who is generally the fastest man on the team, attempts to steal bases. He must be willing to sacrifice himself on a bunt or hit-and-run. His main responsibility lies in advancing the lead-off man into scoring position for the power hitters coming up.

The Third Batter

In my view, he should be the best hitter on the team. He should have power enough for extra-base hits to score a runner from first base and to put himself in scoring position with two outs. He should have good speed to stay out of inning-ending double plays and to score from first on an extra-base hit with two outs. Ideally, if he's a left-handed hitter, he can then pull the ball through the hole at first base when the runner is being held on, and start a step closer to first base to prevent the double play. More than any other batter in the lineup, he can keep the inning going with a base hit, and over a season he'll have as many at-bats as the lead-off man and thus hit hard and often for his team.

The Fourth Batter

He should be a power hitter, capable of driving in runs with the long ball. Often there are two outs when he comes to the plate, so a long ball is needed to score a runner from first base. He should be tenacious and determined, a clutch hitter, because he and the fifth batter will have more RBI opportunities than any of the other batters in the lineup.

The Fifth Batter

His characteristics are very similar to the fourth's. Of the two, the batter with the highest batting average and lowest strikeout ratio should be fourth in the order, the other fifth. The fourth and fifth batters, because they are power hitters, will generally strike out more than other batters.

The Sixth Batter

Since he'll lead off many innings, he should combine some of the same qualities as the first batter in the lineup. Still, he'll have many more opportunities for RBIs than the lead-off man, so he should be a better hitter. Everything else being equal, the better hitter belongs in the sixth slot, the better base stealer and better set of eyes in the lead-off spot.

The Seventh Batter

Similar to the second batter, he wouldn't be called upon to sacrifice-bunt as often as his number two counterpart. The seventh batter should be a good hit-and-run man since he often has to advance the fifth hitter, who generally is not a fast runner.

249

The Eighth and Ninth Batters

Generally the poorest hitters on the team. A coach wants his better hitters batting as often as possible, so he necessarily places them at the top and middle of the order. Sometimes eighth and ninth batters, while not necessarily power hitters, will have good contact ability and keep the ball in play. Having good hitters in both the eighth and ninth spots is a rare blessing for a team, but when it happens it prevents an opposing pitcher from pitching around batters six and seven. I prefer the fastest of my two last batters to be ninth, since if he gets on base, three more fast batters are coming up and I can try short-game strategies.

GIVING SIGNS

As coach, you should disguise how you "talk" to your team while ordering certain offensive strategies from the dugout or third-base coaching box. Batters and base runners should look toward you between every pitch and watch for signs that indicate what their next responsibility will be. I feel that most coaches use unnecessarily complicated and confusing signs that their own teams are likely to miss, causing a strategy to backfire. *Many more signs are missed by the offensive team than are stolen by the defense.*

The four basic and most frequent signs—take, bunt, steal, and hit-and-run —should be simple. The less frequently used signs—squeeze, take bunt, and slash, and double steals—should be more dramatic, so as to capture the attention of the batter and runner. The best method of sign giving is to establish a sign for every strategy and inform the players that these signs will stay the same for the entire season. Keep it simple so the players will have no problem remembering: right hand to the *h*at for hit-and-run; to the *b*elt for bunt; to the *s*hirt for steal; to the *t*ip of the nose for take. Then establish an *indicator sign* after which the sign will immediately follow and be in effect. The indicator, for example, could be placing the right hand behind the back. Immediately following the indicator, a sign *may* be put on. If not, the entire sequence was a decoy to disguise the system from the opponents. Throughout the season, the signs remain the same, but the indicator can change if necessary. There are many different systems of giving signs, but for any of them to be effective, they must be easily understandable for your offense yet disguised from alert opponents.

A Word to the Fan

Those of us with a vested interest in our own performance or the performance of our players tend to read everything we can about baseball, so I suspect that most of you reading this book are players and coaches.

And yet, there is another extremely important audience I'd like to address in this book: you fans. Baseball would not have survived for over a century and a half, nor will it continue to survive, without the millions of faithful fans who, though they may never have played the game themselves, still support baseball. Your support is crucial to the health and welfare of the game.

A good fan's support goes far beyond buying a ticket to a professional game to help pay the salaries of major-leaguers. I do believe that baseball provides the best bargain the entertainment dollar can buy, but there is something baseball needs more than the mere purchase of a season ticket to the Angels, Yankees, Royals, Toros, Diablos, Hornets, or Bulls. Baseball needs mothers and dads willing to coach a Little League team; needs parents and friends to provide rides to games and practices for kids unable to get across town on their bikes; needs sponsors to help provide uniforms and equipment for American Le-

251

Few sports fans are as loyal and long-suffering as baseball fans. Their enthusiasm and team pride are hard to match.

gion, Colt, Pony, Babe Ruth, and other leagues across the country; needs citizens to push through and support municipal bond issues to provide more recreational facilities and fields for youngsters; needs a strong community voice speaking out against dropping baseball and softball from high-school and college athletic programs; needs increased attendance at high-school and college games, if only to show support for the many outstanding players who get so little recognition; needs calm and thoughtful leadership among fans to combat an alarming increase of rowdyism at games. Baseball needs fans whose hearts have been captured by this great sport!

There is no question that interest in baseball is on the rise. Average attendance at each major-league game in 1982 was nearly 22,000, and several teams approached or exceeded 2 million in season attendance. The Dodgers drew over 3 million! Additionally, the minor leagues drew better in 1982 than any other year in the last twenty-five. And college baseball, rapidly gaining its fair share of "baseball fever," increased attendance by 20 percent over the previous year to top out at 11 million in 1982.

Baseball fans come in every size, shape, and color, and there is no such thing as "the average fan." For every San Diego Chicken or "Wild Bill," there are thousands of quiet, unobtrusive, devoted baseball intellectuals who can quote every statistic about the 1954 Cleveland Indians or the 1969 Amazing Mets.

Some fans have played the game; many have not. Some have developed an interest in baseball through their parents or family; others through a friend or schoolmate. There are fans who get their excitement primarily from watching televised games, and there are others who practically live the baseball season at the park. Some follow the box scores of the entire league closely; others recognize the names of only the home team. The majority of fans are men, but among the best and most knowledgeable fans are women. Some bring gloves to the park early for batting practice in hopes of catching a ball; others regularly get to the game in the second inning. Many fans wear T-shirts and sneakers; others wear furs and three-piece suits.

The beautiful fact is that all of you are baseball fans and not one of you is more or less important than any other. Just because you didn't make your high-school team doesn't mean you're a failure or need be a dropout. If you can't pronounce Yastrzemski or Guerrero, who cares? If you can't keep score as well as Alan Roth, what's the difference? Your sustained interest in baseball is all that matters and gives you that honored title: fan.

Being a fan is great fun and pure relaxation. Part of the value of going to a game—any game—is the emotional satisfaction of cheering the home team,

A player's autograph is something cherished by young and old, boy and girl, man and woman alike.

second-guessing the managers, and disputing the umpires. Most of the time, the good fan comes away from the ball park feeling better than when he entered —even though his team may have lost, he's late for dinner, and someone spilled mustard on his shirt.

But along with the excitement, sheer enjoyment, and personal gratification of being around baseball, there come what I can only call "responsibilities." The following is only a partial list of what I consider a fan's "duties." You may disagree with the list, but I'd like to think that such responsibilities are a natural outgrowth of anyone's love for the game.

1. *Make your love for baseball a legacy to pass on to some youngster.* Along with my dad, Harold Kindall, I have Eric and Roger Kammeyer, Fritz Klark, and Hal Younghans—fine men, all of them—to thank for sparking my love for baseball when I was a boy in St. Paul, Minnesota. I forget which one taught me to keep score, which one got me the autographed ball from the St. Paul Saints, and which one introduced me to Walter Alston, but they all loved baseball and left part of that love with me.

2. *Encourage sportsmanship and fair play.* Baseball is a game, not a battle. Sure, players at every level should give their maximum effort, but they should also keep the outcome in perspective, win or lose. No baseball game is so important that it should cause a rule to be broken, a friendship to be destroyed, or a fight to occur. There is a growing concern in America about unruly and abusive spectators at high-school, college, and professional sports

Umpires! The unsung heroes of baseball. Authority and respect will forever rest with "the men in blue."

events; their behavior is inexcusable. A good part of baseball's appeal to the public is that it can be wholesome, clean, family entertainment free from the rowdiness that seems to mushroom when good fans are absent or silent. The classiest teams in baseball have always been the ones that respect both opponents and umpires, and there's no reason why the same can't be said of the quality fan.

3. *Recognize and encourage excellence at all levels of baseball.* The 12-year-old Little Leaguer who raps out five hits in a single game is just as excited and proud as Milwaukee Brewer Paul Molitor was when he set a World Series record with five hits in a single game. The high-school all-conference player feels as pleased for his honor as Cardinal catcher Darrell Porter felt when named MVP in the 1982 World Series. Cracking the starting lineup for his college team is just as important to that sophomore as earning a starting shot in the majors was for Terry Francona. The major-leaguers get their deserved recognition and acclaim through the media, but who besides mom and dad will congratulate those deserving young ballplayers? Fact is, a crowd of 200 good fans at an amateur baseball game can make players feel like they're playing in Yankee Stadium itself. The dedicated young player who spends the necessary extra hours on practice and drills as he aspires to excellence can be made to feel 10 feet tall if someone other than his family recognizes his efforts.

4. *Learn more about the game of baseball so you can appreciate more fully the uniqueness and intricacies of this challenging sport.* The truly good fan will

know why the manager pitched to the left-handed hitter with first base open and the pitcher up next. He may not agree, but at least he'll understand the dilemma the manager faced. The history of baseball is filled with fascinating incidents and captivating personalities that will bring new richness to your love for the game. (Did you know, for example, that there have been two managers in the major leagues who refused to wear a uniform? Each managed his team to a pennant wearing a white shirt and tie!) Most fans will remember a game by its final score—a win or a loss. But there are many who will remember the strategy, the difficult defensive play, or the 3-and-2 change-up with the bases loaded in the eighth inning of a tie game. Like just about anything good in life, the more you learn about baseball, the more you appreciate and enjoy it.

5. *Baseball in the Olympics is next!* At this writing, there are seventy-seven countries with active baseball programs, many of them with national teams eager to send their baseball best to compete for a Gold Medal. Our University of Arizona team has traveled three times to Europe and Asia and

Perhaps a Willie McGee, Paul Molitor, or Joaquin Andujar will come from this group of Little Leaguers. If so, it'll be thanks to three coaches unselfishly passing on their baseball legacy.

Baseball is a family game—for the players as well as the fans. Former American League batting star Tito Francona bestowed his talent and love for baseball on son Terry, now a major-league outfielder.

played against teams from Cuba, the Netherlands, Italy, Germany, Korea, Japan, Taiwan, and Mexico. Impressive baseball talent is developing all over the world, and knowledgeable fans like you are applauding base hits, strikeouts, double plays, hit-and-runs, and squeeze plays in virtually every language. Thanks to the efforts of former Baseball Commissioner Bowie Kuhn, United States Baseball Federation President Dr. Robert Smith, and the venerable Rod Dedeaux, longtime and successful coach at the University of Southern California, baseball will be an exhibition sport at the 1984 Olympics in Los Angeles. This is the final step to being recognized as a fully accredited gold-medal sport in 1988. Join with your counterparts all over the world to encourage continued growth and interest in the game.

"The Great American Game" is not merely a phrase, it's a fact. In no other sport are there such discernible links between a Ty Cobb and a Terry Francona, between the past and the present, between the players and the fans. I am confident that 154 years from now, if our world survives, there will still be baseball, the bases will still be 90 feet apart, players will still have difficulty hitting the curve, and fans will still be captured by their love for this game.